Books are to be returned on or before
the last date below.

2 8 APR 2005

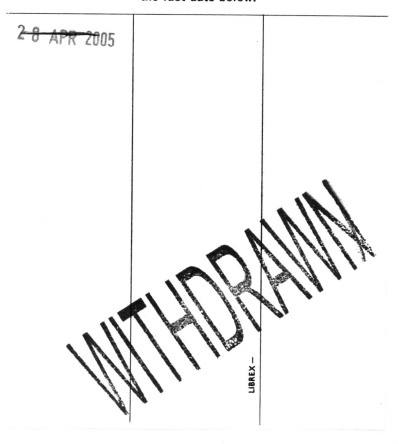

LIBREX —

D1351246

1968
Marching in the Streets

1968
Marching in the Streets

Tariq Ali and
Susan Watkins

BLOOMSBURY

For all those who stayed the course

First published in Great Britain in 1998 by
Bloomsbury Publishing plc
38 Soho Square
London W1V 5DF

Copyright © 1998 by Tariq Ali and Susan Watkins

Sources for materials quoted in the text are given on page 218.

Commissioning Editor Sarah Polden
Designer Tim Foster
Editor Richard Dawes
Picture Researchers Anny Chettleborough, Martha Davidson
Production Polly Napper
Indexer Hilary Bird

A CIP catalogue record for this book is available from the British
Library

ISBN 0 7475 3763 1

3 5 7 9 10 8 6 4 2

Printed in Great Britain by Butler and Tanner Ltd, Frome

Contents

The original Che Guevara poster, distributed in Havana in January 1968.

Introduction

'A time for asking questions of Authority.'

History does not repeat itself, either as tragedy or as farce; but it rhymes. Thirty years later there are still echoes of 1968. Rereading the description of the French strikes and student upheavals during 1996–7 did bring to mind the much more dramatic episodes which paralysed that country three decades ago. The triumphant march of Laurent Kabila across the Congo and the ignominious flight of the Western-backed tyrant Mobutu reminded one that popular anger can still be refracted through an army of liberation.

In the mid-fifties, in his 'Letter to an Imaginary Friend', the American poet Thomas McGrath wrote of those who mocked the past. He was writing then of the thirties, but today it applies just as well to the sixties:

> Wild talk, and easy enough to laugh.
> *That's* not the point and never was the point.
> What was real was the generosity, expectant hope,
> The open and true desire to create the good.
>
> Now, in another autumn, in our new dispensation
> Of an ancient, man-chilling dark, the frost drops over
> My garden's starry wreckage.
>   Over my hope.
>   Over
> The generous dead of my years.
>
>   Now, in the chill streets
> I hear the hunting and the long thunder of money....

Nineteen sixty-eight was a year that those who lived through it, on either side of the political divide, will never forget. It was a year that marked an entire generation on every continent. Long before 'globalization' became a buzz-word in the culture of free-market politics, the events of 1968 had globalized political radicalism as part of a struggle to change the human condition for ever. It was a year of hope, when those who accepted the world as it was were the ones who felt disinherited, while the wretched of the earth, the dispossessed, began to recover their inheritance.

Much has been written about the sixties in relation to sex, drugs and rock 'n' roll. The image of the psychedelic sixties (especially in Britain) has blurred the politics of the period. We live in times which have placed Utopia out of bounds and in a culture strangled by a brazen opportunism. For that reason, here we have concentrated on history and stressed the global aspect of what actually happened in 1968.

Nineteen sixty-eight was an attempt to create a new world, a new starting point for politics, for culture, for personal relations. We believed that people should be measured not by 'success' or material possessions, but by the humanity of their aspirations, that the economy should be reorganized to serve the interests of the many, not the few, and that the destiny of socialism was inseparably intertwined with real freedom and meaningful democracy. The world had to be rebuilt anew so that it served the interests of the majority.

Britain in 1968, as now, had a Labour government whose failures on every level stoked the radicalization and caused tens of thousands to leave the Labour Party while even more refused to join. The following paragraph, from an article in *Black Dwarf* of July 11, 1968 by the economist Sean Gervasi, has a distinctly modern ring, except that New Labour would regard any extension of the welfare state as an ultra-left, Keynesian, 'Old Labour' lunacy. Some things have changed.

The first issue of *Black Dwarf* (June 1968) reflected the spirit of the times.

'What then has happened to the Labour Party's design for a New Britain? It should be said, first of all, that the New Britain had very little to do with socialism. It was merely a glossy version of capitalist society, with a high rate of economic growth and some extension of the welfare state.'

The first edition of the London-based newspaper the *Black Dwarf*, items from which occur throughout this book, appeared on June 1 1968, at a time when the streets of Paris were scarred by the events of May and authoritarian leaders worldwide were reeling from the resonance they set in motion. Taking its name from a Chartist publication of the early 19th century which blended satire with news coverage for the working man, the *Black Dwarf* became, during its two years of life, a valued means of expression for the political underground and the voice of the new Left. More precisely, the editorial board mixed Marxist politics and culture in combining the insights of playwright David Mercer, theatre director Roger Smith, poets Christopher Logue and Adrian Mitchell, feminist Sheila Rowbotham, Fred Halliday, Clive Goodwin and myself.

What united us was, above all, the belief that it was a time for asking questions of authority. A time to first challenge and then break all taboos: political, social and sexual. What was striking was the speed with which ideas of liberation spread throughout the world. The inspiration came from the battlefields of Asia where a poor, peasant country had raised an army to challenge the might of the world's most powerful industrialized nation. The Vietnamese David had dented the American Goliath. The legendary Vietnamese military commander Vo Nguyen Giap, who had defeated the French in 1954, now promised with calm confidence that the same would happen to the United States. He predicted with deadly accuracy that the Americans would lose the war:

'Our people are fighting for our national cause, but also for socialism and for the other peoples in the world struggling for their liberation. The myth of the invincibility of the USA, this colossus supporting itself impotently on the H-Bomb, is collapsing irretrievably. No matter how enormous its military and economic potential, it will never succeed in crushing the will of a people fighting for its independence ...

'Why did the United States think it would be victorious? It deployed an enormous war machine in our country. Westmoreland is a general who has found a way to boost the US expeditionary force from 20,000 men to more than 500,000 without offering Washington anything in return but a light at the end of the tunnel. The Americans based their confidence that they would win the war on their superior numbers, their overwhelming armament, their riches in dollars and in the tons of bombs they are dropping.

Finding themselves in a more and more difficult situation, they are now accusing their generals of trying to settle things arithmetically – for example, in the matter of balance of forces – while the Vietnamese have a trigonometric strategy. That is not correct. Our strategy is neither arithmetic nor trigonometric. It is quite simply the strategy of a just war, a people's war. They will never be able to understand that.'

The effect of the Vietnamese victories was immediate and dramatic. 'We shall fight, we will win: Paris, London, Rome, Berlin', the cover line I wrote for *Black Dwarf* in May 1968, was characteristically one-sided. What about Prague, Warsaw, Dresden and Moscow? The Vietnamese example had shown everyone that no Big Power was invincible. They were all paper tigers.

Another inspiration was the figure of Ernesto 'Che' Guevara, the martyred Latin American revolutionary and the only political icon of the sixties who continues to excite interest. In 1997, the thirtieth anniversary of his execution by the CIA, there was a plethora of books on Che published in various parts of the world.

Che Guevara was an Argentinian medical doctor who became a comrade and confidant of Fidel Castro and joined the small band of guerrillas who were determined to liberate Cuba, to transform it from what it was – a Mafia-run brothel whose dictators were chosen by Washington – into a revolutionary furnace for an entire continent.

In 1960 Castro, Guevara and their comrades were on the verge of a sensational victory. The Cuban peasants, workers, students and a professional layer of doctors and lawyers decided to back the revolution. Cuba threw out the American companies and overnight the bearded figures of Fidel Castro and Che Guevara became Latin American heroes.

Che had been a leading military strategist of the Cuban Revolution. As a guerrilla commander he did not shrink from unpopular decisions, but in post-revolutionary Cuba his interests turned to social and economic philosophy.

The struggle of the Vietnamese continued to haunt this leader of the Cuban Revolution. At the Havana Tricontinental Congress in 1966 Che called for 'the creation of two, three, many Vietnams' to isolate and defeat the armies of the Pentagon. By that time he had already left Cuba to carry on the struggle for a new world order. He did not succeed in the Congo, though he did encourage the efforts of a local guerrilla leader by the name of Laurent Kabila.

In Bolivia, an ill-judged venue by any criteria, he tried to ignite the peasants by repeating the Cuban model in the jungles. His small group was isolated and finally cornered. Che was captured alive and shot dead on the orders of a CIA operative.

Che's failures were outstripped by his martyrdom. His face was as beautiful in death as it had been in life (John Berger compared it to Mantegna's Christ) and he became a role model for hundreds of thousands all over the world and acquired the status of a legend. What made him special was his decision to relinquish the power and privileges that he enjoyed in Cuba in order to resume the struggle on behalf of the oppressed of this world.

One of his last testaments, in the shape of a poem entitled 'Against Wind and Tide', was sent to his wife, Aleida. It is a moving epitaph to a man whose image still haunts both enemies and friends:

This poem (against wind and tide) will carry my signature.
I give to you six sonorous syllables,
a look which always bears (like a wounded bird) tenderness,

An anxiety of lukewarm deep water,
a dark office where the only light is these verses of mine
a very used thimble for your bored nights,
a photograph of our sons.

The most beautiful bullet in this pistol that always accompanies me,
the unerasable memory (always latent and deep) of the children
who, one day, you and I conceived,
and the piece of life that remains for me,

This I give (convinced and happy) to the Revolution,
Nothing that can unite us will have greater power.

Che Guevara had wanted to create a different world and a new state form. Many in the West were hostile to the idea of the state as such and to most of its works. Why should the state regulate personal life? Why had homosexuality been outlawed for so long? Why had abortions not been legalized until 1967? Why should young people be forced to dress in a particular way? Why were women denied equal pay and status? Who decided the architecture of public housing? (Why not those who were going to live in it?) Why were state bureaucrats all over the world so deeply insensitive to the needs and the lives of ordinary people? Why were university students forced to live and work in cramped conditions? Why should the Third World be subjected to a continuous rape by the First? These questions, in different forms, were being asked everywhere, though not by everyone. It was the failure of traditional politicians to provide an adequate response that led to the explosions which marked 1968.

The temperature during that year of upheaval was uneven. In Britain, sex, drugs and rock 'n' roll vied for space with the massive anti-Vietnam War demonstrations in Grosvenor Square. Hedonism jostled uneasily with revolutionary politics, though there were occasional fusions that marked the political culture of the period. Elsewhere it was politics that dominated. London may have had the King's Road and Carnaby Street, but it was Paris which had the star quality of the Latin Quarter.

Looking back, it is difficult to remain unmoved by the generosity of spirit as well as the hope and optimism that dominated the proceedings thirty years ago. Millions, all over the world, believed in the possibility of a better future for all. The strength of such views compelled politicians to respond with a combination of reforms and repression; the mix varied in different parts of the world.

When the year began, the rulers of Western Europe governed their countries with a certain degree of justifiable smugness. The preceding two decades had enabled them to establish social peace. The East had not been so tranquil: there were uprisings in East Berlin in 1953 and in Budapest in 1956, and massive demonstrations in Poland in 1957. It was these early harbingers that made the old men in Moscow nervous of the Prague Spring of 1968.

In the West these earlier uprisings increased the sense of superiority and complacency. Nothing like that could ever happen here. Social-democratic regulation had made the system more acceptable to the majority of citizens than ever before.

The last occasion on which the whole of Europe had been marked by a revolutionary wave was 1848. In that year King Leopold I of Belgium, sick with fear lest the bad habits of the Parisian mob spread to Brussels, wrote to his niece, Queen Victoria of Britain:

'I am very unwell in consequence of the *awful* events at Paris. What will become of us God alone knows; great efforts will be made to revolutionise this country; as there are poor and wicked people in all countries, it may succeed.'

Several months later Victoria replied thus:

'Since February 24 I feel an uncertainty in everything existing, which one never felt before. When one thinks of one's children, their education, their future – and prays for them – I always think and say to myself, "Let them grow up fit for *whatever* station they may be placed in, *high or low*." This one never thought of before, but I *do always* now.'

The Europe of 1968 was different from that of 1848 in most respects. The Second World War had weakened its social fabric and created instability, but the Yalta deal of 1945 between Roosevelt, Stalin and Churchill divided the continent into spheres of influence: the East under Stalin and the West under NATO. The peace was preserved and Western governments believed firmly in full employment and a welfare state. That is why the main inspiration for the radical Left before the May Events of 1968 in France came from Cuba, Vietnam and China. For over two decades the European Left had been admiring events in other continents from afar. Suddenly it discovered upheavals on its own doorstep.

The reforms that followed the Second World War had created heightened expectations. More importantly, they had led directly to a phenomenal increase in education, creating a new intermediate layer in society. In 1967 there were six million university students in the United States, two and a half million in Western Europe and a million and a half in Japan. The generation of students who were on the campuses in 1968 had known neither unemployment nor defeat. They were critical of the previous generation – their parents – who had been unable to defeat unemployment and had permitted the rise of fascism. In Germany, Italy and Japan the students were in open revolt against their parents, who had collectively succumbed to the fascism of Mussolini, Hitler and Tojo. Students everywhere experienced a system incapable of fulfilling its promises, let alone satisfying their intellectual and social needs, a political order reluctant to accept any serious criticism and an imperialist giant engaged in a brutal war against a poor, Third World country.

This new stratum of students, born during or soon after the Second World War, developed a conscience as well as a political sensitivity which soon began to erupt on the streets of every major capital city and on every continent.

That is what makes 1968 such a unique year in the post-1945 period. The Vietnamese victories against the US war machine, the May Events in France and the destruction of Czechoslovak socialism by Soviet tanks represented struggles in each of the three key sectors of the world. Each of these events has left its mark on history.

The defeat in Vietnam has made the United States reluctant to intervene directly in other continents. It prefers to rely on local relays, mercenary alliances and the cover of the United Nations and advanced technology.

The May Events are still part of France's collective memory. This fact was referred to by every commentator in the French press during the big wave of student occupations and workers' strikes in 1996–7. Even the gnarled and twisted observers of the later events smiled at the memory of the original. The rhymes of history.

The decision by the Russians to invade Czechoslovakia and humiliate its reformist leaders was the death-knell of the Soviet system and its network of client states in Eastern Europe. If Gorbachev rather than Brezhnev had been in power in Moscow in 1968, the Prague Spring would have blossomed into a glorious summer throughout Eastern Europe.

It is now common practice by some of the participants of those days to characterize the movements that rose in the sixties as wide-eyed, if wild, attempts to build utopias; to mock them gently (decent, nostalgic liberals) or viciously (unpleasant foot-soldiers of the late Ronald Reagan and Margaret Thatcher or careerists desperate to climb the ladder of influence) and to dismiss the whole period as a spasm. The post-modern fashions of the eighties and early nineties chimed in happily with a generalized scorn for the politics of the sixties.

This critique was not confined to the absurd posturing and in-fighting of far-Left sects, each claiming the mantle of Lenin or Trotsky or Mao. Nor did it single out the decision by some factions within the student movement in Germany, Italy, Japan and the United States to embark on terrorist actions which they hoped would awaken the majority to the crimes of imperialism. That there were excesses of every variety during that period is indisputable, but the critics of the sixties do not confine themselves to these. Their aim is directed at those who were brash enough to challenge the mighty war machine of the United States. There are some who argue that the Vietnam War should and could have been won.

Another major target of recent critics is the movements which achieved the most important gains recorded by that period. This was in the realm of sexual politics. The struggle for the liberation of women and the legalization and 'normalization' of homosexuality is not yet over, but what has been gained is considerable and now part of the common sense of the twenty-something generation.

There were some aspects of the sixties which need and deserve to be criticized. The mindless, sub-anarchist hostility to the state and all its works was not confined to sections of the Left. It was mirrored by the Right. The move from utopian anarchism to utopian capitalism did not require a massive leap. Reagan and Thatcher played on crude anti-state prejudices to proclaim that true hope could be realized only in the conditions created by the free market. What was loose, laid-back and half-baked in the sixties became a deadly and potent virus in the hands of those who followed Hayek and Friedman during the eighties and nineties. And the commissars of free-market fundamentalism have turned out to be as philistine and bureaucratic as their state predecessors. The 'shock therapy' administered by modern capitalism has not just wrecked the lives of millions of ordinary people in the former Soviet Union and Eastern Europe: it has also destroyed the culture of these societies.

Utopian anarchism was not the only philosophy that captured the young. For a whole generation the revolutionary upheavals of 1968 revived memories of the early years of the Russian Revolution. Every small group had its versions of Lenin, Trotsky *and* Stalin. Many left-wing newspapers attached to these groups saw themselves as latter-day versions of Lenin's *Iskra*. Some of those who today denounce and demonize Lenin in the most vitriolic language were, in those heady days, the most servile and sycophantic of Leninists. Needless to add, all those who wanted their weekly paper to be the new *Iskra* ('spark' in Russian), listened avidly to Bob Dylan and the Rolling Stones, watched Godard movies and avidly followed the news from Vietnam on the nightly television bulletins. It was almost as if every activist was leading a double life.

This looking backward to find a future in the past was only a partial abdication of creative thought. Every revolutionary generation looks for a model in what has been won in the past. The Russian revolutionaries themselves were obsessed with the dynamics of the French Revolution of 1789 and Robespierre, Danton and Marat were not unaware of the processes that shaped the English Revolution of the seventeenth century. It was the English who taught the world how to decapitate a king.

While looking back was understandable, it did lead to a romanticization of both the forms and the means of struggle. It is interesting to recall that at an early stage of the student revolt, when the Free Speech Movement was born in Berkeley in California, a target of widespread anger was the computer. It was argued that computers were where secret information was stored, but instead of pressing for the availability of the technology to all, the anti-computer mind-set proposed destruction.

The German poet and cultural theorist Hans Magnus Enzensberger noted this tendency at the time and wrote in 1969:

'During the May Events in Paris the reversion to archaic forms of production was particularly characteristic. Instead of carrying out agitation among the workers in a modern offset press, the students printed their posters on the hand presses of the École des Beaux Arts. The political slogans were hand-painted; stencils would certainly have made it possible to produce them *en masse*, but it would have offended the creative imagination of the authors. The ability to make proper strategic use of the most advanced media was lacking. It was not the radio headquarters that were seized by the rebels, but the Odeon Theatre, steeped in tradition.'

Enzensberger's argument is not misplaced, but what he views as a gesture in the direction of conservative traditionalism was much more an act of solidarity with Third World peasants, primarily the peasants who comprised the guerrillas of the National Liberation Front in Vietnam. There was a conscious hostility to technology since we saw it every night on the screen dropping hundreds of bombs to destroy peasant villages in South Vietnam. Production for use, rather than profit, was seen by some as necessarily a production based on handicraft. Hence the amazing posters produced by the École des Beaux Arts in Paris, which were, naturally, collected and produced as a commodity and sold all over the world. The first edition has become a collector's item. In general, however, the German poet is undoubtedly right. The French students and workers should have, in May–June 1968, taken over the radio station and broadcast their message to the population as a whole.

This book is simply a political calendar of 1968. It reports and describes the events of that year – warts and all. Every single month saw an explosion somewhere in the world. In fact, the biggest success was achieved in Pakistan, where the student movement triggered off a gigantic popular upsurge which led to the overthrow of the military dictator and, ultimately, to the break-up of a state whose very existence was doubted by its own founding fathers.

To those reading about it today, that world might appear to be like a submerged continent. However, it is difficult for us to believe that we live now in a world where hope is gone for ever and where self-contemplation and self-interest have replaced the belief in a world of equality. Humanity still possesses all the facilities to effect such a change, but the system that has triumphed in the last years of this century would rather render our very being null and void than give up its privileges.

TA, January 1998

1968
January

'Hey, hey,
LBJ,
how many
kids did you
kill today?'

A shattered GI during a pause in the Têt offensive in Vietnam. Later in the year GIs like him will be marching in the US streets against the war.

The bodies of Che Guevara and his comrades lie mouldering in the misty Bolivian valley where, three months before, they were secretly buried by a CIA enforcer. But as 1968 begins, the note they sounded of brave-hearted, revolutionary generosity and internationalism is still resounding around the world. Che's call to lift the burden of American bombing on Vietnam by broadening the front, by creating 'two, three, many Vietnams', has found an echo in many hearts. Guerrilla groups are already fighting in Columbia, Uruguay, Venezuela and Guatemala; in Mozambique, Guinea, Angola and Rhodesia (now Zimbabwe); student-led protests are assaulting American embassies in Europe and Asia; while in Vietnam itself the guerrilla fighters of the National Liberation Front are planning an offensive for the New Year's Têt celebrations which will leave the US military reeling and dramatically alter the course of the war.

The year begins with the world's major imperialist power in crisis: the ruling circles of the United States are floundering and openly split about the conduct of the war in Vietnam. It is a crisis that will deepen, week by week, as the fiascos pile up: the huge crowds battling to keep the US aircraft carrier *Enterprise* from docking in Japanese harbours; the US Air Force plane crashing in Greenland with a cargo of nuclear bombs; the chief US naval intelligence ship *Pueblo* blundering into surrender to North Korea; and finally, the trauma of the sight of the Vietnamese NLF flag planted on top of the US Embassy in Saigon at the start of the Têt offensive.

Meanwhile, in the USA, the whole of the young generation seems to be in revolt. Long hair, weird clothes, loud music, wild sex, drugs, Indian religions and psychedelic light shows – the seeds of anarchistic self-discovery planted by the Beats and the Merry Pranksters have blossomed into a rebellion against the whole American Way of Life, and opposition to the government, to 'the pigs' – the police – to the horrors of the US war machine and the bombing and napalming of the people of Vietnam, are all an instinctive part of this.

By the start of 1968 the exigencies of the Cold War are in temporary abeyance, given the upsurge of 'hot war' against imperialist domination in the Third World. The one thing the US rulers fear most is that the Soviet Union or China might put their principles into practice and come into the war on the Vietnamese side, turning a 'local quagmire' into the Third World War. Compared with the revolutionary ferment they see elsewhere, the cautious bureaucrats in Moscow seem relatively safe and reliable to US eyes.

In fact, the Soviet bureaucracy is floundering, too. Krushchev's post-Stalin reforms have given the Soviet intelligentsia some space in which to act, but the Brezhnevites are wary of losing control. The development of Czechoslovakia's 'socialism with a human face' over the coming months will convince some sections of the Soviet bureaucracy that this is the future. Other, more powerful, sections of the élite will be terrified at the prospect of losing power and privilege, and of the dangers of opening up to the West. With the country far poorer militarily and economically than it can afford to admit, the façade of a united 'Soviet bloc' is crucial to retaining the Soviet Union's role on the world stage.

It is impossible not to be struck by the diversity and vitality of the Communist-ruled countries in 1968 – as also by their complete failure to make common cause against the enemy. In China, the Cultural Revolution – the great wave of mass agitation initially sparked off by Mao Zedong to get rid of his critics – has resulted in such civil disorder that Mao is sending in the Army, while the Beijing *People's Daily* speaks of the danger of civil war. American journalist Andrew Kopkind, in North Vietnam early in 1968, asks a government guide

Opposite: Bolivian Air Force Colonel Rene Adriazola shows the world the body of Ernesto 'Che' Guevara, killed by Bolivian rangers in 1967. Above: The year after his death, the USA's *Evergreen Review* draws upon Che's appeal.

how much help the Chinese are giving in the fight against the American bombs. Usually guarded about Vietnam's allies, the guide bursts out: 'They're crazy. They've stopped the trains and they're holding political meetings instead of sending supplies. They're completely hopeless.'

Nevertheless, the mere existence of such a large country, seemingly to the left of the Soviet Union, affects the world's balance of power. In Eastern Europe and the Soviet Union, too, there is diversity and dissent; intellectuals are debating cultural and artistic freedom. Meanwhile Cuba, the newcomer, is still resolutely independent of the Soviet bloc, denouncing the Kremlin's supporters in Havana as 'dwarfs guilty of servility to Moscow's ideas' and determined, like Che, to push for its own internationalist agenda for change, 'a revolution in the revolution'. By the end of January such a revolution will find a new generation of supporters all across the world.

1st **USA** Warriors of the Free World

General Westmoreland, lantern-jawed Commander-in-Chief of US military forces in Vietnam, hands in his New Year's report on the progress of the war to President Johnson, proclaiming: 'There is a light at the end of the tunnel!'

According to Westmoreland, the 'Search and Destroy' strategy implemented by half a million American troops has forced the Vietnamese guerrilla army back to their bases deep in the jungle: there is now no chance of a major attack on the towns and cities. All the General needs in 1968 is more troops, more arms, more bombs, more tanks, more battleships, more planes, in order to finish the job for good.

LBJ's face is tired and anxious, lined with all that he knows – or does not know – about the assassination of his predecessor, John F. Kennedy.

There is a crisis in United States policy, right at the top. The ruling circles are split. The President is trapped between the hawks, like Westmoreland, who want to go for broke in Vietnam, take the war into Cambodia and Laos, go nuclear if need be; and the doves, who point out that, after billions of dollars spent and 20,000 US servicemen dead, the United States is no closer to victory now than it was three years ago. The doves want to negotiate a compromise settlement before the price gets any higher. They argue that the US armed forces are already overextended: 500,000 men are now tied down in south-east Asia, well over half of all US combat-trained troops; more than half of its Air Force fighter-bomber squadrons; and one third of all its Navy combat vessels, including aircraft carriers, are involved in the war. And now even airborne units earmarked for the defence of the United States itself are on their way to Vietnam.

President Johnson rides roughshod over Vietnam demonstrators in a cartoon in the *Black Dwarf*.

Pentagon chiefs are saying that they will win the war before the end of the year; but as the doves point out, they have been saying this since 1965. Meanwhile hundreds of ancestral South Vietnamese villages have been destroyed and the villagers moved to 'strategic hamlets' – barbed-wire compounds guarded by troops. This is supposed to prevent them giving succour to the guerrillas of the Vietnamese National Liberation Front (NLF) in their fight against the South Vietnamese government, whom only the foreigners support.

In reality the strategic hamlets are a breeding-ground for NLF recruits. The stockaded villages of Vietnam have for centuries been run on a communal, self-governing basis. Tending the pools and paddy-fields and of reinforcing the dams and dikes have always been collective tasks. Within the dense bamboo hedges that protect the ancient villages, low mud and brick houses surround the temple complex where village elders confer, collect taxes, settle disputes and recall legends of the ghosts and heroes of days gone by. Once this basic unit of Vietnamese society has been destroyed by the US invaders, the sullen, dispossessed refugees have nothing left to lose. For many, the choice is between selling themselves, their mothers or their sisters to the galumphing invaders, or slipping off to the forests to join the NLF.

January 1968

The United States has been spending $100 million per year on herbicides and defoliant sprays to kill off the dense forest trees that shelter the guerrillas. The most ancient trees, some of them fifty metres tall, pose a particular problem to the chemical industries. And hundreds of thousands of tons of bombs have rained down on the paddy-fields and villages of independent North Vietnam, in an effort to force the people to abandon their southern compatriots.

Yet despite all this, and despite the hundreds of thousands of Vietnamese dead, the 'enemy's' strength still seems to remain the same. The South Vietnamese regime, whose rule the Americans are fighting to support, remains a byword for corruption and inefficiency. The official South Vietnamese Army remains unwilling to fight even in defence of its own government, despite all the American training and guns.

President Johnson has other problems on his plate. The diplomatic community has been unnerved by the protests against the Americans' conduct of the war erupting outside US embassies from Tokyo to Paris, London and Berlin. The President's initials have given birth to a universal chant on the streets of the world: 'HEY, HEY, LBJ, HOW MANY KIDS DID YOU KILL TODAY?'

At home, a whole generation of disaffected American youth is in revolt, blowing their minds, dodging the draft, occupying the colleges to protest against academic links with the big corporations and the war machine. The students, black and white, are angry, their eyes displaying a manic integrity which frightens the establishment, who ask each other in tones of disbelief, 'Are these really our kids?'

A massive budgetary crisis is looming: the cost of the Vietnam War has sent the balance-of-payments deficit out of kilter and the dollar's gold price is way too high.

American students denounce the war as they confront the National Guard.

National Guardsmen drive black rioters away from a torched building on the west side of Detroit, Michigan. Black anger ripped apart the city and several others as the war came home in 1968.

As if this was not bad enough, the past two summers have seen the black ghettos of over half a dozen American cities explode in flames of protest against white cops, the housing crisis and black unemployment, with rioters smashing and looting everything they can grab. To loot is to liberate. The riot police are busy preparing for the summer of '68 by stocking up on high-powered rifles, dum-dum bullets, machine-guns, tear-gas, Mace, armed helicopters and armoured cars.

What's more, in the United States 1968 is also an election year.

5th Moscow, USSR The Heirs of Stalin

The trial of four young intellectuals opens in Moscow. They have been charged with spreading anti-Soviet propaganda in support of two writers, Andrei Sinyavsky and Yuli Daniel, who had been jailed in 1966 for publishing their works, under pseudonyms, in the West.

In the Soviet Union 1968 is to prove a crucial turning point in the cultural thaw that followed Stalin's death in 1953. The poet Tvardovsky wrote in 1960:

> In those memorable moments
> At the grave of the dread father
> We became fully answerable
> For everything in the world,
> To the end.

It was the Soviet intelligentsia – writers, scientists, academics – who found themselves in the forefront of this 'becoming answerable'. After the successive traumas of 1930s Stalinization, followed by the nightmare of the Second World War, the great mass of the Soviet people were not united in any way and were therefore helpless to face the crisis of 1953. There was no hereditary working class (more than half the country's engineering workers, for instance, had been in the industry less than ten years). 'There was no real political and class alternative to the bureaucracy in the country,' the writer Boris Kargilitsky pointed out, 'but a cultural and moral alternative to Stalinism did exist.'

The intelligentsia had preserved some elements of unity, through its formal and informal academic and cultural organizations, friendships and family ties. Literature, as always, led the way. The trickle of new Soviet writing that began with Krushchev's famous reformist speech to the Twentieth Party Congress in 1953 had turned into a flood by 1962, when *Pravda* published Yevtushenko's poem 'The Heirs of Stalin' and *Novy Mir* published Solzhenitsyn's novella, *One Day in the Life of Ivan Denisovich*. 'Literature and criticism,' wrote V. Lakshin, one of the leading theoreticians of *Novy Mir*, 'became imbued with that vivid organic humanism which is nowhere equivalent to pleasing everybody and pardoning everything.'

At the same time a wave of strikes reveals the popular frustration over the rickety Soviet economy: rising food prices and terribly overcrowded housing; the production of poor-quality goods that nobody wants; the shortage of many others; the gross inefficiencies of the agricultural system.

When Boris Pasternak published *Doctor Zhivago* in the West, the Soviet bureaucracy had contented themselves with giving him a mauling in the press; putting Sinyavsky and Daniel on trial for the same error is intended as a warning threat to the intelligentsia. But the government has miscalculated: as so often this year, repressive tactics backfire. The mood has changed. The intelligentsia are united in outrage. A demonstration of 200 gathered in Pushkin Square in

Yuri Gadanskov, Alexei Dobrovolsky and Alexander Ginsburg: three of the intellectuals tried in Moscow for presenting an alternative to Stalinism.

December 1965. The protests – small-scale but highly committed – gather pace after the two writers are jailed. Of the four young intellectuals being tried in January 1968, one, Alexander Ginsburg, will receive a five-year sentence for the *White Book* he has compiled on the case of Sinyavsky and Daniel. Another, Yuri Gadanskov, the young editor of an underground pacifist magazine, will get seven years.

A curious and largely sympathetic crowd gathers outside the court. The protests will continue until the trauma of August 21.

Meanwhile a new wave of Soviet economists (together with like-minded colleagues in Poland, Hungary and Czechoslovakia) are beginning to work out theories of 'market socialism': incorporating elements of market relations (buying, selling, the fluctuation of prices) within an overall planned economy. This would involve a process of economic democratization, more rights for individual enterprises, more control from below. Whether this control would be in the hands of the enterprise managers or in those of the workers is one of the matters for debate. Reformists in the Soviet Communist Party (including the young Mikhail Gorbachev) support these ideas. But they are outgunned by the conservative supporters of General Secretary Leonid Brezhnev, who has taken over from Krushchev. The Brezhnevites are putting their faith in technocratic reform and computerization as the shining solution to all the USSR's economic problems. 'Cybernetic Socialism' will be the bright new dawn – and allow lazy, bloated managers and party bureaucrats to keep their jobs and privileges.

The Brezhnevites stand for conservative stability: they have no wish to return to the terror of Stalin's time, when ruling Party members themselves quaked in their boots. On the other hand, they will make no concessions to democratic political or economic reforms that might threaten their own positions. It is a policy that can only lead to a lethal stagnation.

Brezhnev himself is the epitome of this tendency: a cold, grey, lecherous creature, corrupt, small-minded and incapable of seeing beyond today. He really believes that, provided all dissent is stifled, the rule of the bureaucracy will last for ever. None of his minions has told him that the word he hates, 'intelligentsia', was first coined in his own country, or that numerous Tsars, too, hated the people it describes. Like all bureaucrats, old and new, Brezhnev fears independent minds. Above all, he fears those who refuse to be bought.

Brezhnev is informed that the sentences in today's trial will be harsh, just as he had wanted. After being fellated by a female employee, he returns, sated, to his apartment, a stone's throw from the Kremlin. He sleeps comfortably.

Prague, Czechoslovakia Socialism with a Human Face

It is fitting that the first real challenge to the apparatus in Moscow will come from this city, the most beautiful in Europe, and possessed of a real sense of history. Here it was that, a full century before Luther, Jan Hus fought fiercely for the reformation of the Church and against the sale of indulgences. Hus was executed and the Hussite rebellion crushed. But the memory of that struggle lives on: Moscow is only the latest equivalent of the Vatican.

At last, a victory for the new Hussites, as Alexander Dubcek replaces First Secretary Antonin Novotny at a stormy Central Committee meeting of the Communist Party of Czechoslovakia.

It is the culmination of four years of struggle within the Party over reform of the stagnating industrial and economic system, more say and more autonomy for the minority Slovaks, and greater political and cultural freedom.

The struggle has intensified dramatically since the end of October 1967, when a small student demonstration sets out one wintry evening to protest about the lack of heat and lighting in the University dormitories. The students are in high spirits as they make their way up towards the seat of government at Hradcany Castle. Their young faces are illuminated in the darkness by the flames of the candles that they carry: all they have to study by.

The cobbled streets are blocked by armed police. The students are shoved aside, roughed up, clubbed to the ground and dragged off under arrest. Some fifty of them are hospitalized. Next day the Government press describes them as hooligans who launched the attack on the police themselves.

The sense of shock and outrage at the Government's crack-down and its blatant lies draws many more people into the protest.

What sort of socialism is it that breaks the bones of its young people when they ask for light-bulbs to study by?

What sort of socialism is it that cannot provide light-bulbs for its young?

The students align themselves with the dissident writers who have spoken out against the regime at their 1967 summer congress, and been sacked for it.

Before long debate turns into active protest. The sight of students handing out leaflets on street corners that winter, and getting into intense discussions with passers-by about the police behaviour and the Interior Ministry's role, reminds foreign correspondents of a scene from Berkeley or some other turbulent student campus in the West.

Dissenting students, rebellious intellectuals, industrial modernizers, Slovak representatives angry and impatient with the delay of the reforms and far broader layers, yearning for improvements: Dubcek and the reformers seize the controls of the Communist Party on a crest of popular feeling. Dubcek himself is a surprise choice for some. Josef Smrkovsky, a Central Committee member soon to be elected President of the National Assembly, recalls:

Czech leader Alexander Dubcek in 1968.

'A whole lot of people were tipped for the First Secretaryship; one Novotny opposed, in another case the Slovaks were against, until finally the only candidate with a hope of being accepted was Dubcek. So finally the Praesidium all agreed on Dubcek. Only, as far as I know, Dubcek was unwilling to accept. People told me afterwards how in the night from Friday to Saturday, when the meeting ended, Dubcek protested. Cernik [another leading reformer] begged him to take the job, promising him that they would all back him up. In short, they literally shoved him into it. Dubcek was not prepared for a post like that, and suddenly it fell on his head.'

For the next month Dubcek shuts himself up to read, in an effort to prepare himself for the mammoth tasks ahead. The socialism which he and the others are proposing is one which embraces democracy and economic reform. A socialism which protects the many but does not exclude those who wish to start their own small shops, restaurants or industries. 'Socialism with a human face.'

There is already stiff opposition. Brezhnev himself has flown into Prague on December 8, barely four weeks before, to twist arms in Novotny's favour.

This is not just a matter of political principles. The reformers have made it very clear that they are determined to sort out the huge old party apparatus whose veterans have frustrated so many reforms. Jobs, power and status are at stake. The conservatives have everything to lose. Among the heads of the armed forces there is talk of intervening themselves: Defence Chief General Sejna points out that it would only take a couple of arrests for the Central Committee Praesidium vote to go against the reformers.

(Two months later, on March 8, Sejna will defect to the United States, bringing about Novotny's final fall. Has he already consulted Washington when he proposes blocking Dubcek's rise?)

New York, USA The Rational Mr Spock

Dr Benjamin Spock, world-famous paediatrician and author of the best-selling book *Baby and Child Care*, is indicted by a federal grand jury for sponsoring resistance to the draft and urging young men not to fight in Vietnam. Also charged are William Sloane Coffin Jr, chaplain of Yale University; Marcus Raskin, co-director of the Institute for Policy Studies in Washington dc and a member the White House staff of the National Security Council during the Kennedy administration; and several others.

The US government's decision to attack some of the most respected – and respectable – opponents of the Vietnam War is seen as an indication that the hawks are winning the battle for a head-on confrontation with the anti-war movement at home.

Dr Spock insists that his action is legal in the highest sense: he is opposing his government's

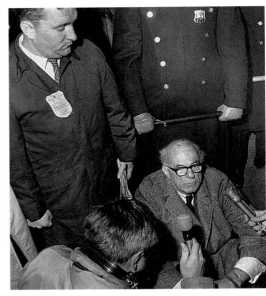

Dr Spock talks to reporters at an anti-Vietnam War demo, after which he was arrested and arraigned.

crimes against humanity, in line with the decisions of the Nuremberg War Crimes Tribunal. Despite this, he will be convicted, although his conviction will be overturned on appeal once the growing protests have turned the tide on Vietnam.

Havana, Cuba Cultural Revolutionaries

A week-long Cultural Congress opens in Cuba, the baby of the non-capitalist world. Post-revolutionary Cuba is a very different place to Eastern Europe. Here there is every colour of the rainbow and a new music and exuberance, instead of the grey monotone and bureaucratic inertia. Fidel Castro and his comrades are very critical of the Soviet model.

The new Cuba attaches a great deal of importance to art and literature, and to the intellectuals and artists who produce them. Castro has personally received Jean-Paul Sartre and Simone de Beauvoir when they visited Havana. According to legend, it was the French philosopher who suggested the idea of a gathering of the radical intelligentsia.

The Cultural Congress is designed to bring together progressive intellectuals and artists from all over the world to discuss politics and culture and how writers could and should intervene to help the struggles of the oppressed. The problem of going beyond a purely backward-looking religious or nationalist culture in the fight for national liberation is one that will still haunt the world thirty years later, whether in Ireland or Tibet, in Yugoslavia or the Islamic world. Nineteen sixty-eight is a moment when it is possible to begin to imagine where an alternative solution might lie.

As the British Marxist historian Eric Hobsbawm reports in the *Times Literary Supplement* on his return from Havana:

'Cuba was, of course, an ideal setting for such a Congress. It is not only an embattled and heroic country, though as Castro himself observed, a long way second to Vietnam, but a remarkably attractive one, if only because it is visibly one of the rare states in the world whose population actually likes and trusts its government. Moreover, the free and flourishing state of cultural activities at present, the admirable social and educational achievements and the endearing excursions into anti-materialist utopia, can hardly fail to appeal to intellectuals.

'The shelves of the shops may show large gaps, but telephone calls are free. Petrol is rationed, but the State provides posadas where couples can go to make love. The visual arts are unexpectedly brilliant, given the unvisual tradition of the country: witty, entertaining and, above all, public.

'Perhaps the most interesting discussion was on the problem of developing a genuinely autochthonous culture in underdeveloped countries; interesting both for the acute analyses of the process of cultural penetration under colonialism and neo-colonialism it produced, and for the very general rejection of the simple nationalist-populist response to it.

'As Mammeri Mouloud of Algeria put it, the intellectual of the Third World finds himself faced with the double necessity of assuming an inherited native culture and using an acquired, colonial culture. Neither can simply be put on like a ready-made suit. Traditional culture, the product of a cultural system which is already in part disrupted, cannot be the basis of the new culture, whatever elements may be preserved of it.

'Attempts to make it so either fail, as in sub-Saharan Africa, or produce the *espectáculos folklóricos* of the modern tourist trade, or the even more dangerous "accelerated indigenization of the violence and tribulations of other times" of which M. Depestre of Haiti spoke with comprehensible feeling.

'On the other hand, certain elements of traditional and popular culture – Dr Belail Abdel Aziz of Morocco suggested that the concept of community in the Maghreb might be one such – could be essential parts of any anti-capitalist society, or any society unwilling to subordinate itself entirely to the logic of technology.'

Also at the Congress is the renowned Mexican painter and muralist, the veteran Stalinist, David Alfaro Siqueiros, notorious for his part in a machine-gun attack on Trotsky's home in Coyoacán, Mexico in 1940. Siqueiros is greeted with cries of 'Murderer!' by young French delegates when they spot him outside the Havana Gallery of Modern Art. The young poetess Joyce Mansour then lands a kick on Siqueiros' backside, crying, 'That's from André Breton!'

Two young delegates, editors of the London-based *New Left Review*, Alexander Cockburn and Robin Blackburn, are confronted with a novel dilemma. Blackburn has written an ultra-left

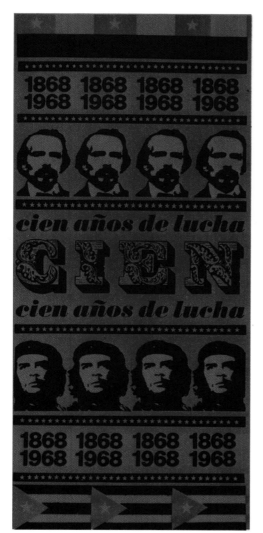

Cuba marks a century of struggle in 1968 by organizing a Cultural Congress in Havana.

Eartha Kitt takes the anti-war movement into the White House. She harangues a bewildered First Lady (centre) and Katherine Peden.

Trotskysant speech, but cannot deliver the diatribe himself. He has no idea that the lovely Cuban comrade he has seduced is the girlfriend of 'Baba Roja', the Cuban Chief of Police, not best known for his generosity of spirit. In Blackburn's improvised absence, Alexander Cockburn delivers the speech, his hands shaking as he realizes the depth of the anti-Stalinist rhetoric. Once finished, he flees the podium.

| 18th | Washington DC, USA | 'No wonder the kids rebel… |

Fearful of the rising tide of violent protest and anxious about the disillusioned and rebellious youth, Lady Bird Johnson, the wife of the President, hosts a Ladies' Lunch at the White House on the theme of 'What Citizens Can Do to Help Insure Safe Streets'.

The yellow and white dining room will be set with five tables, ten women at each. There will be bowls of spring flowers on every table, gold, green and ivory dinnerware, golden spoons, forks and knives, golden ashtrays, golden mint plates and a five-course lunch served from silver trays: crab-meat bisque, Breast of Chicken White House, fresh asparagus, garden salad, white wine, peppermint-candy ice cream with hot fudge sauce, cookies, mints and a demitasse.

In the spirit of the President's new civil rights initiative (currently bogged down in the House by Congressmen objecting to the bill on desegregated housing), black singer and recording star Eartha Kitt is included on the guest list.

Eartha was the daughter of poor sharecroppers, born in South Carolina to a world of Deep South rural poverty and murderous racism. As a teenager she had supported both herself and her aunt, working in a Harlem sweatshop stitching uniforms for the Second World War, before going on to build a career for herself as a slinky cool, multilingual cabaret star among the ultra-sophisticated audiences of Paris's Left Bank.

The singer has not lost touch with her people. Growing more and more impatient as she sits through the set-piece speeches lamenting the criminality of the youth and calling for more pay for police, Eartha stands up during the question-and-answer session.

'Many things are burning in this country,' she begins, and there is a stunned silence from the ladies present at the White House lunch, shocked to be hearing such a different point of view.

Emphasizing every word, Eartha continues: 'Young people and their parents are angry because they are being so highly taxed and there's a war going on, and Americans don't know why. The youth is not rebelling for no reason at all. They are rebelling against something and we can't camouflage what it is.

'Boys I know across the nation feel it doesn't pay to be a good guy any more. They figure that with a criminal record they don't have to go off to Vietnam.

'You're a mother, too, Mrs Johnson. I'm a mother and I know the feeling of having a baby come out of my gut. I have a baby and then you send him off to war. No wonder the kids rebel and take pot. You send the best of this country off to be shot and maimed – so they rebel. They rebel in the street. They will take pot and they will get high, because they are going to be snatched away from their mothers to be shot in Vietnam.'

USA Hell no! I ain't gonna go!

A serious blow to the machismo of the desk-bound Pentagon chiefs: Muhammad Ali, heavyweight boxing champion of the world and the strongest man in the US, is refusing to fight for them in Vietnam.

'I ain't got no quarrel with the Vietcong,' he tells the press.

The American establishment will never forgive the treachery of this uppity nigger.

On January 18 Muhammad Ali's appeal is thrown out of court.

World heavyweight boxing champion Muhammad Ali is barred from the ring and stripped of his title for refusing induction into the US armed forces.

18th–21st **Sasebo, Japan** The Student Samurai

Protests erupt in Japan against the imminent arrival of a 75,000-ton nuclear-powered American aircraft carrier, the USS *Enterprise*, on its way to Vietnam. Demonstrators besiege the US Embassy in Tokyo; students occupy the Japanese Foreign Ministry.

Forty-seven thousand protesters converge on Sasebo harbour, home to the massive US Navy base, where the *Enterprise* is due to dock. In addition to the island of Okinawa, the United States has 147 mainland bases in Japan, including harbours, air bases, supply depots, hospitals and rehabilitation centres: all are being mobilized for the war in Vietnam. Japanese industry has been turned into a massive supplier of equipment for the war: vehicles, ammunition, spare parts, napalm, phosphorus – even body bags for the corpses are stitched in the clothing factories of Japan.

The demonstrations at Sasebo are led by the ultra-militant Zengakuren student faction. They have good reason to protest. In 1941 their parents' generation was dragged into one unjust and murderous war, against their own interests; the young students are determined to make sure that it doesn't happen again. The Japanese know what it is to have American bombers in their skies; why should they side with the US war machine against the Vietnamese?

To have their country used as a major base for the war is both humiliating and dangerous: what if the hawks have their way and the conflict does go nuclear? What if China is dragged in? There is widespread anger at the humiliating terms of the Security Treaty signed with Washington in 1960 which has turned Japan into a virtual military fiefdom of the United States, and at Premier Sato's complete prostration before all the Americans' demands.

To cap it all, the *Enterprise* is powered by nuclear reactors and believed to be armed with nuclear warheads. Sasebo is in the Nagasaki prefecture, in the south-west of Japan. The Japanese government has been under heavy pressure from the US military for many years now to rid its people of their 'nuclear allergy', their total antagonism to all forms of nuclear war. Now the Pentagon has decided to embark on a homoeopathic solution, hoping that persistent small doses of the 'allergen' in the form of nuclear-powered submarines and warships will cure the Japanese.

Japanese demonstrators opposed to the presence of the USS *Enterprise*, on its way to the war in Vietnam, take to the water in small vessels as the aircraft carrier drops anchor.

The protesters are determined that it will not. The Zengakuren have come to Sasebo armed with ten-foot wooden staves, equipped with helmets, and with

Students surge through the streets of Tokyo in one of a series of demonstrations – one of which occupies the US Embassy – against the use of the city's harbour by the nuclear-powered *Enterprise*.

handkerchiefs across their faces to protect them from the gas. They converge on the narrow bridge that leads to the US naval base on the far side of the harbour, chanting and snake-dancing, their helmets glistening white in the pouring rain. Five thousand riot police confront them. They charge forward, armed with clubs, hoses and tear-gas.

Spurred on by the rhythmic whistles of their comrades, the Zengakuren fight to hold their ground but are beaten back. Those who are caught are clubbed senseless by the police. Altogether, there are 450 casualties. The police are ruthless in pursuit: wounded demonstrators trying to escape into the local hospital (from whose windows patients and hospital workers have been watching the confrontation) are chased and clubbed; tear-gas is thrown into the hospital building and the place is flooded by water-hoses. The patients' sympathy is overwhelmingly on the demonstrators' side. One student, wounded in the eye, is deluged with gifts of milk, fruit, toilet paper, even underwear, by the other patients on his ward.

The *Enterprise* docks in Sasebo harbour, a day later than planned. The huge grey hulk of the flat-top, powered by eight nuclear reactors, bristling with warheads, take-off point for up to a hundred fighter planes, dominates the whole harbour, a visible emblem of the subordination of Japan to America's military ambitions.

Makoto Oda, a member of the anti-war Beheiren Peace for Vietnam Committee, circles the aircraft carrier in a tiny dinghy, calling through a megaphone for the crew to desert. He promises them a safe haven: the Beheiren group is already sheltering a group of US Navy men who deserted the previous autumn.

A dozen taxis carrying sailors from the *Enterprise* to the Sasebo brothel district are halted by a crowd of thousands, banging on their roofs and windshields. Riot police have to be sent in to ensure that the sailors can complete the task of military penetration. There is another clash between police and demonstrators on the bridge leading to the base: 150 people are injured. All shore leave is cancelled. The US sailors are restive: they have been promised a good time.

The *Enterprise* leaves Sasebo four days earlier than originally planned. Crowds of protesters along the shoreline shake their fists at her as she steams off southwards, towards Vietnam.

22nd **Greece** Blood on the Acropolis

The long, dark nights of the year are darker and more soul-chilling still in the prisons of the military junta which has seized power in Greece.

At the end of the Second World War it had been the Greek left who stood poised to take power, having built up enormous popular prestige and support through their leadership of the Resistance during the Nazi occupation. But the Great Powers' agreement in Yalta in 1945 (which laid the basis for the division of Europe between the USA and the USSR for the whole of the Cold War period) had allocated Greece to the West. In their moment of need, Stalin abandoned the Greek communists and their allies to their fate, and the forces of the left were crushed first by British and then American arms in a bitter civil war (1946–9) which left hundreds of thousands dead and the country politically traumatized and economically wrecked. Greece was saved for the 'free world' – although not, as it was to prove, for Western-style democracy – and was integrated into NATO in 1952. The old right seemed firmly entrenched in power.

But by the mid-1960s a new spring seemed to be blossoming in Greece. Georgios Papandreou, himself a former anti-Nazi imprisoned by the Germans during the Second World War, united liberals and democratic forces in a new political party, the Centre Union, and swept to power in 1964, largely supported by the villagers who still made up fifty per cent of the Greek population. The Centre Union began a programme of mild reforms, including checks on the power of the police, and began to openly question whether Greece's total subservience to the United States' wishes was always in the interests of the Greek people. Meanwhile the left of the Centre Union, led by Papandreou's son, Andreas, was calling for more far-reaching reforms.

In 1965 Georgios Papandreou clashed with the King, formally the head of the Greek army, over the question of disciplining right-wing army officers. King Constantine dismissed him. This led to such a period of political instability that, by 1967, it was clear that fresh elections would have to be called – elections which only the Centre Union would win. It was to forestall the will of the people that a military junta, composed of the most virulently authoritarian colonels, seized power on April 21, 1967.

The Colonels combined their hatred of the liberals and the left with an abhorrence of sexual tolerance, a vicious religious obscurantism and a belief in the supremacy of physical force, especially torture, in imposing their views. Amnesty International detailed cases of booted interrogators jumping up and down on their victims' stomachs, tearing out fistfuls of their hair, pulling out their fingernails and toenails and administering a variety of electric shocks to the 2777 political prisoners being held in jail without trial.

The petty-bourgeois Colonels have resentments against the traditional right-wing establishment, too, which has kept officers' pay so low in the Greek Army. They also pick quarrels with the monarchy and the old Army and political elite. Nevertheless, Greek big business – the owners of shipping lines, oil refineries and the like – are soon hand in glove with the new junta, while the prisons fill up with all those who dare to stand up for cultural and political freedom. Writers, artists and musicians are well represented in these notorious cells. Mikis Theodorakis, composer of the soundtrack of *Zorba the Greek*, is one of many.

'I am proud to have done my duty as a citizen, politician and artist,' he announces on January 22, 1968, on the way to his appeal against imprisonment for having spoken out against the junta. 'I have always struggled for freedom and dedicated my life to my work as a composer. I should like to be the last political prisoner in this country.'

Thule, Greenland Radioactive Payload

A US B52 jet bomber carrying four hydrogen bombs crashes in Greenland. Local workers are drafted in to help servicemen shovel the radioactive snow into sacks, but no matter how deep they dig, the Geiger counter won't stop ticking ...

23rd | Hamburg, West Germany To Conform is Evil

Radical students in West Germany are fighting for the right to argue, for the right to question their professors at the end of lectures, the right to disagree. Living on the front line of the Cold War, they have begun to question both the myth and the reality of the 'free world' to which they are supposed to belong. Protests over student living conditions, tram fares and hostel regulations have been met with arrests and police violence, leading to wider protests. In June 1967 police in West Berlin opened fire on a demonstration against a visit by the Shah of Iran, killing a young student called Benno Ohnesorg.

It is the authorities' indifference to Ohnesorg's senseless death, as much as the police's behaviour, that has spurred the student movement on to a much greater and more far-reaching radicalism, and a much more deeply felt rejection of all the values of the West German state and the world system of which it is such a cornerstone.

The intellectual left in the Marxist study groups of the SDS (Socialistische Deutsche Studentbund) has been developing a thoroughgoing critique of the whole system, exploring psychosexual, social and cultural aspects of the repressive society as much as political and economic ones.

Theology students, in the land of Luther, are arguing for their right to question the pastors' sermons, especially when these involve support for what many students believe to be an unjust social system and an immoral war. Rudi Dutschke has been one of the theology students in West Berlin trying to turn the churches into discussion forums for ideas about morality and the State. On January 23 the right-wing pastor of the Church of St Michael in Hamburg, Dr Helmuth Thielicke, calls in West German troops to clear his church of students who wish to question the ideas in his sermon. The students have been distributing leaflets with their own version of the Lord's Prayer:

> Our Capital, which art in the West, amortized be Thy investments,
> Thy profits come, Thy interest rates increase,
> In Wall Street as they do in Europe.
> Give us this day our daily turnover,
> And extend to us our credits, as we extend them to our creditors.
> Lead us not into bankruptcy, but deliver us from the trades unions,
> For Thine is half the world, the power and the riches,
> For the last two hundred years.
> Mammon.

North Korea War Games

The key US intelligence-gathering ship USS *Pueblo* is captured by North Korean naval units and escorted under guard into Wonsan harbour after she is discovered operating deep inside North Korean waters.

This is a full-blown crisis for Washington: the *Pueblo* is the only ship equipped to intercept and decipher all US naval codes; its radio transmitters are primed to communicate with US naval units all round the world.

The US Administration comes under heavy fire from the Senate Foreign Relations Committee for permitting the *Pueblo* to operate illegally in North

Arthur Goldberg, US Ambassador to the United Nations, lies to the UN that the *Pueblo* was seized outside North Korean waters.

Korean waters at a time of such high tension. Delighted, the Soviet Foreign Minister, Andrei Kosygin, is piling on the agony by refusing to use his good offices in Pyongyang. The *Pueblo* was, after all, in clear breach of international law.

The USS *Enterprise* is turned around, halfway to Vietnam, and sent steaming north again to the Straits of Korea.

30th-31st Saigon, South Vietnam The Tết Offensive

Night in the South Vietnamese capital. From the roof bar of the Caravelle Hotel, American correspondents can look out across the city that was once the Pearl of the Orient, the Paris of the East, lined with long, shady avenues, pagodas and parks. Saigon, built for 350,000 people, has swollen to three million over the past three years. It is crowded with refugees from burnt-out villages, living in shacks of tin and cardboard, getting by on the street.

The air is dense with the smell of cheap petrol and rotting sewage, the smoke from Vietnamese cooking fires and the sharp, spicy scent of food. It is Tết, the national New Year holiday, celebrated with firecrackers, gifts and flowers. Among the crowded shacks and alleyways, the city is tense with a million hatreds. Beneath the advertising hoardings and the neon lights lies the ever-present menace of war.

January 1968

Left: American Military Policemen examine a Vietcong fighter killed in the surprise attack on the US Embassy in Saigon on January 31. Below: General Westmoreland holds a press conference the day after losing control of the US Embassy.

Suddenly a barrage of gunfire bursts out. Another follows soon afterwards. Then there is a third.

From the South Vietnamese Army barracks, the Presidential Palace, the government radio building, from police stations and arms depots, from the crowded Cholon district and the suburb of Hanh Xanh, the city erupts with sniper fire and machine-guns, artillery and exploding mortar shells.

It is the start of the Tết offensive.

Across a front over 600 miles long, the National Liberation Front launch their assault on 140 towns and cities, from the Seventeenth Parallel in the north all the way down to the Ca Mau peninsula in the extreme south. They attack South Vietnamese Army bases, airfields, radio stations, prisons, naval headquarters and administrative centres.

On the morning of January 31 the world awakes to find the red, blue and yellow flag of the National Liberation Front flying all over the country. The ancient citadel of Hué is taken and a daring team of NLF guerrillas temporarily captures the US Embassy compound in Saigon. The Stars and Stripes is hauled down and, for one glorious hour, the NLF colours fly over the Embassy itself.

One thing is now certain. The United States will never win this war. America understand this and the number of anti-war protesters trebles overnight. General Westmoreland is seen on television throughout the world. The bravado is gone. He is a broken man.

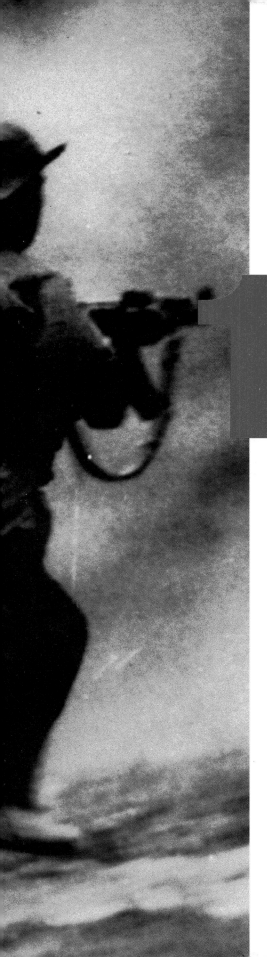

1968
February

'We fight because
we are oppressed,
because we are
exploited…'

Troops of the Vietnamese National Liberation Front go into battle.

Bertolt Brecht wrote in his poem 'In Praise of Doubt', 'The most beautiful of all doubts is when the downtrodden and despondent raise their heads and stop believing in the strength of their oppressors.' This is what is happening in Vietnam. The Têt offensive, unleashed at the end of January, opens the most decisive month's fighting of the Vietnam war: the David of the NLF launches an attack on the Goliath of the US forces that is virtually unparalleled in military history. The home-trained guerrillas and their supporters in the towns attack US and South Vietnamese government bases and administrative centres in over 140 towns, from the Seventeenth Parallel in the north to the Ca Mau peninsula in the extreme south. The historic citadel of Hué is in NLF hands and, for a few glorious hours, their flag flies over the US Embassy compound in Saigon.

The impact of the Vietnamese offensive is global. A wave of joy and energy rebounds around the world and millions more are suddenly, exhilaratingly, ceasing to believe in the strength of their oppressors. In cities everywhere, people are coming out on to the streets, waving NLF flags: 'We stand with them'. FRELIMO guerrillas fighting the Portuguese colonial army in Mozambique cheer as they hear the news over the radio at their jungle base. There is a sense of 'If they can do it, so can we!' In Lisbon, where a senile fascism in the shape of the NATO-backed Salazar dictatorship is still on full display, police with sub-machine-guns are sent to break up a pro-NLF demonstration marching on the US Embassy. Together with the stirring words of Che Guevara come Lenin's: 'The main enemy is at home.' In Pakistan, the popular poet Habib Jalib warns the pro-US military dictator Field Marshal Ayub Khan: 'The cloud of dynamite that covers Vietnam is moving your way.' In Paris, students rename the Left Bank heartland 'the Heroic Vietnam Quarter'. The NLF flag flies over the city's Sorbonne Library.

In the February 23, 1968 edition of the *Los Angeles Times*, Conrad, the influential daily's cartoonist, mocks the attachment of the Pentagon and the White House to the policy of 'escalation' in the Vietnam conflict.

February 1968

In West Berlin, the SDS (Socialistische Deutsche Studentbund, or German Socialist Student Federation) put out a call for an International Congress on Vietnam. Responses come flooding in from the United States, Europe and 'Third World' countries, including some struggling against dictatorships. For the young radicals who assemble in the third week of February in the huge, banner-draped hall of Berlin's Free University, there is an immediate sense of connection and discovery: a sense that the germ of a new International already exist here in this hall, where people laugh and talk with joy and recognition, greeting with ever-growing applause each fresh victory of the Têt offensive. These are the young men and women whose ideas, hope and optimism will be at the forefront of the struggles to come.

At the end of the Congress, some twenty thousand march with steaming breath through the cold streets of West Berlin, carrying portraits of Che Guevara and Rosa Luxemburg as their flags. Che, the Argentinian medical student who became a revolutionary in Guatemala, overthrew the old Cuban dictatorship, fought in Africa and gave his life in Bolivia for the liberation of the oppressed; and Rosa, the lame, warm-hearted, Polish-Jewish internationalist who was murdered in Berlin in 1919 for her fight against German capitalism. The grey walls of Berlin resound to the chants of a new generation.

Some 20,000 demonstrators chanting 'Ho, Ho, Ho Chi Minh' march in West Berlin to express their solidarity with the Vietnamese resistance.

For the US establishment, the shock of the Têt offensive comes as a political defeat of epic proportions. For three years they have been telling both the American people and their allies abroad – the NATO governments in Europe and numerous US-backed dictatorships in the Middle East, Asia and Latin America – that they were on the verge of a big victory in Vietnam. The Têt offensive has confounded their whole line.

The chiefs in the Pentagon, both misinformed and misinformers, are devastated. All their certainties are being destroyed by the determination of some impoverished, ill-equipped peasants in a tiny country, far away. In its entire history the United States of America has never suffered a military defeat before. The sane elements in the American establishment will now begin to speak up against the war in Vietnam and call for an immediate, negotiated withdrawal. They know that they cannot win; what must be avoided now is the unthinkable disaster of being publicly seen to lose. Next month General Westmoreland will be sacked, LBJ will announce that he won't be running for a second term and 'talks about talks' will begin.

1st Saigon, South Vietnam The Beginning of the End

The Têt offensive confounds General Westmoreland's prognosis of imminent victory. His 'light at the end of the tunnel' has turned out to be the flares of the advancing battalions of the South Vietnamese National Liberation Front.

Fighting is still raging in Saigon as the Americans shell and bomb NLF-held areas. Falling flares turn day into night. The Vietnamese are now fleeing the capital with goods piled high on their bicycles, as they have fled countless villages over the past three years. Others plead with US officers to stop the blitz, but the panic bombing continues. Whole streets of homes, shops and warehouses are being destroyed, often simply to crush a mere handful of NLF snipers.

The forces actually deployed by the Vietnamese during the Têt offensive are staggeringly few: the US Embassy compound, ringed with concrete and thought to be impregnable, was taken by a band of twenty guerrillas. It is only recaptured after heavy strafing by American helicopters.

Part of the guerrilla group that attempted the assault on the marble Presidential Palace has retreated to a half-built hotel and keeps government and US troops at bay for three days. The siege ends when a seventeen-year-old girl in black pantaloons leads out a group of nine guerrillas, their hands above their heads. They will all be executed without mercy.

US MPs take an NLF guerrilla into custody after the January 31 assault on the US Embassy.

In Saigon's working-class Cholon district, an area that has a large Chinese population, the NLF

A B-52 Strato-Fortress bomber from the USAF base in Guam carpet-bombs Vietnam. It didn't work.

barricades have gone up against the government forces. Police and military precincts in the area are island fortresses, besieged from the surrounding streets by a sea of the largely NLF-supporting population. It will be weeks before US bombs and napalm make the district 'safe' again. And all this in the capital city of South Vietnam, into which the United States has poured money for over a decade.

8th Ben-Tre, South Vietnam 'The only way to save Ben-Tre is to destroy it'

The destruction wrought by the US and South Vietnamese government counter-attacks far outweighs that caused by the NLF artillery during the Têt offensive.

Ben-Tre, a peaceful little town of 35,000 souls nestling in the Mekong Delta, has been held by a force of some 2,500 NLF fighters since the night of the Têt. Over half of the South Vietnamese government garrison had melted away before the attack, and the NLF had seized the town in a matter of hours. Now the remaining government forces are pinned down in their barracks and the US advisory compound is under attack.

A US officer makes the immortal statement: 'The only way to save Ben-Tre is to destroy it.'

For its population there is no choice. Freedom and Democracy are coming their way, courtesy the US Air Force. The destruction of Ben-Tre takes fifty hours of air and ground attack, using 500lb bombs, napalm, rockets, various anti-personnel bombs and 105mm and 155mm mortars.

Bombers drop burning napalm on two miles of residential districts; the straw-thatched houses are reduced to cinders. Helicopters strafe the market-place in the

The Resistance in Vietnam

Le Vinh, a small, slight, black-haired man in his forties, is a regimental Political Officer with the National Liberation Front. His face is deeply tanned from years of living in the open.

Ten years earlier he was making his living running a small haberdashery shop in Saigon, when he heard by chance that the police of the US puppet, Ngo Dinh Diem, had him on their list of suspects for some very minor part he had played in the anti-French resistance during the fifties. Le Vinh managed to slip away just hours before the police raided his shop. He made his way north-west, to the Tay Ninh forests, and met up with the guerrillas there.

Now, a decade later, the NLF has built up substantial bases in the forests, equipped in part by material smuggled in from the north along the perilous Ho Chi Minh Trail. Even more valuable is their network of contacts and secret supporters in the towns and villages, even in the South Vietnamese Army bases. Vietnamese strategy, too, is split: the militarists, and their Chinese backers, favour an increase in military hardware, enlarging the Trail so that it is capable of carrying tanks and armoured vehicles.

General Giap – the victor of Dien Bien Phu, a name which in the late sixties still sends a shiver down the collective spine of the French Army – and his supporters insist that the struggle must be political as well as military: the war can only be won by involving the people in an uprising against the American aggressors and their 'puppet regime' in Saigon, together with an armed assault by the guerrilla forces. For the moment, the 'politico-militarists' seem to be winning.

Le Vinh tells the Australian war correspondent Wilfred Burchett how recruits come to the guerrilla army: some from the villages that the NLF has taken; some as refugees, escaping to the forest from the Americans' 'strategic hamlets'; while some have deserted from the official South Vietnamese Army, bringing their weapons with them.

There are middle-class boys and girls, students from Hué and other towns, small shopkeepers, artisans, peasants whose ancestral villages have been destroyed, their houses flattened, their families killed, their crops burnt, their animals driven away. Le Vinh

A young woman fighter of the National Liberation Front.

is in charge of their education. All new recruits have fifteen days' training before they are given a gun, and the first five days are spent in political discussions and question-and-answer sessions.

'Why are we fighting? And for whom? These are the first two questions that we need to lead the new recruits to find answers to.

'Why do we fight? We fight because we are oppressed, because we are exploited, both by the foreign invaders and by the Saigon oppressors, by the feudal powers. Everyone who comes to us has some experience of that, however trivial. It is the accumulation of so many trivial-seeming cases that begins to make the pattern.

'Before, cases where fathers or brothers were arrested, tortured or killed by the Diem police, or by the foreign invaders, were viewed as a natural calamity, an act of God – and virtually no family has been spared such oppression. Now they are seen in the context of their side against ours.

'The peasants all know the stories of their forefathers who fought and won against the foreign invaders – from legends and poetry, from the temples to bygone heroes, from wandering storytellers and theatre groups. It is not difficult for them to grasp that they are worthy defenders of the traditions of their ancestors.

'The second point: for whom are we fighting? Who will benefit from the final victory? Above all, the peasants and the workers, the poor and the oppressed. The new recruits soon begin to speak up about their own experiences, at the hands of the landlords or the rent or tax collectors. The idea that it is the poor and exploited who should have the worthiest place in society often comes as a great revelation. The poor soon begin to speak up with pride. Previously, they were ashamed of being poor; they felt it something of a crime and did their best to disguise the fact.

'One recruit recalled how, when he went to Saigon in the old days, he used to grind his hands with pumice stone to remove as many calluses as possible, so that the people with whom he might have to shake hands would not guess at his poverty.

'Why, and for whom? But to these two points it is necessary to add a third one: victory is certain.

'We will win.'

The NLF flag flies over the Citadel in Hué as a thousand resistance fighters defend Vietnam's former imperial capital against an onslaught by US Marines.

centre of the town, destroying the walls and reducing the roofs to heaps of scrap iron. The NLF-controlled radio station is flattened by US bombs. The poor neighbourhoods in the north and west of the town are bombarded by constant artillery, while Commander Chester Brown flies overhead in a small plane, directing the fire. Thousands of families are burnt to death or buried in the ruins of their homes. Thousands of others die from the bombs as they attempt to flee the city. The only way to stop recruits for the NLF is to kill the children.

Hué, South Vietnam The Citadel is Taken

The old imperial city of Hué, 300 miles north of Saigon, was built centuries earlier for the first emperor of a united Vietnam. It was laid out in accordance with the complex demands of Chinese geomancy: elaborately carved and gilded palaces and pagodas are set within a formal garden, a representation of the world in microcosm. A great wall surrounds it, and the whole imperial city itself is set within a still larger citadel, whose walls are twenty feet high and fourteen thick.

Many of the country's most gifted minds have studied beneath the ancient trees of Hué's university. General Vo Nguyen Giap was a student there. North Vietnamese Prime Minister Pham van Dong was the son of an Imperial Court mandarin. Ho Chi Minh's father was a secretary to the Imperial Palace Ministry of Rites for a time, and Ho himself was among the students just before the First World War.

Now the NLF flag flies over the citadel. The attacking US forces have been shelling it incessantly for over a week through thick cloud and driving rain, but they are making little progress. The sight of the blue and red flag with its yellow star seems to drive them crazy. Deputations from the citizens of Hué begging them to spare the old shrines are brushed aside: it may be necessary to destroy the imperial citadel to save Vietnam from communism.

As soon as the clouds lift they will bring in planes to drop napalm and nausea gas over the citadel. The following week US troops will launch a ground assault supported by armed helicopters, dive bombers and planes spreading flaming napalm. Huge orange fireballs will roll above the ancient walls.

Finally the flag comes down. The trees are charred and blasted, most of the buildings are blackened timber and there is smashed porcelain everywhere, the wreckage of the old vases known to ceramists as Hué blue. The Vietnamese people picking among the mud-splattered ruins are sullen and angry. Why? Why destroy the whole citadel for a few hundred liberation fighters? Why not starve them out?

Khe Sanh, South Vietnam Besieged and Isolated

Meanwhile the isolated US base at Khe Sanh, up by the border, is still besieged by the forces of the NLF and North Vietnam. US troops are dug into bunkers, dodging sniper and artillery fire to run from one manhole to another while the NLF tunnels grow even closer. Khe Sanh marks the ultimate defeat of General Westmoreland's Search and Destroy policy. Instead of isolating the enemy forces and cutting them off from the rear, the US Army is itself surrounded and cut off from its supply lines.

Mozambique, Berlin, Paris, Rome Comrades

The daring, heroism and sheer chutzpah of the NLF guerrillas has an electrifying effect as images of the Tét offensive flash around the world. Many are laughing with joy at the sight of the NLF flag on the US Embassy in Saigon.

FRELIMO guerrillas fighting the Portuguese colonial army in Mozambique cheer as they hear the news from Khe Sanh over the radio at their jungle base.

There are huge demonstrations in Berlin, Paris and Rome.

The German SDS put out a call for an International Congress on Vietnam later in the month.

In Paris police attack pro-NLF demonstrators in the Latin Quarter, using riot shields and long wooden batons. A tear-gas grenade causes panic as it explodes inside the Deux Magots café. A young teacher coming out of a cinema is taken for an Algerian demonstrator by the police and beaten unconscious before being taken to the police station.

Chicago, USA Bobby Kennedy for President

Within the United States, the Tét offensive provokes a major crisis. The doves behind him, New York Senator Bobby Kennedy launches a powerful attack on LBJ's policies and the conduct of the war, asking why the Vietnamese people have so significantly failed to defend either their towns or their notoriously unpopular government against the NLF.

'People will not fight to line the pockets of generals or swell the bank accounts of the wealthy. They are far more likely to close their eyes and shut their doors in the face of their government – as they did last week.

'More than any election, that single fact reveals the truth. We have an ally in name only. We support a government without support. Without the efforts of Americans that government would not last a day.

'It is said the Vietcong will not be able to hold the cities. This is probably true. But they have demonstrated despite all our reports of progress, of government strength and enemy weakness, that half a million American soldiers with 700,000 Vietnamese allies, with total command of the air, total command of the sea, backed by huge resources and the most modern weapons, are unable to secure a single city from the attacks of the enemy.

'It is time to tell the truth about Vietnam. A military victory is not within our grasp. A political compromise is not just the best path but the only path to peace.'

Orangeburg, South Carolina, USA Farewell to Non-violence

Three black students are killed and nearly fifty others wounded by white police and National Guardsmen at South Carolina State College after four days of demonstrations outside a whites-only bowling alley. Most students are shot in the back while lying on the ground or seeking cover.

The police and Governor Robert McNair blame the students for the shooting, and more than thirty black youths are arrested.

This same month, novelist James Baldwin writes:

US Highway Patrolmen stand over two men injured when police and National Guardsmen charged firebomb-throwing students during a third night of rioting at South Carolina State College.

'I remember standing on a street corner in Selma, Alabama, early in the Sixties, during a voter registration drive. The blacks lined up before the court-house, under the American flag; the sheriff and his men, with their helmets and guns and clubs and cattle-prods; a mob of idle white men standing on the corner. The sheriff raised his club and he and his two deputies beat two black boys to the ground. Never will I forget the surge in the mob: authority had given them their signal.

'It was a non-violent black student who told Bobby Kennedy a few years ago that he didn't know how much longer he could remain non-violent: didn't know how much longer he could take the beatings, the bombings, the terror. He said he would never take up arms in defence of America – never, never, never. If he ever picked up a gun, it would be for every different reasons...

'That boy has grown up, as have so many like him – we will not mention those irreparably ruined, or dead; and I really wonder what white America expected to happen. Did they really suppose that 15-year-old black boys would remain 15 forever? Did they really suppose that the tremendous energy and the incredible courage that went into those sit-ins, wade-ins, swim-ins, picketlines, marches was incapable of transforming itself into an overt attack on the status quo? I remember that same day in Selma watching the line of black would-be voters walk away from the court-house which they had not been allowed to enter. And, I thought, the day is coming when they will not line up any more.

'Let us attempt to face the fact that we *are* a racist society, racist to the very marrow, and we are fighting a racist war. No black man in chains in his own country, and watching the many deaths occurring around him every day, believes for the moment that America cares anything at all about the freedom of Asia. My own condition, as a black man in America, tells me what Americans really feel and really want, and tells me who they really are. And, therefore, every bombed village is my home town.'

11th Chicago, USA Daley's Gangsters

Chicago is chosen over Miami as the site of this summer's Democratic Party Convention after the White House decides that the Chicago Police Department is better equipped to suppress a riot than its Miami counterpart.

No one doubts that there will be trouble. The black community in Chicago is bitter about slum housing conditions and zero prospects in education and employment. Black Civil Rights leader Martin Luther King has already called for demonstrations against the Democratic Party over its Vietnam policy and its failure to respond to urban poverty. Students groups, anti-war protesters and the New Left are recruiting for a mass march on the Convention and Black Power leaders are planning their own protest.

For Mayor Daley's Chicago riot police, drills with rifles, tear-gas and shotguns are now a standard part of police training. All the 12,000 policemen assigned to the Convention will be issued with siphons of Mace nerve gas. A liaison system has already been set up between the police, the army, the National Guard, the State police, the FBI and the secret service.

Alastair Cooke writes in the *Guardian*:

'The plan is that the President himself will be whipped in and out in a helicopter,

and his brief presence at the Convention will receive an armourplate protection never before given to the leaders of a democratic nation. It will be quite a spectacle for the "free peoples" of the west to watch by satellite and ponder at leisure.' The war is coming home.

A Question of Definition
Is a democracy
in which one may not say
that it is not
a real democracy
really
a real democracy?
Erich Fried

13th Bolivia Wedding Bells

Régis Debray, a French left-wing intellectual and author of *Revolution in the Revolution*, was arrested by the Bolivian Army after a meeting with Che Guevara's guerrilla band in 1967. He has been kept in solitary confinement in the small oil town of Camiri. An international campaign demands his release and succeeds in preventing the Bolivians from killing him. To show their humanity, the Bolivian military junta permit him to marry his Venezuelan lover, Elizabeth Burgos. They are joined in wedlock in Camiri prison.

14th London, UK Counter-culture

Joseph Berke, a twenty-nine-year-old American poet and psychiatrist, announces the opening of the Anti-University in London, 'to counter the intellectual bankruptcy and spiritual emptiness of the educational establishment'.

Cornelius Cardew will be lecturing on experimental music, R.D. Laing on Psychology and Religion, Allen Krebs on Sociology and the World Revolution, Obi Egbuna on Black Power and Barry Flanagan on Space. Charles Marowitz, Jim Haynes, David Mercer, Asa Benveniste and Juliet Mitchell are also on the faculty.

Berke claims: 'The antiuniversity is as much part of the counter-culture as hippy communes or underground newspapers. All of them – antihospitals, antiuniversities, antifamilies, antitheatres, antistates, are form of a cultural guerrilla warfare. We have to step out of Structure A in order to be able to see it. But one can't step out if there's nowhere to step to.'

Despite repeated requests, the Anti-University refuses to allow 'The Art of the Higher Bullshit' to be taught as a formal discipline.

15th Paris, France The Stars are Marching in the Streets

Police clash with demonstrators, including Jean-Luc Godard, Simone Signoret, Marlene Dietrich, Luis Buñuel and Jeanne Moreau, who are marching with banners flying to the Cinémathèque Française. They are angered by the Ministry of Culture's decision to sack the Cinémathèque's founder and director, Henri Langlois.

It is a protest against the high-handed and coldly authoritarian style of Gaullist rule. The bureaucrats have no idea of the value and richness of Langlois' obsessions. As a young journalist in Paris in the thirties he had developed a passion for the old silent films just at the time when they were considered only good for being turned into nail varnish. He began to give his first screening in a thirty-seat cinema club in St Germain-des-Prés in 1934.

During the Nazi occupation he had to hide films from the Germans, who wanted to use them for the manufacture of explosives. His driving idea was to preserve everything that looked like a film. 'How are we to know what will be a classic? We are not God, we cannot play at being infallible.'

One result was the amassing of a vast collection of American 'B' movies, thrillers and *films noirs* that, without Langlois, would certainly have disappeared: they have an enormous impact on the new generation of French directors of the *nouvelle vague*, who owe so much of their film education to Langlois' Cinémathèque. Now Godard, Truffaut, Chabrol, Demy and Varda are joined by an older generation: Bresson, Chaplin, Fuller, Kazan, Losey, Minnelli, Reisz, Clair, Renoir, Rossellini, Welles – all rally to defend the cause of imagination against the dead hand of bureaucracy. Langlois will be reinstated amid much celebration, after the glorious events of May 1968.

17-18th West Berlin, West Germany Class of '68

The International Congress on Vietnam called by the SDS opens at the Free University in West Berlin. The political situation is highly fraught: tensions have been running high between the left-wing students and the authoritarian city authorities. The demonstration that the SDS has called for the next day has been banned; the SDS are appealing against the injunction.

The atmosphere at the Congress is electric: the hall is packed for a non-stop session lasting twelve hours, with an overflow of thousands in the huge portico of the Polytechnical Institute and two further halls. Some 10,000 militants attend, with contingents from France, Germany, Italy, Greece, Norway, Denmark, Austria, Canada, the UK and the USA. The central hall is dominated by a huge NLF banner and Che Guevara's slogan 'THE DUTY OF A REVOLUTIONARY IS TO MAKE A REVOLUTION.'

What is Che's appeal to the class of '68?

He represented a rejection of rotten compromises and Cold War diplomacy. He put his theory into practice and fell in a brave, if quixotic, attempt to come to the aid of the Vietnamese people. He became a symbol of the purest form of internationalism, recognizing no frontiers. His actions represented an uncompromising and absolute rejection of the system. His image became a flag of students in Europe and *campesinos* throughout his own continent, to be defended against all enemies.

The speeches are urgent, stirring and militantly internationalist, throwing down the walls of the nation-state to reveal an innately interconnected world. Each speech is hotly debated and ruthlessly questioned from the floor. Kurt Steinhaus speaks from the SDS, Tariq Ali is from the Vietnam Solidarity Campaign, Robin Blackburn from *New Left Review*, Jeannette Habel from the French Jeunesse Communiste Révolutionnaire; also to speak are Gaston Salvatore, a Chilean nephew of Salvador

Allende studying in Berlin, the playwright Peter Weiss, the poet Erich Fried, Iranian revolutionary Bahman Nirumand, Rostango from Italy and Alain Krivine from France.

Ernest Mandel, Marxist economist and Trotskyist, puts the Vietnam War in a global perspective, assuring the Congress that the United States is absolutely certain to be defeated.

Rudi Dutschke is in his early thirties, the oldest of the German student leaders. He is of medium height, with an angular face, long hair and a gentle smile. He always smiles with his eyes. He is a powerful orator, but his audience is only too aware of its history. Dutschke's orations are spellbinding efforts but are rarely greeted with thunderous applause. Memories of Hitler's demagogy have made the radical students wary of all orators. A comrade advises Dutschke to moderate his style. These students are the children of parents who served the Third Reich. They refuse to forget the crimes.

Dutschke links the struggle in Vietnam to the battles against class rules in Europe. He talks of extending the student movement by a 'long march through institutions', gaining experience on every front: education, computers, mass media, the organization of production, while simultaneously preserving one's own political consciousness.

Top: Rudi Dutschke at an international anti-Vietnam War demonstration in West Berlin. Above: Two US citizens burn their draft cards.

'The aim of the long march will be to built counter-institutions, liberated zones in bourgeois society, which will be the equivalent of the areas freed by Mao's partisans in China during the Long March of the Chinese communists.'

Two black American Vietnam veterans mount the platform, giving the clenched-first salute. They describe the war as they have known it and tell how the black soldiers are being used as cannon fodder. Then they link arms and begin to chant:

> I ain't gonna go to Vietnam
> Cos Vietnam is where I am
> Hell no! I ain't gonna go!
> Hell no! I ain't gonna go!

While Erich Fried is speaking, the news comes through that the injunction against the next day's demonstration has been overthrown on appeal. There is little doubt that the judge has received reports of the mood of the Congress – and its size. One condition remains: the marchers will be banned from approaching the area of the US Army garrison.

Dutschke seizes the microphone: 'Comrades, this last restriction is the one we must try to overthrow. We must try to speak to the soldiers. If the enemy fixes the rules of the game, and we accept them, we have lost already – as Marcuse says. It means we play by *their* rules.'

The Congress is divided. The Berlin riot police are well known. Neubauer, their political boss, has told their chief: 'It doesn't matter if a few people are killed, a thousand heads must be bloodied.'

Erich Fried, who, as a teenager, had opposed the Nazis on the streets of his native Vienna before being forced to flee abroad for his life, quickly scribbles a note and hands it down the platform to Dutschke.

Dutschke pauses, reads the message to himself, then turns to the Congress and reads it out aloud.

'"Our victory lies in the fact that we got the demo. No provocations, please! I have spoken and saved my soul. Fried."

'Comrades, I was wrong,' Dutschke continues. 'This *is* our victory.'

The crowd that gathers on the Kurfürstendamm the next morning is 20,000 strong, with thousands of red flags and portraits of Karl Liebknecht, Rosa Luxemburg, Lenin, Ho Chi Minh and Che Guevara. Since the previous day dozens of coachloads of demonstrators have been converging from all over West Germany for the banned demonstration. The city authorities have forbidden the use of schools and other official buildings, but an impromptu solidarity throughout the city has found food and lodging for them all.

On this winter's morning in West Berlin there is a sense of breaking the ice that has frozen over Europe's history. The marchers sing and shout their way triumphantly through the streets, chanting as they go: 'HO, HO, HO CHI MINH!', 'CHE, CHE, CHE GUEVARA!' *'FNL vaincra!'* all the way to the rally outside the Opera House, to the spot where Benno Ohnesorg was killed by a policeman's bullet while demonstrating against the Shah of Iran's visit the previous summer. The march then pauses near the Berlin Wall. More speeches to people on the other side to make common cause. It is difficult to gauge who is more hostile to the marchers: the bureaucrats in the East or the NATO politicians in Bonn.

Mao Zedong, the 'Great Helmsman' of China's 'Cultural Revolution'.

18th Rishikesh, India High as a Kite

Apparently unconcerned by the state of the world, the Beatles fly to India to start a meditation course at the Maharishi Mahesh Yogi's retreat in the Himalayan foothills. Here they can literally stay as high as kites.

23rd Czechoslovakia Stalinism Called to Account

Ivan Klima, Antonin Liehm and Ludwik Vaculik are reinstated as editors of the Writers' Union newspaper, *Literarni Listy*, after a tough struggle on the Central Committee. They had been expelled by Novotny the previous autumn.

There are calls in the Czech press for a full calling to account of the postwar Stalinist era. One paper publishes a list of government ministers who played a role in sending oppositions to prison or to execution, and a list of their innocent victims.

Meanwhile Novotny is trying to drum up support among local party leaders in the factories, representing himself as the workers' champion against the intellectuals and white-collar reformers. Pressure has been mounting for Novotny to resign as President as well as General Secretary.

25th | West Germany Fighting Collective Amnesia

There are widespread calls for the Christian Democrat President of West Germany, Dr Heinrich Lübke, to resign following fresh revelations in *Stern* magazine that the architect's signature on plans for a Nazi concentration camp is his. He appears on TV to refute the allegations but fails to deny that he was the signatory. 'Naturally, after a quarter of a century, I cannot remember every paper I signed…' he says.

It is against the collective amnesia contracted by Lübke's generation with the blessing of NATO that the students of the SDS will fight. They are ashamed of what their fathers and mothers did during the Third Reich. Their anger, like that of their counterparts in Japan and Italy, will stray into acts of violence against oppression and new forms of authoritarianism.

Lübke will resign early in 1969.

28th | Madrid, Spain Deaf Ears

Franco's police temporarily withdraw from Madrid University, which they have been occupying after student protests against the fascist regime during the previous month. When asked if their spell in the University has taught them anything, the Chief of Police blocks his ears.

It is over thirty years since the Generalissimo broadcast his declaration of war against the democratically elected government of the new Spanish Republic and marched on Madrid. It took three years of bloody civil war and massive military aid from Hitler and Mussolini before the popular forces could be crushed, and mass executions of oppositionists by the Spanish military continued for several years.

Franco is old now, sick and hated. The whole country is waiting for the old man to die – some with a burning impatience for change, others with a mounting terror at what change may bring. For them, the future is a Pandora's box out of which a whole series of spectres arise, holding exaggerated terrors for an administration used to the comfort of Falangist repression, bolstered by the mystique of the fatherland and the stranglehold of the Church.

The students who have grown up under this regime sense the loosening grip as sections within the *franquista* elite – Army, Church, Falangist apparatus; the banking world of Madrid; Catalan big business; the 200 families who control everything – begin to jostle with each other for their place in the post-Franco world. The students have known no other opposition to the regime than that provided by the left. They are their parents' children. Their rebellion against the anachronistic, underfunded, overcrowded Spanish universities often wins their professors' support. In Catalonia and the Basque country, this is buttressed by regional feelings and the population's general hostility to Madrid centralism. At this stage the question of a popular explosion after Franco's death cannot be ruled out.

Meanwhile, the thin-lipped butcher continues to sit and smile, while all around him the whispers grow. He is thinking of appointing Juan Carlos, the son of the nominal pretender to the Spanish throne, as his successor when he goes.

1968
March

'The Cossacks
are here!'

Grosvenor Square: Hostility to the US war in Vietnam erupts in Britain.

In March the fever hits Poland. The immediate cause of the unrest that sweeps through the country this month is the banning of a new production of Adam Mickiewicz's classic nineteenth-century play *Dziady*. Yes, a play. The role of culture in helping to preserve and encourage dissent has been a hallmark of the former Soviet Union and its satrapies in Eastern Europe. When Osip Mandelstam died in a Stalinist concentration camp, one of his contemporaries remarked that the regime really appreciated poetry. It understood its power, and for that reason it executed recalcitrant poets. Vice paying homage to virtue.

With virtually all political dissent banned during the Stalin era, culture became the only outlet for social expression. The classics found huge readerships. Theatres and concert halls were packed. Whereas most of the contemporary products of the State Publishing Houses spoke in the dull, worthy tones of official literature everywhere, readings of Dostoyevsky, Tolstoy, Pushkin, etc. could be used to encourage and preserve a critical, anti-authoritarian spirit throughout the region. The theatre, above all, was a place where people could truly experience their solidarity with their fellow-citizens as entire audiences erupted into applause over the pointed delivery of particularly appropriate lines from Shakespeare or Sophocles, Molière or Aeschylus.

With the cultural thaw that was Krushchev's main legacy to the region came a new renaissance of the East European cinema. Mainly in black and white, the 'new wave' films have a visual freshness and unstrained clarity that feels subversive while still retaining links with the pre-Nazi cinema of the twenties and thirties. They are as sensitive to the play of shadows as they are to the emotions of their characters – 'ordinary people', for the most part: history is seen through the eyes of typists and railway clerks.

Poland is no exception. Here, too, there had been a thaw in 1956–7 and critical poetry and essays had been permitted a brief airing in semi-official publications. The censorship had been relaxed. A new leader, Gomulka, had replaced an old bureaucrat and the Polish people had been promised reforms. Nothing changed. Very soon the new leaders had reverted to the irresistible pull of the bad old ways.

The troubled mix of religion and politics that marks the unrest of 1968 here is, however, unique to Poland, where the Catholic Church has collaborated with every regime, however repressive, while at the same time attempting to dominate the leadership of every opposition. The only political current with which the Church seems to have no truck is reform communism, the type of 'socialism with a human face' that is beginning to open up so many possibilities in next-door Czechoslovakia.

Ironically, it is the most authoritarian communists who will be inflaming die-hard Christian prejudices against the reform movement in Poland this March by tarring it with the age-old brush of anti-Semitism: the democrats will all be 'Zionists' and the mass protest movements that erupt first among Warsaw students and then spread throughout the country, to Cracow, Poznán, Lublin, Gdansk, Lódz, Szeczin and Wroclaw, will be denounced as a Jewish plot. Sadly, the tactic seems to work. The students are isolated, and tear-gas does the rest.

It is worth recalling that after the Second World War, when Poland was bequeathed to the Soviet 'sphere of influence', there was a short period of genuine enthusiasm for the new regime by workers and the intelligentsia that had survived the war. This was perhaps best symbolized by

Warsaw students attack 'Press lies'. Jewish students are accused of writing the anti-Semitic slogans themselves that appear on the walls of the University and Polytechnic School.

Andrzej Wajda's trilogy of films celebrating the Resistance and the defeat of German fascism. The whole process of how this enthusiasm was cynically manipulated by the state was subsequently portrayed by Wajda in his 1977 film *Man of Marble*. By this time Solidarnosc was already knocking on the doors of the old system. The new enthusiasm for a better deal for Poland's large, and socially important, working class, and for a more democratic and open society all round, was again exploited just as cynically by the Catholic Church. This process and the corruption and subsequent fragmentation of Solidarnosc has, so far, not been filmed by Wajda or any other filmmaker.

Culture, which played such a vital part in the construction of an alternative in Eastern Europe, is currently paralysed by the advent of the free market and the world of MTV and American and Australian soap operas. It was not always thus, as a look at Poland in 1968 reveals. And the fact that a British newspaper, the *Guardian*, published a full-length review of the banned Mickiewicz play reminds us that the press in Britain, too, had rather different priorities during this period of upheaval.

1st Czechoslovakia A Spring Wind Blows

It is spring in Czechoslovakia, and change is in the air. The reforms are becoming visible; editors who were sacked for demanding a new political order are being reinstated. In the first new edition of the Writers' Union newspaper, *Literarni Listy*, Jan Prochazka expresses the mood of a ferment that is no longer restricted to tiny circles in Prague but is spreading throughout the country.

'If we are on the threshold of a new era and making this new start, perhaps we should do so under the leadership of new people. To keep the same set of guides and leaders for Hell, Purgatory and Paradise is surely too costly an economy, even for a nation as small as ours.'

'We should recognize the unique nature of this moment and grab the chance that history is giving us to combine the two things which ought to flourish together: socialism and freedom,' says Writers' Union chairman Goldstücker.

But there is well-grounded fear mixed with the hope. History has not been kind to the peoples of Czechoslovakia: 'The present phase may just be a thaw between two winters.'

Left: Prague students mock the city's 'most secret police'.
Below: Celebration in Prague of the Czechoslovak state's twentieth anniversary. Left to right: Brezhnev (Soviet Union), Dubcek, Dolansky, Novotny (Czechoslovakia) and Ulbricht (German Democratic Republic).

Prochazka adds: 'In the last years, many people did not dare to use the telephone openly and they are still not sure that they can. Silent fingers reach for your correspondence. Watchful eyes follow everywhere. It was better to avoid some people because they served more than one employer.

'We have often heard the word "democratization" in the past years and it was always described as a gift from above. It was never a real democracy. It was only an adaptation of the length of the reins.'

Prague Radio reports the view of a German newspaper: 'Something like a spring wind is now blowing through Czechoslovakia.' 'This is true,' adds the commentator, 'but the state of the weather suggests that winter will not give way so easily.'

Yet the thaw is happening: the icicles are beginning to melt and the birds to sing. Alexander Dubcek and the reformers who back him inside the Communist Party launch a series of mass meetings around the country to build up support for their Action Programme, which has still not been approved by the Central Committee. Debates are going on in the factories, clubs and bars. What will the new economic programme mean? Will it bring fresh insecurities or new hope? Will 'flexibility' apply just to the management or will there be new scope for workers' initiatives? The pros and cons of 'self-management' in Tito's Yugoslavia are hotly debated.

And if the Soviet line is no longer to determine domestic policy, what should Czechoslovakia's foreign policy be?

During Majales, a traditional student celebration of spring banned by the Czech regime, students poke fun at communist rallies by marching with banners which mock the zenophobia of communism (left) and quote Hasek's satirical novel *The Good Soldier Schweik* (right).

Literarni Listy editor Alexander Kliment calls for 'a foreign policy of active neutrality – a socialism of our own type, according to our own needs, according to our possibilities and according to our choice'.

Here the Dubcek leadership knows that it is treading on the most delicate ground. At one mass rally, attended by 16,000 young people, Dubcek's colleague Josef Smrkovsky is jeered when he criticizes a proposed resolution for failing to welcome Czechoslovakia's alliance with the USSR.

In the end a compromise resolution is passed, agreeing that 'Czechoslovakia's geographical position in Central Europe makes it essential that she maintain equal and good relations with all neighbours, especially the Soviet Union.'

Already it is becoming clear that only a ruthless campaign of repression will succeed in re-gagging the Czechoslovakian people, now that they have begun to talk.

A student newsreel is showing in the cinemas that gives the students' version of the previous November's demonstrations, which were broken up by the police. It includes eyewitness accounts, interviews with professors, and the evidence of hospital staff who tended students who were beaten up. A police statement admits that some of the students' complaints against the police are justified.

There are calls for free elections, for a functioning parliament with a real opposition, for a recognition of the role of public opinion. Radio broadcaster Milan Weiner is one of many intellectuals beginning to argue that the nation's future should be decided by the entire population, not just by the Communist Party.

Prague Radio has become a platform for the new democracy. In a surreal moment it denounces its own censorship, announcing: 'Citizens: Everything you have so far heard on the radio news, everything you are listening to now, and every item about to be broadcast *bears the stamp of the Central Publishing Administration!*'

Radio journalists meet the new Deputy Justice Minister and argue that censorship is at odds with the Czech Constitution's guarantee of freedom of speech. The Minister agrees, revealing that under Novotny the communist censorship authorities had even banned a century-old article by Karl Marx that attacked Prussian censorship .

However, Novotny still retains the presidency. He has substantial support in the lower echelons of the Party, the army and the security forces, not to mention the massive backing of the Soviet Union and all those in Eastern Europe – Ulbricht in East Germany, Gomulka in Poland – who stand to lose if the spring winds start to blow around them.

Italy Educating the Educators

A stormy wave of student sit-ins erupts in the most violent street fighting yet seen in Italy as police and students battle for control of the Architectural Faculty in Valle Giulia, Rome.

The past year has seen an extraordinary wave of university occupations by the volatile and highly politicized students: Turin, Pisa, Naples, Trento and many other universities have seen protests against student conditions turn into strikes against the whole Italian university system. Students at La Sapienza in Pisa have produced a set of theses arguing that the university belongs to the students and that the student assembly should become the sovereign body in governing it. They demand not simply the right to study, but also the right to have a say in what they study. In Trento students occupy the Institute of Social Sciences, demanding (successfully) the right

Above left: Democratic and leftist students clash with neo-fascists at Rome University.
Above right: Italian police in riot gear defend themselves against a student armed with a book.

to take degree courses in sociology. (The Institute is the only place in Italy where sociology is studied at all.) They want to be able to use the tools that will enable them to construct a critique of society, the role of the family and the values and content of the education system itself.

In Milan and Turin students militating against the antiquated university curriculum set up their own study groups and counter-courses; student assemblies take over the decision making.

At Turin University it had been impossible to study any developments in psychology after 1879. Now the students invite Musatti, the founder of Freudian psychoanalysis in Italy, to come and talk to them. They read Marcuse's *Eros and Civilization* and the anonymous *Viennese Diary of a Schizophrenic*, and debate the validity of a Freudian-Marcusian stance on psychoanalysis and social repression. There are counter-courses in the philosophy of science, the pedagogics of dissent, capitalism and counter-culture. Architects are studying imperialism and social development in Latin America; engineers are reading Marx.

When Christmas comes the students refuse to go home for the holidays. They prefer to stay on in their 'liberated zones'. With the New Year come police evictions, then reoccupations; with each new move, tempers on both sides rise.

The movement is spreading to the secondary schools. In Milan striking school students protest at the lack of access to their school for working-class students. They want to be able to work in more informal study groups, to extend the curriculum to include social problems and to study outside the classroom. Their headmaster, the noted Dante scholar Professor Daniele Mattalia, refuses to call the police, saying: 'The students have voted to strike in a general assembly. I believe them to be mature people. The authorities consider them a bunch of savages, whereas I have been educating them in the principles of self-government and self-discipline.' The Christian Democrats in the Ministry of Education are enraged by his dissent and suspend Mattalia. The students strike in support of their headmaster.

Rome University students have been occupying the Faculty of Letters since the previous day and negotiating with the professors on the conditions in which examinations should be held – in Italy they are traditionally viva voce, by oral interview.

Finally students and faculty agree that the examinations should be held in public and that everyone should be permitted to attend; that the examinees should be allowed to discuss the professors' final decisions with them and that all present should be allowed to enter into the discussion; that the students be free to reject the professors' judgement by leaving examinations; and that the examinations should become a process of continuous assessment, taking place every month.

The Rector and the Education Minister, Gui, are faced with either accepting the students' victory or opposing the faculty itself. Completely validating the students' Marcusian outlook, the authorities decide that social control is more important than education. They send in the police to clear the building and lock out the students.

The students gather on March 1 and resolve to take the Architectural Faculty in Valle Giulia instead. Their spirits are high: they feel totally justified in what they are doing, in their right to question and to learn. Their only weapons are a few crates of overripe tomatoes for hurling at the police. Before they even get into the park where the faculty building is situated, they are attacked by the police, who have set up cordons of jeeps and are armed with tear-gas and clubs. There is a moment's panic as the students run for cover amid the tear-gas: they had been expecting some resistance, not outright war. Then they start to fight back, prising up cobblestones to hurl at the police, ripping up wooden park benches and using the planks as clubs.

The battle for Valle Giulia lasts for over five hours: Rome is in a state of siege, with tear-gas hanging in the air, sirens wailing and policemen hunting down students in the streets. The following day twice as many students gather to protest.

8-9th Warsaw, Poland 'The play's the thing...'

Four thousand students march through Warsaw University in protest against the jailing of two of their number. 'No study without freedom', 'Long live the writers' and 'We want *Dziady*!' read their placards. Twenty-five truckloads of armed militia surround the University buildings. Truncheon-wielding militiamen seal off the streets and break up the demonstration, clubbing students to the ground.

The trouble had begun at the end of January, when the Polish authorities closed down an enormously popular production of the nineteenth-century play *Dziady* (Forefathers) by Adam Mickiewicz – a Polish classic, known to every school child.

Tumultuous applause has always greeted such lines as 'We Poles have sold our souls for a couple of silver roubles' or 'The only thing Moscow sends us are jackasses, idiots and spies' whenever *Dziady* has been performed. What is new about this 1968 production is its emphasis on the mystical Christian elements of the play, powerfully dramatized with all the expressionist virtuosity and flair of sixties theatre. A rather cautious, if didactic, review published in *Trybuna Ludu*, the main Party newspaper, well before the play was banned, took issue with the stress on altars, priests and devils in director Dejmek's production:

'Dejmek has tried to reconcile the two elements, political and mystical, and mysticism got the upper hand. And so long as we start from the assumption that Mickiewicz's mysticism constitutes just as important an element of *Dziady* as his political passion, and that in consequence we must take both factors equally into account when staging the work, so long will defeats dominate success.'

But it was the audience's ecstatic reception of the play that led to the sudden shortening of its run. The last performance of *Dziady* at the Naródowy Theatre was

Dziady at the Naródowy Theatre

Harry Stevens reviewed Dejmek's production of *Dziady* at the Naródowy Theatre for the London *Guardian*:

'The staging of *Dziady* has always presented the producer with almost insoluble problems ... it is a terrible hotchpotch. It begins as a play of romantic love, in a setting of peasant religious superstition – the opening scene in a churchyard presents a calling up, and exorcism, of the dead, the "forefathers". Then, suddenly, it switches to a drama of romantic, but highly political, revolutionary content: a transformation symbolized in the report that the hero, Gustav, has died in prison, only to be "resurrected" as the revolutionary Konrad. From that point the play acquires a new, violently denunciatory, anti-authoritarian note which is sustained ... to the end.

'But interwoven with it is still a religious element, in the person of a priest as well as the presence of angels and demons. The producer's problem, therefore, has always been how to cut so as to resolve this dichotomy: whether to try to fuse the two elements into a unity or, as the Polish "left" would prefer, to eliminate the religion and concentrate on the political element. At the Naródowy, Dejmek ... attempted to keep both elements. And, in doing so, he seems to have come a political cropper.

'The political elements in the play consist of the prison scenes, especially when the "revolutionary" Gustav/Konrad and his friends discuss their fate and that of Poland; and the later "senatorial" scenes, in which a Russian senator and governor is the central character. Dejmek set the revolutionaries and the "powers" in contrast: the prison scenes were fairly naturalistic (though in an impressive modern set), with earnest discussion among fellow-conspirators, Konrad astonishing and finally shocking his comrades by his bitter objurgations, culminating in his soliloquy when the others abandon him – the "improvisation" – which ends with blasphemies.

'The "senatorial" scenes were played mainly in grotesque, the senator himself asleep half the time, waking up to deal with 'affairs of state' such as Polish political prisoners. At the close, a striking piece of mime: the stage clears and darkens, and from the backcloth Konrad, spotlighted, emerges in chains, seeming to grow larger and larger as he advances down the ramped platform. The symbolic political prisoner – of whom?

'The part of Gustav/Konrad was played by one of Poland's finest actors, Holoubek; he brought to it a new vision. Gone was the traditional, romantic harangue, rising in a crescendo of fire and fury to a tirade in the "improvisation". This most romantic poem in Polish literature, essentially a product of the Enlightenment and ... the French Revolution, was played down by Holoubek ... it became ... the soliloquy of a man struggling with himself, yet still retaining its note of arrogance, of egotism, of the belief that he is the new Prometheus, man greater than God.

'But in this production the religious element was just as challenging, partly by the producer's striking exploitation of the author's text, partly because of some fine acting. From the first, as the vigorous press controversy that followed the first night showed, it was realized that this essentially religious note was coming across very powerfully. Thus a strong connecting thread linked the first graveyard scene with all that followed. A prominent character in the play is a priest, in sympathy with the conspirators but anxious as to the way Gustav/Konrad's mind is working: he remonstrates with Gustav, but to no effect. The end of the "improvisation" is followed by a physical struggle between angels and demons for possession of the "dead" Gustav. But the priest comes between the body and the demons, and they are baffled ... the next scene enacted a kind of apotheosis of the priest, in which the mass was indicated, before an altar with choir, organ and attendant ministrants: an unprecedented interpretation.'

packed to the rafters, with prominent Polish theatre figures returning from abroad to attend. The final applause was a fifteen-minute standing ovation during which the cast stood, unmoving, taking no bows.

After the play a spontaneous demonstration of about 300 students marched through the darkened streets to the memorial statue of Mickiewicz, a national hero. The night-time gathering was broken up and two students, Adam Michnik and Henryk Szlajfer, were arrested. (Michnik, a left-wing communist, had previously been expelled from the University for supporting left-dissident philosopher Leszek Kolakowski's outspoken attack on the Gomulka regime; Szlajfer, the son of one of the official censors, is arrested for attacking the censorship.)

On March 2 the Warsaw Writers' Union had called a special meeting to protest against the clamp-down. The students are now following suit. On March 9 Warsaw University students march through the town chanting 'Freedom, democracy' and 'Warsowians, support us.' Public opinion seems massively on their side. Police chase demonstrators from the streets and make a baton charge up the steps of the Holy Cross Church, to seize a group of fifty students taking refuge there.

11th Warsaw, Poland A New Gestapo

On the third day of protests 10,000 mainly young people gather outside the University to support the students after the street clashes on Friday and Saturday. They chant slogans and burn copies of the Party newspaper's reports of the previous days' demonstrations, in which the troubles are attributed to the children of the élite – dubbed the 'banana youth', owing to their penchant for imported fruit.

Steel-helmeted riot police launch a baton charge to clear the crowd, driving the protesters into the side-streets, where more auxiliaries are waiting. The protesters respond with chants of 'Gestapo! Gestapo!' from the steps of the Holy Cross Church. The police fire tear-gas grenades into the vast crowd. A section of the demonstration breaks away, heading towards the Party headquarters, but the huge building is surrounded by police and they are driven back towards the Ministry of Culture in Krakowskie Przedmiescie Street. The demonstrators pour in and sack the building, attempting to fight off the police with bits of broken furniture.

13-22nd Poland The Party Plays the Anti-semitic Card

The Warsaw protest movement spreads to the rest of the country, with solidarity meetings in Cracow, Poznán, Lublin, Gdansk, Lodz, Szeczin and Wroclaw.

In Cracow the demonstrators' placards read: 'Warsaw is not alone. We want justice.' Police attack with truncheons in the city centre, driving the crowd out of the medieval market square and down the narrow side-streets of the old city, where many are ruthlessly beaten. In Prague a rally of Czech communist youth adopt a resolution in support of the Polish students and condemn the official Polish press attacks on them. A group of students ask for radio and TV time to broadcast their 'solidarity with the Warsaw students' but their request is denied, at least temporarily.

Meanwhile government officials are attempting to whip up popular hostility by pandering to ancient prejudices. They accuse 'Zionist' elements of instigating the riots. In a country where the bulk of the Jews were destroyed in the Holocaust and some killed by good Catholics when they returned to their homes, the Polish Communist Party plays the race card.

March 1968

Top: West Berlin students demonstrate in favour of Poland's students. Peter Brandt, son of West Germany's Foreign Minister, Willy Brandt, is second from right.
Above: An official party meeting is held to counter the protests of Polish students.

It is claimed that the demonstration's organizers met in the Jewish Babel Club in Warsaw to plan their activities. *Trybuna Ludu* prints a list of names of prominent Jewish students, and identifies one young man in particular as 'a Babel Club activist and son of a well-known newspaper editor': it is obvious that the boy's father can only be the editor of Poland's sole surviving Yiddish paper.

Official counter-demonstrations are organized, with banners reading 'Clean the Party of Zionists' and 'Away with the new fifth column'. Factory workers are ordered to attend rallies against 'the enemies of People's Poland'. The war veterans' organization, Zbowid, chaired by the hard-line Interior Minister, General Moczar, is particularly rabid.

First Secretary Wladyslaw Gomulka, under pressure from the liberals for being too hard and from Moczar for being too soft, makes a speech on March 19 trying to restrain the anti-Semites and to get the students to call off their protests.

The Polytechnic School students' response is to occupy their school. By evening the administrative building is draped with banners: 'Warsaw with the Students', 'Democracy and Socialism', 'Workers, Your Cause is Ours', 'Truth from the Press', 'Don't Lie to our Fathers, Workers and Peasants', 'Higher Wages – Not Security Police'. Supporters pass money and food in through the spiked railings. Students hand out leaflets to the crowds outside, calling for Czechoslovakian-style reforms and 'freedom of expression, assembly and demonstration'.

By the evening of March 22 some 10,000 people have gathered outside the Polytechnic. At seven o'clock a large contingent of riot police arrives and the crowd begins to thin out. Then comes a dramatic government ultimatum, delivered over the radio and television channels: unless the students end their strike in one hour, by nine o'clock, they will face expulsion from the school. Immediately the vast crowd reassembles in Workers' Unity Square, outside the Polytechnic. At nine o'clock one of the students comes out on to the balcony overlooking the square and announces that some 4000 of the students have voted to defy the ultimatum. Cheers go up from the crowd. The whole square joins in singing the *Internationale*. The students defy the ultimatum for several hours more and then come out in their own time, escorted to safety by the vast mass of Warsaw citizens. But the Polytechnic occupation turns out to be the last mass action of the Polish movement before government repression and anti-Semitic propaganda succeed in defusing the protests.

15th   Prague, Czechoslovakia   The Autumn of the Dictator

Another victory for the reformers in the Czech capital as the hard-line Prosecutor-General and Interior Minister responsible for the crack-down on the previous November's student protests are forced out of office.

'Few people know how to leave on time,' is the scathing comment of the reformist Trade Union newspaper *Prace*. 'It is an art better mastered by athletes than by politicians.'

The defection of Czech Defence Chief General Sejna to the USA the week before has been a body-blow for the old-guard Stalinists. The following week will see the canny old Novotny himself obliged to bow to public pressure and resign from the Presidency, followed by a flurry of other high officials.

Czech TV panel discussions now show free, uninhibited political debate. Former political prisoners confront their jailers on screen.

The Prague newspaper *Mlada Fronta* receives letters from readers 'disoriented by so much open discussion'.

Deputy Prime Minister Cernik replies: 'I think it is because people are not used to it. After so many years, we don't know how to express our opinion publicly. When people were not allowed to express anti-official opinion on radio, television and in the press, they became unused to hearing contrary news.'

The Brezhnevites are also unused to hearing such contrary news. An emergency summit meeting of the Soviet bloc is called in Dresden, East Germany, on March 23. The situations in Poland and Czechoslovakia are top of the agenda. Dubcek ducks and weaves. The pressures on him are immense, but he has some friends inside the Soviet Union too.

USA   Democratic Gain

Three days after the US Presidential Primaries begin with a crushing defeat for LBJ – thrashed into second place in New Hampshire on March 12 by the left-field, anti-war candidate Eugene McCarthy, who takes 42.4 per cent of the vote – Bobby

Above: Eugene McCarthy – 'Clean Gene'.
Above right: Bobby Kennedy on the campaign trail.

Kennedy breaks cover and declares that he too will challenge Johnson for the Democratic nomination. Kennedy is a far more formidable contestant: an anti-war candidate with a real chance of winning the Presidential race.

17th Washington DC, USA The Chickens Come Home to Roost

General Westmoreland's request for 206,000 more troops to 'finish the job' in Vietnam is rejected. The war is now costing the USA $30 billion a year. It is the cause of a major balance of payments deficit and a currency crisis now looms.

The overvalued dollar leads to a 'gold rush': US gold reserves are draining out of Fort Knox at an alarming rate. Emergency legislation is rushed through Congress to free the entire US gold reserves 'down to the last ounce' to defend the gold price of $35 an ounce and the US Treasury Secretary announces: 'There will be no devaluation of the dollar.'

The currency markets lick their lips and recognize the last flailings of despair.

The only solution Johnson can see is a ten per cent income-tax surcharge and an austerity programme which will set a thousand torches to the already tinder-dry inner-city slums.

The President's movements have to be shrouded in secrecy, to avoid the protests that erupt wherever he goes.

All the crises – military, economic, social and political – are closing in.

London, UK Vietnam Solidarity Campaign

> 'Fortunately, in England at any rate, education produces no effect whatsoever. If it did, it would prove a serious danger to the upper classes, and probably lead to acts of violence in Grosvenor Square.'
> (Lady Bracknell in *The Importance of Being Earnest* by Oscar Wilde)

Twenty-five thousand people gather in Trafalgar Square for a Vietnam Solidarity Campaign march to the American Embassy in London. 'VICTORY TO THE NLF' read the banners. The huge crowd surges down Oxford Street, huge NLF tricolours of red, yellow and black waving amid a sea of red flags. The whole street echoes to the chant of 'HO HO HO CHI MINH!' Behind the leaders of the Vietnam Solidarity Campaign comes a helmeted contingent from the German SDS.

The demonstration turns into North Audley Street and then enters the great open rectangle of Grosvenor Square. Across the central gardens lies the vast, bunker-like Embassy building. There has been much discussion among the organizing committee as to whether the demonstrators should try to occupy it. Now the police lines suddenly give way. Hundreds of people make a dash across the open ground, towards the Embassy.

The cry goes up: 'The Cossacks are here!'

The mounted police move forward. Demonstrators, tense, link arms for support as the police horses mow into the crowd. A hippie trying to offer a mounted policeman a bunch of flowers is truncheoned to the ground.

Two demonstrators grab a horse's reins and pull it down. The police lay into them with boots, fists and knees. Other demonstrators rescue the pair, dragging them clear. The square has become a battlefield, full of smoke bombs, screaming, whistles blowing, demonstrators beaten to the ground or dragged away by their hair. A group of striking building workers from the Barbican are holding the front

The heart of London's elegant Mayfair: police seize and spank a woman demonstrator, one of 30,000 protesters outside the American Embassy in Grosvenor Square.

line. After two hours the demonstrators decide to evacuate the square, shaken by the confrontation with the police violence but hugely heartened by the massive numbers on the march and the spirit they had shared.

In the USA Senator McCarthy uses the London demonstration to demonstrate how his nation is totally isolating itself, with its embassy 'in the country of its closest European ally permanently under siege'.

22nd . Nanterre, Paris, France   The Birth of a Movement

Nanterre University, on the north-western outskirts of Paris, is a bureaucrat's solution to the educational problems created by the massive growth in student numbers since the Second World War. A brutalist construction of glass and steel cubes, set down where industrial wasteland meets the ready-built slum housing of the Spanish and Algerian immigrant workers, it was opened in 1964 and already houses over 15,000 students. It is a breeding ground of discontent. There have already been militant protests about the petty regulations in the student hostels, the nature of the teaching and the content of the courses. In the Sociology Department, students and teachers have been embroiled in furious disputes.

In January the University authorities had called in plain-clothes police to spy on the students and photograph the most militant. The students had responded by 'spying' on the police: they took photographs of the plain-clothes men, blew them up and displayed them as 'Wanted' signs on placards. The administration called in first the gendarmes and then the riot police to break up the protest.

Simmering tension and mistrust continue to build throughout the spring term. On the evening of March 22 news flies round the campus that five comrades have been arrested for anti-Vietnam protests. An emergency meeting is called. What should the students do to support their comrades? What pressures can they put on the authorities to get them freed? A vote is taken. In the chilly darkness of the March night the students charge up the staircase to the eighth-floor offices of the University administration, burst open the locked doors and occupy the place. Several hundred of them spend the night there, discussing with a growing sense of purpose, excitement and intensity the links between the University bureaucracy and the French state, the nature of class rule and repression, the nature of power.

In the morning they will be evicted but, for the authorities, it will be too late. The experience of their togetherness has bonded the students into a new force. What will become known in the months ahead as the March 22 Movement has been born.

Washington DC, USA Adieu, Westmoreland

President Johnson announces that General Westmoreland is to be replaced as Commander-in-Chief in Vietnam. The wild-eyed general is dragged away screaming, 'I was just about to win!'

30th South-east England and Paris, France The Cinemas are Revolting

The Palace Pier in Brighton resounds to the sound of marching feet as Richard Attenborough begins filming the anti-militarist classic 'Oh! What a Lovely War!' Not far away, in Kent, Lindsay Anderson is shooting 'If ...', a stunningly surrealistic attack on the British public-school system.

'In one scene, senior boys fire Sten guns from the chapel roof while old ladies, choir boys and members of the school [military cadet] Corps counter-attack from the quad below. I find this film relates to a great many things I read in the paper every morning,' Anderson explains.

Meanwhile Jean-Luc Godard's new film, *Weekend*, opens in Paris.

'People are prostituting themselves all week long, working at jobs they don't like, selling things they don't believe in, and all for what? To buy a car and spend the weekend at the sea,' says the director. The film homes in on the traffic jams and blocked highways as capitalism's lemmings bolt for the coast. It features a brilliant single shot, no less than seventeen minutes long, tracking along a line of stalled cars and the bloodied victims of car crashes, accompanied by a symphony of car horns that rises over the background music composed for the film by Stockhausen.

President Johnson announces to the American nation that he will not seek re-election.

31st Washington DC, USA 'Hey, hey, LBJ, we didn't let you stay!'

'I shall not seek, and will not accept, the nomination of my Party for another term as your President.'

Heavy, lined and lugubrious in defeat, President Johnson goes on TV to announce that he will be standing down.

Cheers erupt all round the world from the joyous opponents of the American military machine.

1968
April

'The dry grass
will set fire to
the damp grass'

African proverb brought to North America by slaves

**National Guardsmen, equipped to counter a riot, block Beale Street,
Memphis, Tennessee, against campaigners for civil rights for blacks.**

Martin Luther King and Malcolm X: one aim, but two very different responses to discrimination against US blacks.

Sometimes I wonder, huh,
Wonder if other people wonder, huh,
Sometimes I wonder, huh,
Wonder if other people wonder, huh,
Just like I do, oh, my Lord, just like I do!

Negro folk song

The assassination of Martin Luther King on April 4 marks the end of the 'non-violence' strategy of the Black Civil Rights movement in the United States. King had always known that, like thousands of his fellow-citizens, he could be stepping out into the path of a white racist's bullet when he raised the banner of black Americans' rights.

'I would rather die today on the highways of Alabama than make a butchery of my own conscience,' he had told the crowd in Selma, Alabama in 1965, before leading them out on a march to Montgomery to demand a law on voting rights.

The cancer of racial prejudice which continues to poison the United States today has its roots in genocide and slavery, two of the key foundation stones of the American Republic. The virtual extinction of the native population in the name of a superior civilization paved the way for the violence that characterized the slave trade. It was these uniquely American factors that created what became known as the black condition.

Despite the defeat of the Southern Confederacy in the Civil War, the abolition of slavery and the limited gains permitted to blacks during the Reconstruction that followed, the situation at the beginning of the twentieth century was dire. The black population was cruelly exploited. The communities were stagnant and lynch mobs were active in ensuring that blacks knew their place in American society, forcibly preventing them from exercising their right to vote. The effects of this institutionalized discrimination which replaced slavery had equally damaging psychological consequences. Novelist Richard Wright comments in his autobiography, *Black Boy*:

'Color hate defined the place of black life as below that of white life; and the black man, responding to the same dreams as the white man, strove to bury within his heart his awareness of this difference because it made him lonely and afraid. Hated by whites and being an organic part of the culture that hated him, the black man grew in turn to hate in himself that which others hated in him. But pride would make him hide his self-hate, for he would not want whites to know that he was so thoroughly conquered by them that his total life was conditioned by this attitude; but in the act of hiding his self-hate, he could not help but hate those who evoked his self-hate in him. So each part of his day would be consumed in a war with himself, a good part of his energy would be spent in keeping control of his unruly emotions, emotions which he had not wished to have, but could not help having. Held at bay by the hate of others, preoccupied with his own feelings, he was continuously at war with reality. He became inefficient, less able to see and judge the objective world. And when he reached that state, the white people looked at him and laughed and said: "Look, didn't I tell you niggers were that way."'

The struggle for black civil rights provided a forward-looking release for that energy, even as it drew down upon itself the murderous hatred of the white racists. But even before King's assassination, black Americans had been divided over his Gandhi-inspired strategy of 'non-violence'. Black Muslim preacher Malcolm X argued that violence was as American as apple pie and that it might be the only way of defeating the structures of white power.

By 1964 Malcolm X had publicly broken with the primitive black separatism advocated by the Nation of Islam. He began to argue for a unified struggle by blacks and whites against racism and war. His assassination in that year shook Black America. King himself paid warm tribute to his slain rival.

The wave of riots that engulfs over forty cities after King's death in April 1968 is a sign of the new mood of rage and despair within the black communities that threatens to pass beyond politics altogether. The Black Panther Party, based in Oakland, California, is treated as the enemy within and destroyed by the FBI and the police in a series of gun battles. Black communities also accuse the FBI of deliberately encouraging hard drugs and armed gangsterism in an effort to depoliticize and split the ghettos. The fragmentation of black political consciousness will continue with the emergence during the Reagan years of a new brand of right-wing, xenophobic nationalism under the leadership of Louis Farrakhan. Thirty years after King's death, the blacks are still at the bottom of the heap that is the United States of America.

Chicago smoulders after the black ghetto erupts on the nights of April 5th and 6th.

1st | Brazil Hour of the Furnaces

In Brazil, young students and workers are learning how to outwit the forces of the military dictatorship that came to power in 1964. In the fifties Brazil's rapid post-war development, fuelled by US investment, had led the *Wall Street Journal* to ask: 'Is there any other place in the world where such profits can be obtained?' But it had also unleashed new social forces who were unwilling to bear the brunt of the anti-inflationary policies and vast foreign debt repayments that the IMF and the US government began demanding by the early sixties.

Rio de Janeiro students opposed to Brazil's military regime hurl rocks at riot police who counter with tear-gas.

By 1963 the civilian government of President João Goulart was being buffeted this way and that by the conflicting demands of the multinational corporations and the Brazilian masses. There were waves of strikes in the industrial areas in support of wage claims, growing agitation for agrarian reform among the peasants of the drought-ridden north-east, and discontent over pay and conditions within the Army itself. The Cuban revolution had brought fresh hope and enthusiasm to the left, and the students had plunged into a campaign for mass literacy and basic education in a crusade against Brazil's vertiginous social inequality.

Thrashing around for some solution to its problems, the Goulart government began promising radical social and economic reforms. In March 1964, in front of an audience of 150,000 workers at a rally in Rio de Janeiro, Goulart signed a decree to nationalize the oil refineries and another authorizing the peasants' expropriation of unused land. He also announced plans for rent control, tax reform and the extension of the suffrage to illiterates (half the population) and to soldiers.

Before the month was out the Brazilian Army High Command had gone into action, with the tacit backing of the US Ambassador, the old oligarchy and the politicians of the right. The Generals ordered their tanks out on to the streets.

Some thousands were assassinated in the first days of April 1964, especially in the countryside, where a landowners' militia unleashed a campaign of terror against peasant militants. The Military Police were given powers to enter homes and interrogate citizens with no need of a warrant or suspicion of guilt. Over 15,000 people were arrested in the period following the coup, and the political and civil service hierarchies were heavily purged: over 10,000 government employees were fired or forcibly 'retired'.

Yet it proves hard to impose a monolithic military order on a society as alive and as heterogeneous as Brazil's, and 1968 sees a growing challenge to the military regime. At the end of March soldiers have shot dead a seventeen-year-old student who was demonstrating against the dictatorship. One hundred thousand people attend his funeral. Now, with armed police on every corner, the students wait for nightfall before taking the risk to run through the packed streets shouting, 'Down with the dictatorship!'

They organize lightning political meetings under cover of the traffic jams, disappear into the side-streets and then reassemble, ten minutes later, at a prearranged location.

The police are being outmanoeuvred. The city governor calls in the army to occupy the city. Tanks and armoured personnel carriers take up their positions, combat troops chase the students through the streets. There is a burst of machine-gun fire. Another protester is dead.

In São Paulo, Belo Horizonte, Goiânia and many other cities and towns a wave of revolt erupts against the regime. A military commander announces that all necessary steps will be taken against further demonstrations. Protesters will be treated 'like an enemy attacking the fatherland's territory and threatening the nation's basic institutions'.

Nevertheless, memorial meetings go ahead for the dead seventeen-year-old, and masses are held for him in churches throughout Brazil. Two weeks later 15,000 striking metal workers will join the students in their defiance.

4th Vietnam 'Limited Bombing'

In an attempt to defuse the peace movement – or to gain time to redraft military strategy – President Johnson has called for 'serious peace talks' with North Vietnam. As an earnest of goodwill, he announces that from now on there will only be 'limited bombing' of the North.

Hanoi announces that it will participate in the talks. The hunt begins for a suitable venue.

Villagers of Dai Lai recount their experience of 'limited bombing':

Tran Thi Sai, aged thirty:

'At the time of the air-raid I was with friends. We were on our way to the fields. When I heard the planes, I took

> •US bombing raids carried out on North Vietnam in March 1968, before the declaration of limited bombing: 2,500.
> •US bombing raids carried out on North Vietnam in April 1968, after the declaration of limited bombing: more than 3,500.

shelter in a dugout. As soon as the bombs had fallen, I ran home to see what had happened. Even from a distance I could see that the whole village was ablaze.

'My second child, a boy, managed to escape from the fire. His little brother, aged five, tried to follow him but couldn't keep up; he got trapped in the courtyard. My mother picked up my twelve-month-old baby and tried to dash from the building: they were burnt alive in the doorway. My ten-year-old daughter was out minding the buffalo, so she was spared. My husband was husking rice, right here in the village. He stayed in the open till the very end, to make sure the others got into the shelter. That was how he got killed. The shrapnel split his head open.

'I stood screaming and sobbing while some of the other workers rushed into the flames in an attempt to save their families. I tried to do the same: hurl myself into the blaze and rescue my mother and children. But I was stopped and led away so that I shouldn't see their bodies as they were brought out.

'I lost my mother, the baby she held in her arms, my five-year-old son and my husband. There are only three of us left: my two children and myself.'

Bui Van Nguu, aged forty-six:

'At the time of the air-raid I was at home, making brooms for the co-operative. My two daughters were in the kitchen. They were busy with the pestle and mortar. Their two small brothers were in the kitchen with them, playing games. My wife had left our youngest child, a girl of eighteen months, asleep in the hammock while she went to do some washing at the pond.

UNTERSTÜTZT DIE WELTWEITE FORDERUNG:

Schluß mit den US-Bombenangriffen auf Nordvietnam!

KOMMUNISTISCHE PARTEI ÖSTERREICHS

A powerful Austrian poster condemning US bombing in North Vietnam.

'When my wife saw the planes coming, she started running towards the house, but before she could get back, she was blown off her feet by the blast of a bomb. Another high-explosive hit the kitchen, burying our four children. And then the house collapsed and caught fire. The roof fell in on me. The baby girl in the hammock started to cry. I scrambled up and caught her in my arms, and ran through the flames with her. When we got to the yard I saw my wife lying flat on the ground, half buried beneath the remains of the wall. She called out to me. I put the baby in the dugout and went to her aid. By the time I reached her, she was trying to get up of her own accord. Her clothes were badly torn and her face was bleeding. I handed the baby to her and told her to carry it to safety. Then I hurried off and tried to free my other four children.

'I searched among the debris. I could piece three of their bodies together. There was no trace of my eldest daughter. I didn't find her body until the next morning. It had been blown into a vegetable plot about thirty feet away. It was buried under a pile of ashes. At first we thought it was someone else, but I looked and there could be no mistaking the shape of her ear. She was thirteen.'

Hoang Ban, aged forty-four:

'We had finished lunch and were about to return to the fields when we heard the sound of aircraft engines and the roar of exploding bombs. I was at home. I didn't even have time to get to the shelter: I just flung myself flat on the floor. I could see flames and smoke at the other end of the village, and I realized that the bombs must have fallen near my mother-in-law's house. I got up and started running towards it. Hers was the end house, and it was in flames. My wife's brother had escaped, followed by his son. But suddenly the blaze had spread to the whole house, and the walls had collapsed.

'We did our best to fight the fire, and when it was out we searched among the ruins and found the charred bodies of my mother-in-law and my wife's young sister. My mother-in-law's neighbour was in the shelter with them. She had been expecting a child in two months' time; now she was dead and her body was like theirs, black and broken from burning.

April 1968

'After we got them out from the shelter, they were put in coffins, at about five in the afternoon, and buried that same day. Every time I look at my wife, I think of her mother and her young sister and I say to myself, "How can they possibly do such things?"'

Memphis, USA   He Had a Dream

Martin Luther King and a couple of friends comes out on to the balcony of their room at the Lorraine Motel in Memphis, Tennessee, just after 6p.m.

King is in town to lead a demonstration and rally in support of the three-month fight for union recognition by 1300 local garbage collectors. The whole black community of Memphis has rallied behind the strike: the week before, King had led a march of 15,000 through the town in support of the men. White Memphis police and National Guardsmen had broken up the protest with tear-gas, clubs and chemical sprays. One black boy was killed. The following day's march will be a stand against intimidation.

King leans over the railings to chat to a friend in the car park below. It is a pleasant evening: the smell of a Southern spring is in the air. Everything is friendly and relaxed. The friend has with him a musician who has made a version of 'Precious Lord, Take Me by Thy Hand'. King asks him to play

Above: Martin Luther King, the charismatic champion of black civil rights and ardent advocate of non-violent means.
Below: Military police patrol Washington DC after riots in reaction to the murder of King.

it at the rally that evening. 'I really want you to play that tonight,' he says.

A gunshot rings out and King slumps down on the concrete terrace, the blood frothing from his jaw and gaping neck.

It takes a quarter of an hour for the ambulance to arrive. A friend has stuffed a towel into the open wound, but King is losing blood fast. He is taken to the emergency operating room in St Joseph's Hospital. Half an hour later he is pronounced dead. He was thirty-nine years old.

The Mayor of Memphis declares a state of emergency. The Governor orders 4000 National Guards to take up positions in the city, but they cannot stop the crowds pouring out on to the streets, raging, distraught, crying and screaming out their rage.

For the next four days TV news coverage is saturated with footage of Martin Luther King talking on the theme on non-violence in an attempt to keep black Americans safe at home watching, rather than out on the streets protesting.

It fails.

In New York, Washington, Baltimore, Chicago – in all in over forty cities across the USA – young blacks are taking to the streets in pure rage, smashing, burning, looting, exchanging gunfire with the police sent in to stop them.

In Cleveland, Floyd McKissick, the director of the Congress of Racial Equality, says: 'Dr King was the last prince of non-violence. Non-violence is a dead

Opposite: Chicago's West Side burns as blacks express their rage at King's murder.
Below: Mourners pack the streets of Atlanta, Georgia on April 9 to see mules draw a caisson bearing King's body from the church to a memorial service at the city's Morehouse College.

philosophy. It was not the black people who killed it. It was the white people, and white racialists at that.'

In Washington DC smoke billows up behind the Capitol and tongues of flame lick the sky. Sirens are screaming over the sounds of shouting, smashing glass and running feet. Jeeps and tanks line streets of smashed shop fronts, and everywhere there is broken glass and blackened, burnt-out cars.

6th Oakland USA Soul on Ice

In the San Francisco suburb of Oakland the Black Panther Party have been trying to stop the kids from rioting after the assassination.

'Don't let the cops set you up to get killed,' Bobby Seale and the Panthers tell them. 'Don't start no trouble. Go home. Throwing rocks and bottles is irrelevant to the real revolution.'

The young kids out smashing and burning don't usually listen to anyone outside their own age group, but the Panthers are an exception. The Black Panther Party had been set up three years earlier by Huey Newton and Bobby Seale, two young residents of West Oakland's black ghetto, as an organization to police the police. The Black Panthers follow police patrol cars through the ghetto. When the police stop blacks on the street for questioning, the Panthers are there behind them, checking out what's going on, advising the suspects on their legal rights and offering what they can towards raising bail or getting counsel.

Newton has done a year in law school and the Panthers are careful to stay inside the law in what they advise. But beyond that they make no secret of their attitude to the police. For their part, the Oakland police make no secret of their attitude to the blacks.

The Panthers are within the law when they carry guns, too. Whatever the other results of their being armed, there has been a distinct drop in police harassment in West Oakland since the Panther patrols have been operating.

For most of the young ghetto kids the Black Panthers are objects of adolescent hero worship. So when the word goes round that the Panthers are telling everyone to cool it, the kids go home. There is no riot in the Bay area following the assassination of Martin Luther King. But the police are all geared up for one.

Officers Nolan R. Darnell and Richard Jensen are driving through West Oakland in a squad car when they spot a man apparently hiding behind a parked car. According to the police version, as they get out to investigate there is a burst of gunfire. Officer Jensen is superficially wounded. Darnell radios for help.

Strangely, not only the Oakland police but a large force from neighbouring Emeryville appear almost immediately on the scene. A two-block area is cordoned off. It is reported that some Panthers have taken refuge inside a house at 1218 18th Street. The police surround the two-storey frame house and begin firing.

During the ninety-minute siege that follows they pour a couple of thousand rounds into the house, riddling the shabby wooden structure. As darkness falls, they bring in floodlights, illuminating the target and the surrounding area, lighting up the little house like a movie set, while a crowd of about 200 residents from the cordoned-off area stands around to watch.

In the basement Eldridge Cleaver and Bobby Hutton are lying as flat as they can on the cement floor, holding their breath while bullets whistle through a thin partition less than a foot above their heads. Cleaver is one of the foremost strategists of

Eldridge Cleaver, the Black Panthers' Minister of Information, displays his 'passport' while on the run in Moscow in 1969.

the black liberation movement. It is he who has been arguing for the Black Panther Party to come out of the ghetto and into the white political arena, making alliances with other radical groups. Seventeen-year-old Hutton is still at school.

A tear-gas canister is fired in, scoring a direct hit on Cleaver. His shirt catches on fire. With Hutton's help he tears it off to see if his body hair is smouldering. The tear-gas grows thicker in the basement. A round of tracer bullets rip through boards, setting the house on fire, and Cleaver knows they will have to get out.

He tears off the rest of his clothes. 'We go out butt-naked,' he tells Hutton. 'And then the pigs can't claim they shot us because they thought we had a gun.' But Hutton is too inexperienced, too shy. He takes his shirt off, but cannot bring himself to take off his pants. There is no time for Cleaver to convince him. Flames are starting to lick the house, the tear-gas is thickening; they have to get out right away.

Cleaver yells that they want to surrender. The police bellow back that they must throw their guns out first.

Cleaver is unarmed but Hutton has a rifle. Cleaver throws it out of the window at the rear of the burning basement. His foot is full of shotgun pellets. The two of them make their way out, Cleaver limping and leaning heavily on the younger man's arm.

The back of the basement leads out into an alleyway. The two Panthers are surrounded in the glare of the floodlights. They are ordered to sit down on the pavement with their hands on their heads.

'Then,' says Cleaver in his affidavit, 'an army of pigs ran up from the street and started kicking and cursing us, but we were beyond feeling any pain. The pigs told us to stand up and Little Bobby helped me to my feet. Then the pigs pointed to a squad-car in the middle of the street and told us to run for it. I couldn't run because of my foot, but they snatched Little Bobby away from me and shoved him forward, telling him to run for the car.

'It was sickening… Little Bobby, coughing and choking from the tear-gas, stumbled forward, best he could, and when he had got about ten yards from me, the pigs cut loose on him with their guns. And then they turned back to me…'

But now the watching crowd intervenes, screaming and shouting their abuse at the cops for the murder in cold blood. This may be what saves Cleaver's life. Or it may be that he survives for the reason that he will suggest in a note to a San Francisco newspaperman that will be smuggled out of Vacerville Prison the following week: that it was his decision to come out naked that saved him:

'This decision is based on long and continuous observation of the pigs while imprisoned. Conclusion: all pigs are homosexuals. When confronted with a naked male body, totally by surprise, the homosexual's basic impulse is to caress it. Instead of shooting me, the Oakland pigs kicked and stomped my naked body. In those circumstances, a kick or a stomp can be interpreted as a caress when contrasted with shooting. There were about 50 frantic pigs around me with guns in their hands. Had just one of them been straight, I'd be a dead black cat.

'In their rage against police brutality, the blacks lose sight of the fundamental reality: that the police are only an instrument for the implementation of the policies of those who make the decisions. Police brutality is only one facet of the crystal of terror and oppression. Behind police brutality there is social brutality, economic brutality, and political brutality. From the perspective of the ghetto, this is not easy to discern.'

(from *Soul on Ice* by Eldridge Cleaver)

Rudi Dutschke, the East German who galvanized the opposition of young West German students to the American military presence in Vietnam.

11-14th West Germany Tabloids Kill!

Axel Springer, the press baron, controls Germany's largest publishing empire courtesy of the occupying armies of the West, in particular the USA. His newspapers are slavishly loyal to US global policies, much more so than the *Washington Post* or the *New York Times*. Most of Germany's industrial barons were supporters of the Third Reich. And just as they did not wish to offend Hitler, so now they seek to serve their new protectors. Their loyalty, like their products, is solid and efficient.

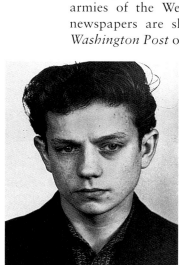

Joseph Bachmann, the would-be assassin of Rudi Dutschke.

Springer's newspapers, with *Bild Zeitung* in the lead, unleash a barrage of bile against the protesting students. Rudi Dutschke is vilified as an agent of East Germany a filthy, dirty red who is polluting the minds of nice, decent West German kids. The propaganda is reminiscent of the hate-filled and inflammatory attacks that were the hallmark of the Nazi rag *Der Stürmer*. Dutschke is branded 'PUBLIC ENEMY NO. 1'. 'DON'T LEAVE ALL THE DIRTY WORK TO THE COPS!' urges another Springer headline.

Joseph Bachmann, a 23-year-old unemployed house painter from Munich, reads these papers every day. Embittered and frustrated by his own situation, he gets satisfaction from reading about the attacks on students in *Bild Zeitung*.

Rudi Dutschke is waiting outside a chemist's shop in West Berlin to buy medicines for his baby son. The atmosphere in the city is ugly, heavily polarized between the new left and the vengeful resentments of the old right.

Joseph Bachmann steps up to the student leader in the street and fires three bullets at him: one hits him in the chest, one hits him in the face and a third lodges in his brain.

As Dutschke fights for his life in hospital, the man who tried to murder him is arrested and boasts to his police captors: 'I heard of the death of Martin Luther King and since I hate communists I felt I must kill Dutschke.' The irony is that Dutschke, a former theology student, is a refugee from East Berlin.

Within hours of the shooting thousands are marching on the Springer Press offices in the Kochstrasse in the heart of West Berlin: this is the target of all their anger and grief.

'This is not the act of one lonely crazed individual. The Springer Press with its systematic hate campaign against the left opposition has produced the climate in which a man can plan and carry out this deed,' reads one red-printed leaflet being distributed on the streets.

The next day a wave of angry student demonstrations attacks Springer offices all across Germany. In West Berlin thousands march with arms linked, twenty abreast, towards the Springer building – now encircled with barbed wire and a heavy police

In West Berlin and cities across West Germany, the attempted murder of Rudi Dutschke sparks off attacks on the Springer empire whose newspapers have created a hate-filled atmosphere.

cordon. The chants echo back from the surrounding buildings: 'RUDI DUTSCHKE, RUDI DUTSCHKE', 'SPRINGER, MURDERER.'

Blasts from police water hoses drive the protesters back until they turn on the clumsy mobile water-cannon themselves, reminiscent of squat Martian monsters in their dark-blue armour-plating. One of those dragged off under arrest is Peter Brandt, the Foreign Minister's son.

In Munich demonstrators manage to break into the Springer Press building and run amok inside it. In Frankfurt protesters march into the church of a right-wing pastor and drown out the singing of the final hymn with the *Internationale*. There are protests in support of Dutschke outside the Springer buildings in Paris and New York.

In London a breakaway group from a huge rally for Martin Luther King in Trafalgar Square, carrying Vietnam Solidarity Campaign and German SDS banners, marches, arms linked, down the Strand, chanting, 'RUDI DUTSCHKE, RUDI DUTSCHKE,' heading for the Springer press offices at the *Daily Mirror* building in Holborn Circus. Police try to seize their placards and banners and arrest Tariq Ali, who is addressing the crowd atop friendly shoulders, but they are pushed away by the demonstrators. A delegation goes into the building. Sympathetic *Mirror* journalists, backed by a worried proprietor, offer the demonstrators next day's front page to argue their case.

Dutschke survives. His wife, Gretchen, receives a moving letter from Axel Springer's son. The press magnate's heir is ashamed of his father's politics and the strident tone of his newspapers.

From now on he will maintain a regular correspondence with Dutschke, who in turn writes to his would-be-assassin, trying to explain what German socialist students are fighting for.

14th Mexico Truth is a Prisoner

US black athletes announce a boycott campaign of the 1968 Olympic Games to be held in Mexico City this September, in protest at the Olympic Committee's decision to let whites-only teams from apartheid South Africa take part. Many of the African countries and some white athletes also join the boycott.

Mexico's government, desperate to avoid the boycott, lobbies hard to get South Africa excluded again. Meanwhile hundreds of political prisoners languish in its own jails.

'Free the political prisoners'

The Mexican Political Prisoners' Defence Committee is struggling to bring to light cases such as that of Valentin Campa, jailed in 1960 for helping to organize a railway workers' strike. After eight years behind bars for this legal act, Campa has been denied parole on the following grounds: 'Because he is sixty-three years old, although strong and in good health and sound from a physical standpoint, he exhibits a certain rigidity and difficulty in remoulding his way of thinking. We conclude that he has not repented, nor has repentance been proved, and that imprisonment has not changed his personality as far as the political ideas he holds. Valentin Campa's request for benefit of parole must therefore be denied, and is denied herewith.'

19th London, UK *Kali Anastasis!*

Greek actress Melina Mercouri, stripped of her citizenship by her country's military junta, arrives in London and leads a protest demonstration to the Greek Embassy. She sends an Easter message home on the first anniversary of the Colonels' coup:

'Greeks, my brothers, I speak to you from a country that is far away. May you have a good Easter – *Kali Anastasis!* – and freedom in Greece, where the gangster colonels will soon be a forgotten nightmare.

'Here is London, the London you listened to in the black years of Hitler's occupation. In this new occupation, imposed by these poor and ridiculous relatives of Hitler, unite as we Greeks always have in times of crisis. We give you our word of honour that we shall never stop our unconditional fight until the last prisoner is free, and democracy flourishes once more in Greece.'

Melina Mercouri denounces the Greek dictators at a London rally and calls for international solidarity.

23rd New York City, USA Against the Corporate University

Columbia University is one of twelve universities working hand in glove with the US Defense Department's Institute for Defense Analysis, carrying out research for the Pentagon and the CIA.

As a prestigious, massively funded Ivy League institution situated on the edge of Harlem, its class role is glaringly obvious. When the University puts forward its plan to build a new gym in Harlem's Morningside Park, taking over public land to expand its exclusive facilities, black liberationist students join forces with local residents to fight it.

A group of militant SDS students has also been fighting to expose the links that exist between the University and its President, Grayson Kirk, and the Pentagon war machine.

The SDS, Students for a Democratic Society, is a radical student group that has grown through its involvement with the early-sixties black civil rights campaigns in the Deep South to number over 30,000 members. It represents the most political end of the spectrum of American youth that embraces hippies and flower-power types, freaks, yippies and the whole student counter-culture.

Mark Rudd, chairman of the Columbia University chapter of the SDS, polemicizes with Grayson Kirk:

Kirk: 'Our young people, in disturbing numbers, appear to reject all forms of authority. I know of no time in our history when the gap between the generations

Black Power leaders Stokely Carmichael and H. Rap Brown face reporters during the Columbia University occupation.

has been wider or more potentially dangerous.'

Rudd: 'You call it the generation gap. I see it as a real conflict between those who run things now – you, Grayson Kirk – and those who feel oppressed by, and disgusted with, the society you rule: we, the young people. You might want to know what is wrong with this society since, after all, you live in a very tight, self-created dream world. Here is what is wrong: the war in Vietnam and all the other unimaginable wars of aggression you are prepared to fight to maintain your control over your empire. Using us as your cannon-fodder to fight your war. The ghetto that you've helped to create below your mansion window, through your racist university expansion policies, through your unfair labor practices, through your city government and your police. This university, your university, which trains us to be lawyers and engineers and managers for your IBM, Socony Mobil, IDA, Con Edison and all the other cogs in the wheels of your genocidal military-industrial complex.'

The SDS campaigners have called a mass rally, one spring evening, to protest against the threatened expulsion of some of their members. The Black Power students show up too. The mood is exhilarating. The whole student body is coming together to challenge Columbia University Inc at every level: as slum landlord, racist expropriator, mis-educator and Defense Department stooge. The decision is taken to occupy the administration buildings and demand that Columbia withdraw from the Harlem residents' park *and* the napalming of the people of Vietnam.

The students throng through the University, occupy five of the buildings and declare them a liberated zone. For eight days there will be creative chaos throughout the campus: teach-ins, workshops, light shows, music making, partying and love. The black students contact the Harlem community for food and supplies. They insist on having their own space, the Hamilton building. With entire black communities under siege in America, they declare that they will work with the white students but will cede neither space nor authority to them. This is what the revolution is about.

Within the SDS other questions are being asked. What of oppression *within* the movement? Is the SDS itself simply replicating the power relations of the outside world?

Ex-SDS activist Marge Piercy writes, in *The Grand Coolie Dam*, of the typical student movement male supremacist:

'The male supremacist tends to exploit women new to the movement or on its fringes. His concept of women is conventionally patriarchal: they are for bed, board, and babies and, also, for doing his typing and running his office machines, and doing his tedious research. By definition women are bourgeois: they are housewives and domesticators. A woman who begins to act independently is a threat and loses her protected status. He can no longer use her.

Such a man will sit at his desk with his feet up and point to a poster of a Vietnamese woman with her rifle on her back, telling you, "Now that is a truly liberated woman. When I see you in that role, I'll believe you're a revolutionary."

He has all the strength of the American tradition of Huckleberry Finn escaping downriver from Aunt Polly, down through Hemingway, where the bitch Brett louses up the man-to-man understanding, to draw upon in defense of his arrogance. Not only are women losers, but for a woman to think about herself at all is bourgeois subjectivity and inherently counter-revolutionary. What the movement needs is more discipline and less middle-class concern with one's itty-bitty self!'

29th UK 'A National Danger'

A wave of white racism erupts in the UK in the wake of a spate of inflammatory press reports that have accompanied the Labour Government's Commonwealth Immigration Bill. Predictions that the scare stories whipped up by the press could only serve to swell the 'Keep Britain White' tendency are vindicated as white dockers, car workers and immigration officials from Heathrow Airport lend support to MP Enoch Powell's attack on British citizens with brown skins, whom he refers to as 'a national danger'.

Kenyan diplomat Dr Joseph Karanja – a brilliant young history don from University College, Mombasa – is jostled and jeered by Powellite dockers while entering the House of Commons. 'Go back to Jamaica!' they shout.

On the same day Britain's first black policewoman, Sislin Fay Allen, starts work in Croydon, near London. She is already thinking about leaving the force because, she says, she has received dozens of threatening and abusive letters. 'I don't know whether I will stick with this job or not. It is not an easy decision to make.'

Meanwhile Shenval Press, in Harlow, Essex, refuses to publish the new radical paper, the *Black Dwarf,* as it contains an attack on Enoch Powell. An editor comments: 'People who support Enoch Powell claim they should have freedom of speech – but we find ourselves unable to publish something quite mild about him.'

Top: Conservative politician Enoch Powell.
Above: Twenty-nine year-old Sislin Fay Allen,
London's first black female police officer who
did not last long in the force.

Revolution is the ecstasy
of history

When the finger points at
the moon, the IDIOT looks at
the finger (Chinese proverb)

Beneath the
cobblestones,
the beach

Open the gates
of the nurseries,
the universities
and all the other
prisons

We shall hang
the last capitalist
with the entrails of
the last bureaucrat!
Ugh!

How can one think freely in the
shadow of a steeple?

Society is a plastic flower

SHOUT

Be realistic – demand the
impossible

FREE OUR COMRADES

Defend the collective imagination

The tears of a philistine are the
nectar of the gods

1968
May

ACTION = NOT REACTION –
BUT CREATION

Commodities are the opium
of the people

Among the cobblestones,
I come alive

I take my desires for reality
because I believe in
the reality of my desires

Defiant Paris protest hits the streets – and the walls as graffiti.

The events of May in Paris have crystallized in the world's imagination as *the* images of 1968: the bare-headed students in their darned sweaters and jeans, the barricades, the riot police, the tear-gas in the air. The student uprising shatters the 'You've-never-had-it-so-good' complacency of postwar Western Europe. '*Métro-boulot-dodo*' is one of the slogans scribbled over and over on the walls of the underground rail system: 'Métro-work-sleep'. The students digging up the cobblestones of Paris to find the beach want something more than this.

The form the rebellion takes draws upon a long revolutionary tradition. Barricades were thrown up in these self-same streets in 1848 and again in the Paris Commune of 1871, when workers shot out all the clocks whose hands had so tyrannized their daylight hours. The French student leaders of 1968 know their revolutionary history: not just the storming of the Winter Palace in 1917, but also the crushed Berlin and Munich uprisings of 1919, the Hungarian Soviet of the same year, the insurrectionary resistance movements of the Second World War in Greece, Italy and Yugoslavia, the anti-colonial struggles that they themselves have lived through, in Algeria and Vietnam.

'He is the shit-in-the bed':
students respond to de Gaulle.

But the causes of the student revolt lie closer to home: in the frigid, hierarchical social order of postwar France in which deference and conformity are the most highly valued traits; in the cold, élitist contempt of Gaullism and the French ruling class for the conditions of its working people and its youth. It is against this status quo that the French students first raise the banner of revolt in the escalating series of confrontations with the police that culminates in the 'Night of the Barricades' of May 10–11.

With the country in a state of shock and outrage over the police brutality against the young in the storming of the barricades, with hospitals and police stations besieged by anxious parents, the trade unions call a one-day general strike and a demonstration – which in turn will lead to all-out strikes and factory occupations that bring the country to a halt. As strikes and occupations spread beyond the students into the population as a whole, and militant young workers in the car factories and aeronautical industry take over their factories, May '68 becomes a movement that shakes French society to its foundations.

Informed by his sycophantic aides that the students have triggered off a wider rebellion, President Charles de Gaulle, the general who has run the country for the last ten years, shrugs his shoulders and mutters, 'Cette chienlit.' 'This shit-in-the-bed.' The students occupying the École des Beaux Arts respond immediately: overnight Paris is covered with posters of de Gaulle's big-nosed silhouette and the caption 'La chienlit c'est lui!' 'He is the shit-in-the-bed!'

The crisis deepens. Ten million workers are now on strike. The government is paralysed, out of control of events. Prime Minister Pompidou negotiates a deal with the trades union leaders, promising pay rises for all; but although the CGT leaders are happy to accept, the strikers themselves reject the settlement out of hand. They are protesting about far more than just cash.

France seems, and not just to the students, to be on the verge of a revolution. De Gaulle leaves the country under cover of darkness and flies to the French Army base in Baden-Baden, in

Paris: the Latin Quarter, the morning after the 'Night of the Barricades'.

West Germany. Here he meets the real shits: the ultra-conservative generals who are still smarting from their losses in Vietnam and Algeria. De Gaulle gets them to agree that if the student rabble combine with the plebeian filth, they will cross the border with their troops and cleanse the Fatherland for him. In return, he bows to their demands: the release of General Salan and his friends in the OAS, currently serving life sentences for atrocities and treason during the Algerian War of 1954–62.

French society is split in half. Conservatives are appalled by the breakdown of society as they know it and rally immediately to de Gaulle on his return. Included in the ranks of loyal Gaullists are the Communist Party leaders of the CGT trade union, who will spend half of June bullying, cajoling and pleading with their members to call off their strikes and occupations and get back to work before the elections called for 23 and 30 June.

'It is the *French* Communist Party, after all,' remarks de Gaulle, with a knowing sneer. But it takes more than arrogant words to end the strikes: tear-gas, baton charges and even bullets have to be employed to put an end to the factory movement.

De Gaulle wins the June elections, but his presidency is now broken-backed. He is evidently not the man for the times: it would be too easy for him to provoke the still inflammable French people. The following April he loses a referendum and retires, defeated, paving the way for the blander, more emollient Georges Pompidou to assume the presidency.

1st Moscow, Beijing, São Paulo, Prague, Havana, Hanoi, Paris May Day

> Hurray, hurray,
> The First of May!
> Outdoor sex begins today!
>
> Anon

May Day is also International Workers' Day, a commemoration of May 1, 1899, when Chicago police shot dead a group of striking workers. For the first few decades after the Chicago killings, May Day was celebrated as a spontaneous display of international working-class solidarity in cities around the world.

Now, in 1968, the images shown on the world's television screens are of the big parades in Moscow and Beijing, where workers bussed in from factories are dwarfed by giant missiles, tank displays and giant march-pasts by the two armies. These are carefully orchestrated state occasions, a public flexing of the muscles in the face of the Cold War enemy.

But some spontaneity remains.

In Brazil, the State Governor of São Paulo himself is the guest of honour at the May Day rally organized by the state-sponsored trade unions – stooges of the military regime – when protesting workers decide to stage their own 'demonstration within the demonstration'. As the Governor begins his speech, a hail of eggs, tomatoes and official placards comes flying towards him. The Governor and his 'union leaders' are forced to flee to the shelter of the city's nearby cathedral as several hundred workers and students storm the platform and begin making their own firebrand speeches to the noisy and appreciative crowd.

In Prague, too, the pictures are different this year. Instead of a military parade, May Day is a genuine civilian demonstration of popular support for the new, reform-communist regime. Families with their children crowd past the platform in the sunshine, talking and laughing. Many throw flowers as they pass by. Dubcek is seen to wipe a tear of emotion from his face. In Moscow, Brezhnev's hard-nosed bureaucrats fume at the Czechoslovaks' cheek.

In Havana, Fidel Castro tells a crowd of half a million that the murder of Che Guevara the previous year will never intimidate the revolution or curb its internationalism. In Hanoi, General Vo Nguyen Giap declares that, unless the USA withdraws voluntarily from Vietnam, it faces military humiliation in the field. Few commentators in the Anglo-American press take this remark at face value.

It is an ordinary May Day in Paris, with the traditional march organized by the large unions, among which the Communist-controlled CGT (Confédération Générale du Travail) is firmly in charge. Here, too, there is little spontaneity; but although the demonstrators dutifully chanting their May Day slogans are not aware of it, their country is on the brink of eruption.

2nd Paris, France Davids and Goliaths

It is announced that the 'peace talks' between the United States and the Democratic Republic of Vietnam will begin in the French capital the following week. Australian journalist Wilfred Burchett comments: 'The mightiest ever of the Western giants, at the apex of its nuclear-muscled power, has to sit down with a small, backward, truncated nation to discuss terms of war and peace. History has scarcely a parallel for such high-tension dealings between two such unevenly matched opponents.' Meanwhile the French students of the March 22 Movement occupy a lecture theatre at Nanterre University, on the northern outskirts of Paris. The Dean had closed the University the previous week, after a growing wave of student protests. Now the students are reclaiming the University as their own.

Daniel Cohn-Bendit addresses a student rally. His audacity symbolized the mood of 1968.

The atmosphere among the students of Paris is becoming more incendiary each day. This is a city where the left has always had the best of the new ideas. The role of the French Communist Party and the Socialists in the anti-Nazi Resistance movement during the Second World War, and the vitality of the Left Bank intelligentsia since then, have together created a large space for radical, left-wing thinking. Besides, there is a universal awareness of a long revolutionary tradition in a country whose memory is already stamped with the events of 1789, 1793, 1848, 1871 and 1936; 1968 will be another such.

A significant minority of the students have already been radicalized as school students in the early sixties. Above all they were inspired by the protests led by Jean-Paul Sartre and others against atrocities committed by France during the eight-year Algerian War. Even after Algeria gained independence in 1962, the knowledge of what the French state was capable of still remained, confounding complacency and making unquestioning obedience impossible.

Added to this, the students find themselves living and working in impossibly overcrowded, outdated institutions. Student numbers have expanded in Paris, as in other countries since the Second World War, but facilities have barely increased and the university authorities remain, for the most part, as cold, forbidding and patriarchal as the Gaullist regime itself.

The students on their meagre grants are poor and sometimes hungry but, compared to the rest of the population, they are free. They have time to live, to think, to argue, to make love. The mere fact of living together, crowded in communal dormitories and lodgings, of eating together in the student canteens, gives them the chance to search for common solutions to the problems they face.

3-9th Paris, France *A bas les flics!*

On Friday May 3, the Nanterre students appeal to their fellows at the Sorbonne for support. Five hundred students crowd the stone-flagged central courtyard of the Sorbonne to hear the speeches from Daniel Cohn-Bendit, a Nanterre sociology student, and others from the March 22 Movement. Outside, a group of neo-fascists (some of whom will be active supporters of Jean-Marie Le Pen's fascist National Front in the eighties and nineties) are roaming the Latin Quarter, looking for left-wing student skulls to crack; there have been many such attacks over the past months. More students are gathering outside the Sorbonne. All are refusing to

Jean-Paul Sartre at the Sorbonne.

disperse. At this point the Rector of the University telephones the Minister of Education, and they agree that the police should clear the courtyard by force.

At 4.45p.m. a mass of armed, helmeted, black-clad members of the CRS (Compagnies Républicaines de Sécurité), the state security police, pour into the courtyard. Dozens of students are arrested by the flics and piled into their waiting vans, packed on to the wooden benches. The students' faces, glimpsed through the wire-mesh windows, are white with shock. Others, crowding the square outside, surge forward at the sight of them, blocking the way, pounding with their fists against the sides of the vans. Shouts ring out, are taken up by the whole crowd and swell into a great rhythmic chant: 'A bas la répression!' Down with repression!

Some students are lifting parked cars out into the street, to block it: the first barricade. A boy in jeans leaps on to a car bonnet, shouting out battle orders. From the gas-masked ranks of the CRS tear-gas grenades are fired out into the crowd. Clouds of acrid smoke swirl up from the pavements, students run screaming, weeping, for the café doorways, spilling out of the little square into Boulevard St Michel.

Barrages of black-clad *flics*. Leather and steel and plastic.
Forgotten nightmares. Masks of blindness. Lines of fear.
Sweet and sickening taste in the mouth. Dry palate. Bowels.
The first wave.
The black-clad army is now a wave of black-clad men, inflicting pain with white clubs. To be left alone is to be grabbed and clubbed; it is falling down and being kicked by many converging on the prey. A girl lies unconscious.
Grenades make bangs and blue clouds.
Cobblestones. Stones found near the trees.
Nauseating gases impregnate streets and lungs. Protection, regrouping, embryos of barricades, then – barricades.
Captured students are taken to Notre-Dame-des-Champs police station.
At ten it starts to rain.
At eleven, the flics are masters.
The Sorbonne – ringed in black.

(Angelo Quattrocchi in *The Beginning of the End*)

'The struggle goes on'. Paris students and their supporters keep up the pressure.

The Sorbonne is closed. Scores of students are under arrest. The narrow streets of the Latin Quarter seethe with *flics*, ready to beat up anyone with long hair or jeans. The shaken student leaders call for support: a huge demonstration will be held on Monday, May 6.

The sight of armed security police clubbing young protesters has sent a shock wave through the French people. There is a groundswell of revulsion against the brutality of the state. In the *lycées*, radical school students come out on strike in support of their older peers.

On May 6 crowds in Paris – where 30,000 demonstrators gather – and in a score of cities across the country, protest against the security police. They demand that the police should be withdrawn from the Latin Quarter, the Sorbonne reopened and the arrested students released.

From the government comes a grim refusal to give way. President de Gaulle sits stony-faced in the Élysée Palace: the CRS will clear up this nonsense.

Every day this week the demonstrations grow larger: tens of thousands take to the streets. An opinion poll shows four-fifths of Parisians support the students.

French broadcasting is under tight government control, but the independent pop stations, Radio Luxembourg and Radio Europe, have their reporters down in the streets, offering their microphones to the students in mobile radio vans.

Young people rush across Paris to join the demonstrations as the students are broadcast live on a million transistor radios, their voices raised above the sounds of

May 1968

Iron bars, scaffolding, bricks are all to hand, but the *pavés,* the cobblestones of the Latin Quarter's ancient streets, are the weapon of choice for many students as they defend themselves against the riot police close to the University of Paris.

Armies of the night: gun-totting police stand firm to stop protesters seizing control of the Boulevard St Michel, the Boul' Mich', a main artery of the students' Latin Quarter stronghold …

street fighting in the Latin Quarter all around them: the screams of tear-gassed demonstrators, running feet, the crash of cobblestones, the swelling chorus of *'Libérez nos camarades'* ('Free our comrades') rising again and again from the student ranks, falling back into the insistent jungle chant of 'CRS equals SS' as the baton-wielding security police move forward again.

10th Paris, France The Night of the Barricades

News comes through on Friday night that the government is prepared to withdraw the security police and reopen the Sorbonne. But the students refuse to capitulate without the release of their comrades. From the huge demonstration which has gathered that evening in the sunshine in the big square at Denfert-Rochereau there comes a roar of defiance: *'Libérez nos camarades!'* Jean-Jacques Lebel, the Paris correspondent of the *Black Dwarf*, files a report to the magazine:

'The crowd is asked by Cohn-Bendit and other leaders where it wants to go. They decide upon the ORTF, the state broadcasting corporation, which has been insulting and disgustingly untruthful in its reporting.

'We circle the Santé prison which is defended by thousands of armed police, then turn towards the Right Bank and the ORTF. But the route has been blocked off by the police. The enormous demonstration is halted in Boulevard St Michel by gigantic forces: we are encircled.

'The decision is taken to occupy the Latin Quarter, peacefully – not to provoke the police, but to defend ourselves if they attack.'

The huge crowd spreads through the labyrinthine streets, heaping up cobblestones, traffic signs, scaffolding and rubble from the building sites – anything that comes to hand to build up defences against the *flics*. The atmosphere is exhilarating, electric: a night-time carnival, thirty thousand strong. 'It's the Commune,' they say. The Commune: the insurrectionary power that arose in Paris during the French Revolution, and again during the revolutionary attempt of 1871. The power that consists only of the people in the act of governing themselves.

For Daniel Cohn-Bendit, the student leader at Nanterre, 'It's a moment I shall never forget. Suddenly, spontaneously, barricades were being thrown up in the streets. People were piling up the cobblestones because they wanted, many for the first time, to throw themselves into a collective, spontaneous activity. People were releasing all their repressed feelings, expressing them in a festive spirit. Thousands felt the need to communicate with each other, to love one another. That night has made me for ever optimistic about history. Having lived through it, I can't ever say, "It will never happen."'

By 10p.m. the students hold the Latin Quarter. A few hours later Jean-Jacques Lebel pens this dispatch from Paris:

'1a.m.: Our group organises the barricade at the corner of Rue Gay Lussac and St Jacques. We are composed of 6 students, 10 workers, some Italians, bystanders and 4 artists who joined later. Most have never seen the others before. We never even knew each other's names.

'A hundred people help carry the stuff and pile it across the street. From then on I was so busy coordinating work at our barricade that I don't know what happened elsewhere. Witnesses say it all happened at the same time and more or less in the same way all over the Latin Quarter.

'Our barricade is double: one three foot high row of cobblestones, an empty space of about 20 yards, then a nine foot high pile of wood, cars, metal posts, dustbins. Our weapons are stones, metal, etc, found in the street.

'A great deal of spontaneous help is given from inhabitants of nearby houses who offer water, sugar and cloth as protection against gases and warn us of police

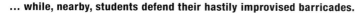

... while, nearby, students defend their hastily improvised barricades.

movements. It is their support which keeps our enthusiasm from flagging in the seemingly endless time of waiting for the inevitable police attack.'

Negotiations are going on. From the back of a mobile radio van, student leaders are conducting a discussion with the Rector, live on air on Radio Luxembourg. The students are refusing to disperse until their comrades are freed, the *flics* are withdrawn and the Sorbonne reopened.

The radios report heavy *flic* reinforcements flooding into the Quarter.

Shortly after midnight Cohn-Bendit speaks to the press: 'We told the Rector that what is happening on the street tonight is a whole generation rising against a certain sort of society. We told him blood would flow if the police did not leave the Latin Quarter. We know the demonstrators will stay behind the barricades until our three demands have been met.'

The Rector telephones the Ministry of the Interior, pleading for permission for more talks. His hands are tied: in an inner sanctum at the Ministry, de Gaulle's hard-line security and intelligence adviser, Jacques Foccart, and Bernard Tricot, the President's key aide from the Élysée Palace, are urging on the Education and Interior Ministers the necessity of taking a firm stand. This is insurrection. It must be crushed. The Defence Minister is also present.

Lines of armoured black CRS vans glimmer in the dark streets. The massed ranks of the security police seem barely human in their insectoid, goggle-eyed masks and helmets. They are sheathed in black leather, armed with batons, shields and tear-gas grenades. This is the naked face of the power wielded by the Fifth Republic. Lebel reports:

'2a.m.: It is now obvious that the police are preparing a powerful attack. The radio announces that we are surrounded and the government has ordered the police to attack. We continue building up barricades, organising a supply of rocks and medical centres every 100 yards. I try to coordinate runners between different barricades near ours but we lack time and are caught by attacks before we can get it together. Practically no news comes from other points of our territory.

'Someone finds a French flag – we tear off the blue and white parts: the red flag now flies over our barricade. I am told many red and black flags flew on other barricades. In front of us we turn over cars to prevent police from charging with their buses and tanks. (The radio said tanks were coming but we never saw any.)

'The police attack Place de Luxembourg. Their tactics are simple: at 100 yards distance they launch gas grenades which blind, suffocate and knock us out. The gas is MACE (Vietnam and Detroit mace), tear-gas and phosphorus grenades which set fire to the cars. Also small explosive grenades: one student near us picked one up to throw it back and it tore his whole hand off.

'We defend as best we can and later we find out that practically every barricade withstood the police at least an hour, sometimes four hours, regardless of blinding and suffocating gases. The police are slowly advancing up Gay Lussac (crowds are running away, we have a hard time calming them down and channeling them towards the exit down Gay Lussac where the police are fewer).

'Then the police attack at three points simultaneously: at two extremities of Gay Lussac, at our barricade and at Rue d'Ulm. Casualties are heavy on our side, mostly

Going over the top. Riot police of the CRS, the Compagnies Républicaines de Sécurité, storm a cobblestone barricade in the Place de Luxembourg district, close to the University.

people knocked unconscious by gas, some temporarily blinded. Thousands of voices shout together: 'De Gaulle assassin', '*Libérez nos camarades*', 'Revolution'. Some make Molotov cocktails. I try to dissuade them for fear of police massacre, not so much of us but of thousands of onlookers, just standing there, fascinated. The general feeling is of a trance. We feel liberated. Suddenly, we have turned into human beings and we are shouting "WE EXIST, WE ARE HERE."

'One boy, in an incredibly heroic gesture, grabs a red flag and leads us towards the cops, through the gas and grenades. To our utter surprise we outnumber the enemy and they retreat. Crowds behind us cheer wildly. We come back behind our barricade, only one slightly wounded. But gases are our worst enemy, we can't breathe, we can't see.

'Finally we are forced back. Our barricade burns. At this point all I can remember is that I fainted from lack of air. I come to in a corridor with two girls slapping my face and putting wet cloths on my eyes. Water is the only thing that helps. They tell me that a student carried me there.

'I look outside: police are everywhere, our barricade across the street is burning. Yellow gas fumes are so thick you can't see.

After rounding up two students in the Boulevard St Michel area, riot police, unmoved by the presence of a member of the Fourth Estate, add a deft finishing touch to the operation.

'I try to run out, thinking to rejoin our forces further down, but police are charging from both sides with grenades and big lethal truncheons: we are cornered.

'We organise inside the apartment building: there are at least 60 students, some wounded, others fainting. We try to barricade the street door. Some desperately ring doorbells of the flats; nobody dares answer. We crowd staircases. The police arrive, break down the door, grab a few and beat them to pulp, then throw in three gas grenades which are murder to our lungs and eyes. They go on down the street.

'A girl on the second floor tells us to come in. We crowd into her flat and she gives us water. Outside: explosions, explosions, explosions.'

A well-known French football commentator is sent to the Latin Quarter to cover the night's events for one of the radio stations. He reports:

'Now the CRS are charging, they're storming the barricade – oh, my God! There's a battle raging. The students are counter-attacking, you can hear the noise – the CRS are retreating ... Now they're regrouping, getting ready to charge again. The inhabitants are throwing things from their windows at the CRS – oh! The police are retaliating, shooting grenades into the windows of apartments ...'

The producer interrupts: 'This can't be true, the CRS don't do things like that!'

'I'm telling you what I'm seeing ...' His voice goes dead. They have cut him off.

(At 5a.m. university students in Strasbourg who have been following the street fighting in Paris all night on their radios, take over and occupy the University's administrative building.)

At 6a.m., exhausted and unshaven, security boss Foccart and the three Ministers leave the Interior Ministry and drive to the Élysée to report to President de Gaulle that the insurrection has been crushed.

Lebel carries on writing:

'6a.m.: Still fighting outside. We all vote to call the Red Cross anyway because one of us is bleeding badly. The police are searching house by house, room by room. Anybody with black hands or wounds or gas spots on clothes (gas attacks leather) is beaten and arrested. We 60 decide to leave together in case we have to fight our way down the street. Helmets are given to the girls. The sun is up.

'We run into the open in a body: fantastic: what a sight! Smoking barricades everywhere, overturned cars, streets unpaved, for half a mile. Painted words on walls: *Vive la Commune du 8 Mai, A BAS L'ETAT POLICIER* ...

'I can't help it, I run over to see our barricade. It still stands, deserted; some onlookers, stunned, the unbelievable sight of the empty battlefield. This Rue Gay Lussac was ours all night till about 4.30a.m.

'I ask a student for a piece of his dirty red shirt, we tie it to a stick, put it back on our barricade and run: police are charging on the other side of the street.

'I can hardly walk from pain. We circle round to Rue d'Ulm, to find police arresting everybody, including those in the medical centre. Barricades and cars are smoking in every street, on every corner. Passers-by warn us where the police are. Many people in cars and taxis volunteer to take us out of the police zone. Everywhere we see enormous police buses full of our people: tired, beaten, bloody prisoners.

'The revolution has begun. If you want to help us there is one way.

'DO THE SAME THING.'

In a broken voice, Daniel Cohn-Bendit goes on the radio and calls for a general strike in protest against the state's behaviour on this night.

Members of the CRS – 'We're students too' – learn about the value of 'sensitive areas' in the suppression of riots.

11th Paris, France *Bonjour, M. Pompidou*

France awakes to a social crisis. Hospitals and police stations are besieged by parents trying to find their missing children. The opposition newspapers rush out special editions condemning the police brutality. The two great trade union federations, the CGT and the CFDT (Confédération Française et Démocratique du Travail), call for a nationwide strike and demonstration to protest against the repression on Monday, May 13 – the tenth anniversary of de Gaulle's accession to power.

Prime Minister Pompidou, returning from a trip abroad, attempts to defuse the situation with concessionary promises: the Sorbonne reopened, the *flics* withdrawn. It is too late.

13th Paris, France The Marching Million

An immense demonstration, one million strong, blocks the streets of Paris in protest against the government. The students have given voice to a much deeper sense of grievance and injustice against the cold, hierarchical, class-dominated social order.

After the demo, a massive contingent gathers at the Champ-de-Mars, the ancient parade-ground at the foot of the Eiffel Tower. News comes through that the government is in retreat, has pulled the CRS back from the Sorbonne. The cry goes up: 'Everybody to the Sorbonne!'

The gates are open. Twenty or thirty thousand people throng inside, crowding the ancient courtyard and the chapel steps. Every room is occupied. There is non-stop political debate in the Grand Amphitheatre. Within hours, the walls are covered with joyful graffiti, festooned with red and black flags, bedecked with revolutionary posters.

The Sorbonne Soviet

The Sorbonne is packed with people, red flags, slogans. In every classroom, and often spilling onto the landings and corridors, Action Committees sit debating their next moves. These committees cover every aspect of revolutionary activity – from guerilla groups for contacting the workers to the organisation of food and medical supplies. In almost every faculty building in Paris it is the same scene.

In the middle of the Sorbonne is a vast amphitheatre. It must hold about five thousand people. All day and all night the debate on the future of the revolution goes on. The speeches were calls for greater unity amongst the factions, demands for the students to declare their objectives, assurances from militant workers that whatever the trade union leadership might say, they were behind the students.

The Odéon was taken over by three thousand young students and workers and has remained 'occupied' ever since. It will not be easily given up. Backstage in the dressing rooms and corridors hundreds of young people work, talk, plan. It looks chaotic but things get done. There seems to be no leadership.

In the auditorium the debate goes on. The audience is less academic and more bourgeois than the Sorbonne and the discussions are often rowdier and jollier. But the atmosphere is the same; De Gaulle's stable regime has blown its lid. For the first time everyone feels they have something to say and a place to say it.

This is a young revolution and most of the work is done at night. The best speech I heard was at two in the morning delivered to the packed amphitheatre. It was given by a typical young *révolutionnaire*: pullover, black trousers, long untidy hair, eyes gleaming with fatigue and lack of food.

'This revolution,' he said, referring to the flags behind him, 'is for the red flag of socialism and the workers' state, and for the black flag of anarchy and the individual'. There was a joyous shout of approval.

In the person of Che, the spirit of revolution oversees the student sit-in at the Sorbonne's Grand Amphitheatre.

I spoke to him afterwards but he could hardly talk for exhaustion and the hacking cough that betrays all those who were brave enough to stand up to the Mace fumes of the night of 10 May.

These young revolutionaries may not win this time but they have struck another blow against Western Society and for their belief that this society is rotten, that it has been rotting for years and that the time has come to change it before it changes them.

Clive Goodwin, *Black Dwarf*, June 1, 1968

For the next five weeks the occupied Sorbonne will become a centre of revolutionary activity, a playground, a festival. Every night the Grand Amphitheatre is packed by a General Assembly that will decide on the issues of the day and elect a fifteen-strong Occupation Committee whose power will be limited to a single night and a single day, so that no bureaucracy can develop. Anyone may enter the huge chamber, anyone may speak.

Together with the occupied Odéon Theatre, the Grand Amphitheatre is one of the powerhouses of thought and command centres of activity. The atmosphere there is intense and extraordinary.

14th | Nantes, France — The Spark Ignites

Young workers from the Sud-Aviation aircraft factory who have been marching with the students the day before, strike and occupy their factory.

Supporters bring blankets and food from the nearby student hostel as they prepare to hold the factory through the night: amid the silent machines, for the first time, people can now hear themselves talk.

De Gaulle, completely isolated from the mood that has gripped half the nation, leaves France on a state visit to Rumania.

15th | Paris, France — The Workers are Angry

Renault workers strike and occupy their factories. At the Renault car factory in the Paris suburb of Boulogne-Billancourt, four thousand workers spend their first night in the occupied plant. Their wives and children flock round, bringing them bedclothes, food and drink.

'The students' struggle to democratize the university is like the workers' struggle to democratize the factory': workers take over the massive Renault plant at Boulogne-Billancourt.

Within forty-eight hours the strike-and-occupy movement has spread across the whole of France. The occupations are not just about better pay; they are against the whole factory system: the power and hierarchy of the management, the submission of humans to the machine. The leadership of the CFDT trade union declares: 'The students' struggle to democratize the universities is of the same nature as the workers' struggle to democratize the factories.'

18th | **Paris, France** We will Write our own Scripts

News editors, broadcasters and scriptwriters at ORTF, France's state broadcasting corporation, announce that they will no longer take orders from Ministers and political parties.

De Gaulle cuts short his visit to Rumania and flies home. By the next day, two million workers are on strike.

École des Beaux Arts: The People's Workshop

'To challenge the cultural system from the inside rapidly leads from challenging art to the art of challenge.'

The walls of the Latin Quarter are plastered with posters, a new art of comment and intervention that has grown up overnight in the explosively creative atmosphere of May. The great, grimy baroque edifice of the École des Beaux Arts is occupied by students, workers, architects, artists, designers and *enragés* who meet every night in a general assembly to discuss the developing political situation and the themes, ideas, designs and slogans for that night's posters.

Once the votes have been taken, the work begins: the silk screens stretched across their wooden frames on the work tables of the huge, white studio, the designs are traced on, the solids blocked out with gum, the varnish is coated, all amid the oily smell of ink, white spirit, linseed oil and a night-time's worth of cigarettes. One person whooshes the printer's ink across the screen, one lifts the frame and pulls out the freshly printed sheet, two more hang up the still-damp posters to dry.

In the small hours, more comrades will turn up, coming on from meetings, discussions and events to collect armfuls of posters for fly-posting overnight. Lookouts are posted against the *flics*, paint pots full of glue and big decorators' brushes plaster the new images across the massive walls in the darkness. As day breaks, they gleam with fresh ideas.

A notice has been pinned up at the entrance to the lithographic studios:
'PEOPLE'S WORKSHOP YES
BOURGEOIS WORKSHOP NO'
The artists distribute an explanatory leaflet:
'If we try to be precise about the words we have written at the entrance to the studios and to comprehend what they mean, they will dictate to us the main lines of our future action.

'The words indicate that it is not in any way a question of reforming, that is to say of bettering, what already exists. Any improvement implies that basic principles are not to change, hence that they are already the right ones. We are against the established order of today. What is this established order? Bourgeois art and bourgeois culture. What is bourgeois culture? It is the means by which the forces of oppression of the ruling class isolate and set apart the artists from the rest of the workers by giving them a privileged status. Privilege locks the artist in an invisible prison. The fundamental concepts which underlie this act of isolation which culture brings about are:

'-the idea that art has "gained its autonomy" (Malraux – see the speech made at the time of the Grenoble Olympic Games).

'-the defence of "creative freedom": culture makes the artist live in the illusion of freedom.

1. He does what he wants to do, he believes that everything is possible, he is accountable only to himself or to Art.

2. He is a "creator", which means that out of

23rd France *Adieu, de Gaulle, Adieu*

Ten million workers are on strike: factories, shipyards, oil refineries, railways, offices, banks, department stores, post offices, administrative buildings, schools and colleges have all ground to a halt and many have been occupied by the striking workers, with red flags flying from the gates. The opposition is baying for Gaullist blood. On a huge anti-government demonstration in Paris, young workers and students sing '*Adieu, de Gaulle, adieu, de Gaulle,*' and wave their handkerchiefs as they march. The Cannes Film Festival collapses as the technicians go on strike, supported by the directors who withdraw their films. The airports are shut, and there are no trains, buses or Métro. The coalmines are silent. No rubbish is being collected. The student protest has turned into something huge and spread throughout France.

In the midst of all this the North Vietnamese/US 'talks about peace talks' are proceeding. The Vietnamese delegation enjoy themselves enormously in the

all things he invents something unique, whose value will be permanent and beyond historical reality. He is not a worker who is at grips with historical reality. The idea of creation gives his work an unreal quality.

'In giving him this privileged status, culture puts the artist in a position where he can do no harm and in which he functions as a safety-valve in the mechanism of bourgeois society.

'This is the situation of every one of us. We are all bourgeois artists. How could it be otherwise?

'This is why when we write "People's Workshop" [Atelier Populaire] it cannot be a question of improvement, but of a radical change of direction. 'It means that we are determined to transform what we are in society.

'Let us make it clear that it is not the establishment

of better contacts between artists and modern techniques that will bind them closer to all the other categories of workers, but opening their eyes to the problems of other workers, that is to say of the historical reality of the world in which we live.

'No teacher could help us to become more familiar with that reality. We must all teach ourselves. This does not mean that there does not exist objective, therefore admissible knowledge, nor that older artists and teachers cannot be very useful. But this is on condition that they themselves have decided to transform what they are in society and to take part in this work of self-education. 'The educative power of the bourgeoisie thus challenged, the way will be open to the educative power of the people.'

The graphic arm of the protest movement: image and words combine to punch home the message.

insurrectionary atmosphere of Paris in the spring. The French Communist Party have put the country villa once owned by Maurice Thorez at their disposal, where they host a cocktail party to mark Ho Chi Minh's seventy-eighth birthday. A diminutive Vietnamese diplomat in a pair of extra-thick glasses smiles up at a tall American, taps him on the chest and says, amiably but insistently, 'Always remember that you are the aggressors.'

25th Paris, France Behind Closed Doors

Prime Minister Pompidou meets trade union leaders at the Ministry of Social Affairs in an attempt to buy off the strikes. His tactics are to take each union leader in turn into a side room, ask him what he is really after, and promise that he shall have it.

'The walls of this ministry are thick,' comments one CFDT leader. 'The clamour from the factories and the street does not seem to penetrate them.'

Both sides emerge from the talks looking immensely relieved. They have cut a deal: huge pay increases in return for calling off the strikes.

But to the consternation of the union leaders, the striking workers reject the deal. CGT boss Georges Séguy is booed by tens of thousands of strikers at the Renault plant in Boulogne-Billancourt. They don't just want the money. Their protest is about more than that.

There are rumblings in the security police against being used to attack factory workers. Now even the CRS chiefs tell the government: 'Our loyalty can no longer be taken for granted.'

Gaullists surge along the Champs-Élysées towards the Arc de Triomphe, in a march in support of the embattled President on May 29.

Workers and students unite against the state.

29th Baden-Baden, West Germany General Panic

De Gaulle panics at the state of the crisis and flies in secret to the French Army base at Baden-Baden to ensure he will have the military behind him. The generals demand the release of Raoul Salan, former head of the OAS (Organisation de l'Armée Secrète, which committed innumerable atrocities in Algeria). Two weeks later Salan and other OAS ringleaders will be freed.

The next day de Gaulle returns to Paris and broadcasts to the nation, announcing that France is threatened with communist dictatorship, calling for civic action 'in defence of the republic' and hinting at the use of force.

A massive right-wing demonstration blocks Paris in his support, chanting 'France for the French' and 'Cohn-Bendit to Dachau' as it marches up the Champs-Élysées, spread out across the width of the magnificent avenue.

31st Paris, France Imagination in Power

There is a troop alert around Paris. All reservists are called up.

Le Nouvel Observateur publishes a long interview by Jean-Paul Sartre with Daniel Cohn-Bendit, in which he writes:

'What is interesting about your action is that it puts imagination in the seats of power. You have a limited imagination like everyone else, but you have a great many more ideas than your elders. We have been made in such a way that we have a precise idea of what is possible and of what is not. A professor will say: "Do away with exams? Never. One can rearrange them but one cannot do away with them!" Why? Because he has taken exams for half his life.

'The working class has often imagined new means of struggle, but always as a function of the precise situation in which it found itself. In 1936, it invented the take-over of factories because that was the only weapon which it had to consolidate and to exploit an electoral victory. You have an imagination which is much more rich and the slogans chalked up on the walls of the Sorbonne prove it. Something has emerged from you which surprises, which astonishes and which denies everything which has made our society what it is today. That is what I would call the extension of the field of possibility. Do not give up.'

1968

June

Their nightmares
are our dreams

Paris graffiti

Another month begins and the people of France carry on marching.

While events in France continue to unfold throughout June, the countries of Eastern Europe witness a growing ferment. Yugoslavia has always been different to the rest. Here the victory against the Nazi's Second World War occupation was achieved not by the entry of the Red Army under Stalin's command but by an audacious and courageous resistance struggle, backed by both Moscow and London. The communist partisans were not angels but they were the only force capable of uniting Serb and Croat, Montenegrin, Bosnian and Kosovan against the common enemy: the Nazis and their collaborators. It is this unity of the different Balkan communities that preserved the unity of the Yugoslav state after the end of the war.

Even during the Resistance, the leadership of the Yugoslav Communist Party had known how to play their allies off against each other – Moscow against London, and vice versa. It was this same leadership which refused, at the end of the war, to accept that section of the Yalta Treaty wanting to reintroduce a monarchy to Yugoslavia. Tito told Stalin and Churchill that any such notion was anathema to those who had fought for victory. The Big Two retreated, though Stalin was irritated by the real independence demonstrated

President Tito (right) meets India's leader Dr Zakir Hussain just before the start of Yugoslav–Indian talks on June 11.

by the leader of Yugoslav's Communists. The Yugoslav Press, for its part, denounced Moscow, and Tito privately warned Stalin: if you dare to invade us, our people will be armed to resist you. Another Communist leader, Milovan Djilas, published a scathing critique of Stalinism entitled *The New Class*. The Yugoslav press was suddenly filled with debates on the real nature of socialism. Moscow kept up the propaganda barrage, but the bombers and tanks remained stationary. Tito's refusal to become a pawn in the Cold War gave him a new prestige throughout the world.

But, despite the rhetoric and despite the much greater literary freedom than that which exists in the Soviet Union or Eastern Europe, Yugoslavia in 1968 is still run on authoritarian lines. The Party controls society, the Politburo controls the Party and Tito controls the Politburo. The personnel in Belgrade are more enlightened than their counterparts in Moscow and East Berlin, but the basic governmental structure is the same. This clashes with the regime's rhetoric and the students prise open the contradictions between the propaganda and the reality.

In Belgrade, students want real democracy, real workers' self-management and an end to unemployment. They oppose the enrichment of the managers who control the working class.

Tito is not a de Gaulle. He is an old Communist and he is shaken by the students on the streets. He defuses the protests by defending the demands of the students. He declares that he supports all their demands and that Yugoslav communists have to face up to the new challenge. The police disappear and there is dancing on the streets.

Much could have changed. But very little will. If the structural reforms demanded by the students had been implemented and institutionalized, the citizens of Yugoslavia might have been spared the traumas inflicted on them by their leaders after Tito's death and which led ultimately to the disintegration of the Yugoslav state.

The break-up of the country, over twenty years after the events in Belgrade, was neither necessary nor inevitable, but was brought about by the collapse of the economy under the friendly guidance of the IMF and the World Bank, intra-state jostling for economic gains within the European Community and, above all, by the cynical decision of the scoundrels in charge of the party in Belgrade to strengthen their power base by playing the nationalist card. Add to this the irresponsibility of the European Union which proved incapable of resisting Austro–German intrigues in Slovenia and Croatia and the pieces of the puzzle began to take a clear shape.

In Yugoslavia, if anywhere, the contrast between the ideals of the '68ers who marched in the streets of Belgrade and Milosevic's disgusting appeals to Serbian chauvinism in the same city, a quarter of a century later, is very clear. The first engendered Hope, the second was designed to create a climate of Fear. This new poisonous force ultimately destroyed the Yugoslav state. Today, the very idea of Yugoslavia has been extirpated. In its place, differences are stressed and the old national, utopian imagination is smothered, repressed or instrumentalized by those in power. A tragic end to what was once a hopeful song.

As Yugoslav police charge demonstrators outside the US Consulate in Zagreb in the winter of 1968, the authoritarian face of President Tito's rule shows itself yet again, after months of unrest.

1st France On the Brink of Revolution?

Hot sunshine, and the whole of France has come to a halt.

The rubbish lies uncollected in streets where people have replaced the cars, where the roar of the combustion engine has been replaced by a hubbub of conversation. Wherever you go, people are talking, talking to complete strangers as they never have before.

In Nantes, in the rural region of Brittany, the shopgirls have occupied the big, cut-price department store, Prisunic, and are sleeping in the management's easy chairs. There is no petrol: the sole pump in town has been reserved for doctors only by the strike committee that runs the town. Neighbourhood food cooperatives are selling cheap bread and vegetables in conjunction with the local peasant farmers, with free milk to the under-threes. Teams of students and strikers go out to the farms to help pick the new potatoes. Teachers are setting up communal nurseries for the strikers' children.

The machines have fallen silent. Instead of their noise, the sound of children playing in the sunshine fills the factory courtyards. Men and women sit around, breaking bread, smoking, talking, on and on, beneath the red flags and hand-painted banners that proclaim the occupation.

An effigy of the hated head of security has been strung up outside the huge occupied Citroën plant in Paris. Inside, a communal canteen has been organized, and is providing free meals. Artists, musicians and theatre groups have come in to perform. The occupying strikers sit outside in the sunshine, sharing cigarette-fuelled discussions with outsiders about the plant and its management. A pall of heavy smoke drifts in from the waste ground nearby where an army unit has been given the job of burning the uncollected rubbish.

Other soldiers have been organizing in the barracks in support of the workers who are occupying the factories. Their message is clear: now is the time for the whole country to unite. Their leaflet reads:

'Soldiers,

'The entire people is now rising up against the anti-popular Gaullist regime of unemployment and want.

Capitalism's Discontents

In the second issue of the *Black Dwarf*, published on 1 June in London, the Marxist historian, Eric Hobsbawm, wrote:

'The students rebelling against a society which offers them all its prizes, the workers forgetting about their HP debts to establish, by their spontaneous mass action, that life is more than overtime earnings and holidays in Palma: these are not French but potentially international phenomena.

'We knew – though the politicians didn't – that people are not contented. They feel that their lives are meaningless in the consumer society. They know that, even when they are comfortable (which many of them are not) they are also more powerless than before, more pushed around by giant organisations for whom they are items and not men.

'They know that the official mechanisms for representing them – elections, parties, etc. – have tended to become a set of ceremonial institutions going through empty rituals. They do not like it – but until recently they did not know what to do about it, and may have wondered whether there was anything that they could do about it. What France proves is that when someone demonstrates that people are *not* powerless, they may begin to act again. Perhaps even more than this: that only the sense of impotence is holding many of us back from acting like men and not zombies.'

'The students are struggling in the streets against the CRS. The workers are occupying the factories. In the countryside, the poor peasants are in revolt against the rural exodus and the monopolizers of farmland.

'Soldiers,

'You are the children of the people; your place is at the side of the workers, peasants and students.

'The government wants to use you as a repressive force like the CRS.

'It is using you (WITHOUT PAY) to undercut the strike in public transport.

'It is confining you to barracks in order to isolate you from the people.

'You are the sons of the people. Your place is at their side.

'The government wants to use you to crush the people's revolt.

'You must oppose this.

'ORGANIZE.

'Refuse to suppress the people.

'ALL TOGETHER AGAINST THIS GOVERNMENT OF REPRESSION AND WANT.

signed: The Soldiers' Committee of Vincennes.'

Respectable Man

'The international crises of the past ten years may come to seem relatively mild compared with the rifts and dissensions which now threaten many countries internally. France is on the edge of a civil war. We have seen American cities burning, and Negroes expressing through their violence that desperation and anger which is the consequence of the United States' total failure to come to terms with their predicament. In West Germany students have been on the streets and confronted Herr Springer and the Bundestag with their rejection and contempt of a social system which is politically moribund and only precariously democratic. This too resulted in violence, as did the Vietnam demonstration in Grosvenor Square.

'Everywhere 'respectable' citizens are bewildered, anxious, frightened or angry – or perhaps more commonly a combination of all four. The word respectable requires quotes in this context, since the character and identity of those who believe or acquiesce in the economic and power structure of modern capitalism, are under serious challenge. It is the decent solid citizens who call for harsh authoritarian measures against students; whose hate mythology is one of 'long-haired pinkoes'; who in England find sanction in Enoch Powell's inflammatory racism for their own bigotry and prejudice against coloured people....

'We live it seems in a period when several major strands of history are drawing together. The Soviet revolution has failed genuinely to revolutionise human relationships and whereas it has created a materially socialised basis for living, the humane objectives which should justify its very existence seem as remote as ever. Post-war capitalism on the other hand has produced a society which must appear morally revolting to many people whether they understand its mechanisms or not – this at the expense of large underprivileged sections of each country, and more so at the expense of what is now known as the Third or Underdeveloped World.

'It is time the 'Respectable Citizen' began to understand the real standards by which he lives, as opposed to the cherished delusions he believes to be standards.... He lives relatively unmolested and in comfort whilst most of the world lives in oppression and misery. He votes for his system because his system gives him what he wants, yet it withholds from him the means of understanding that what he is getting is trivial even when it is not plainly squalid. When things go wrong, he reaches for the nearest scapegoat – and there is usually a coloured man, or a Jew, a pinko or even simply an underling to take the brunt of his rage and frustration. He makes money out of everything and everyone, given the chance – not stopping short at the most barbarous means of destruction. He produces and consumes at random, and wastefully. He builds ugly cities and makes the air stink and throb from the pursuit of his wretched palliatives, looted territory, petty power....

'That is Respectable Man.'

David Mercer, *Black Dwarf*, June 1, 1968

A *Black Dwarf* poster-poem by Christopher Logue exhorts the oppressed to open their eyes to their condition:

'Know thy enemy.
He does not care what colour you are
provided you work for him;
he does not care how much you earn
provided you earn more for him;
he does not care who lives in the room at the top
provided he owns the building;
he will let you say whatever you like against him
provided you do not act against him;
he sings the praises of humanity
but knows machines cost more than men;
bargain with him – he laughs and beats you at it;
challenge him
and he kills;
sooner than lose the things he owns
he will destroy the world.'

THE BLACK DWARF 13.2

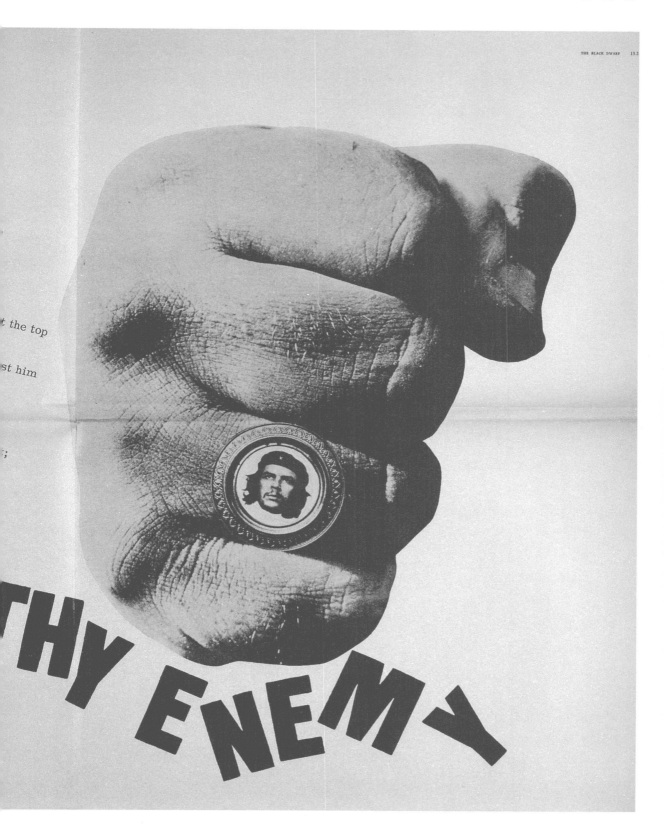

t the top

st him

;

THY ENEMY

| 2nd | **Belgrade, Yugoslavia** *Strictly Reserved for the Working Classes* |

A summer evening in Belgrade: swallows are wheeling overhead and the pavement cafés on the broad, tree-lined streets are packed. But at the new, large university complex on the outskirts of town, known as New Belgrade, the students are agitated. A popular theatre group has been booked to play, and the students have requested that the performance should take place in the university's large, open-air amphitheatre, so that everyone can attend.

Now it turns out that the authorities are restricting the event to youth members of the ruling party, the League of Communists, attending a summer camp nearby. Only a small theatre has been booked.

Resentments about the privileges of the party élite have been running high. The summer before, the students had put on a risqué satirical revue called *Strictly Reserved for the Working Classes*.

An angry group of students try to push their way in as the performance begins, but are thrown out again by the police. As news of the confrontation spreads, a crowd of over a thousand students converges in the street outside the theatre. They have seen the TV footage from the universities of Nanterre, in the suburbs of Paris, and Columbia, in New York City, and their blood is up.

Within a few minutes they have begun to attack the theatre itself, a symbol of privilege: doors are battered down, windows are broken, and when police reinforcements drive up with a fire-engine to control the crowd, the fire-engine itself is overtaken and set on fire.

The police charge into the crowd and the students overturn cars as barricades against them, defending themselves with stones against the police attack. The students retreat to the university itself and hold a mass meeting all through the night, trying to decide what to do. In the morning, some 4000 students assemble for a march on the centre of Belgrade, some ten kilometres away. Halfway there, they are met by a force of thousands of police, drawn from all over Serbia, lined up against them like an opposing army. The police open fire. Nearly seventy people are injured in the violent battle that ensues.

A mass meeting of over 10,000 students gathers at New Belgrade in the afternoon and resolves to take the protest further. The Philosophy and Sociology Faculty is occupied and its façade hung with posters and hand-painted banners proclaiming 'TOMORROW WITHOUT THOSE WHO SOLD YESTERDAY!' and 'DOWN WITH THE RED BOURGEOISIE!'

Students distribute leaflets through the streets and cafés, reading:
'DEMANDS
1. The rapid solution of the employment problem facing new university graduates, most of whom have to go abroad if they want to find any sort of employment.
2. The suppression of the great inequalities in Yugoslavia.
3. The establishment of real democracy and self-management relations.
4. The immediate release of all arrested students.
5. The resignation of the chief of police.
6. The resignation of the directors of all Belgrade newspapers, radio and TV for having deliberately falsified the events of June 2.'

Steel-helmeted riot police pour on to the streets of Belgrade, with orders to prevent all demonstrations, while party directives go out that there must be no fraternization between students and workers. In fact, many of the students *are* workers, seconded on to courses from their workshops and factories: this is perhaps what gives the Belgrade uprising its particularly militant character.

The next day, some of the professors come to join the students in the occupied faculties, helping them to draw up an Action Programme and an open letter to the workers of Yugoslavia that begins:

'We are not fighting for our own material interests. We are enraged by the enormous social and economic differences in society. We do not want the working class to be sacrificed for the sake of "reforms". We are for self-management, but against the enrichment of those who depend on and control the working class.'

The crisis escalates. All the newspapers are screaming for a hard line to be taken against the occupying students. The police close in on the faculties and cut off all entry. On June 9 it is announced that President Tito will address the nation the following day.

Tito's intervention takes everybody by surprise. Alone among the world leaders in 1968, he welcomes the dynamic criticism that the students have to bring:

'It is a challenge to Yugoslav communists, to turn our words into deeds. Yes, there are extremists among the students. Yes, their use of violence is wrong. But their political consciousness itself is not wrong. On the contrary, it is the fruit of our new self-managed socialist relations. All communists should strive to make a reality of the students' Action Programme.

'I pledge myself to resign as your President if the students' programme is not carried through.'

The students storm out of their faculties and parade jubilantly through the streets of Belgrade, cheering and laughing, dancing and singing. Miraculously, the steel-helmeted police seem to have melted away.

Tito's intervention defuses the protest. Only the Philosophy Faculty remains occupied, the students there continuing to work on developing a radical critique of society as a whole until the faculty is closed by the police and the start of the summer vacation disperses the students again.

Meanwhile the sociology students go out into the streets to conduct interviews, trying to determine what the significance of the June events has been for the various segments of Yugoslav society.

– A group of workers from a tyre factory are asked whether they have spoken with any students since the beginning of the events?

'Sure we have. We went after work to see them. After checking we were not reporters they let us in. They wanted us to tell them how self-management really works. We told them that only the director and his friends self-manage the factory. Besides that, the workers' council meetings are so damn boring that we don't go unless we are forced to. We told the students that they had proved themselves to be part of the working class and that all us workers know it. We told them that it isn't possible to reform this bunch of leaders that we have got.'

'What did they say to that?'

'They agreed!'

– A peasant woman selling tomatoes and peaches in a large open-air marketplace on the outskirts of Belgrade is asked what she thinks of the students' demonstration in the city.

'I just don't know what those city kids are up to, but God knows, my life is hard enough without kids wrecking and tearing things up in the streets. If those children go on they'll be shot down in the streets. The police will knock on their doors and shoot them down in their homes, mow them down in their schools. Those children had better rest easy with what they've got, because there is no playing around with Them.'

A man selling live chickens in the market-place is asked if he has seen the posters calling for unity of students, peasants and workers.

'Yes, I saw a poster like that in front of that big school near the park. But I don't pay heed to things like that. All they want is power and if they get it, they'll be just like all the rest. Did you hear the story of the peasant kid that joined the partisans and after the revolution got a position as a Communist official? Well anyway, he went to one of those colleges and graduated, got a villa on the hill, fancy furniture, big car, and a summer house by the sea. Well, one summer he comes back to his village to see his old mother. After listening to his bragging for a while, the mother says, "Son, you have done really well. Live in a big house with fancy furniture. Got a big black car. Even got a summer house on the coast.... But, son, what are you going to do when the Communists come and take it all away?"'

6th | USA Another Murdered Kennedy

Bobby Kennedy is storming through the Democratic primary elections. He is a young, attractive candidate who speaks out against poverty, race discrimination and prolonging the war. He comes to California with a string of brilliant victories behind him and sweeps home in Los Angeles with fifty-three per cent of the vote. It's starting to look as though the American people may elect a crusading liberal as President, next November.

The press are all waiting to meet Bobby after his victory speech, in the ballroom of the Ambassador Hotel. Kennedy stops to shake hands with the kitchen staff as he comes through. The chefs and busboys flock around him, as black Americans have throughout the campaign, as the one white politician to ever talk about their plight.

Sirhan Bishara Sirhan, a twenty-four-year-old Palestinian, steps forward and sprays the Presidential candidate with bullets.

At a stroke, the 1968 US Presidential election is reduced to a choice between lacklustre Vice-President Hubert Humphrey, for the Democrats, and Republican Richard Milhous Nixon. For many of the rebellious young – black and white – this merely serves to confirm their cynical view of the bankruptcy of the whole American political system.

6-13th | France All Good Communists, Come to the Aid of the Fifth Republic

De Gaulle has backed down on his call for a referendum and instead a general election has been called for June 23.

Now a frantic struggle begins to get the strikers back to work. Georges Séguy, head of the CGT trade union federation, is leading the return-to-work movement, travelling round the country from one occupied factory meeting to the next, bullying, pleading, coercing local trade union leaders to call for an end to the strikes.

Another CGT leader, André Barjonet, resigns in protest, declaring:

'For years the CGT has never missed an opportunity for saying to the workers that one must get rid of Gaullism and move towards socialism. For years we have never hidden the fact that our aim in the CGT was not only defence of your interests but also, and above all, to get rid of the power of monopoly of the Gaullist regime.

Above left: Minutes after making his victory speech in the Democratic primaries, Bobby Kennedy is gunned down – an act that ends both his life and the chances of the Democrats in 1968.
Above right: America's poor people march to the Lincoln Memorial in Washington DC on June 9.

'Then, when the time is ripe, Georges Séguy gets up and makes a speech declaring that the CGT does not intend to go beyond day-to-day union demands …

Riot police are sent in to occupy the Renault factory at Flins, near Paris, and evict the striking workers. Day-long running battles ensue. At the Sochaux Peugeot works in eastern France, the workforce is split after an extremely narrow majority at a mass meeting backs the union call for a return to work. The Peugeot management call in the police, fearing that the more militant strikers may be planning to reoccupy the works.

The following day strike pickets are waiting to dissuade the early-morning shift from returning to work. Riot police move in to clear the factory gates with teargas and baton charges. Thirteen are injured and a twenty-four-year-old, M. Beylot, is shot dead by the police. That afternoon the entire second shift joins the strikers and the local population surround the factory gates, booing and jeering at the police. A one-hour total stoppage is held all over France the following day, to protest against the repression.

Meanwhile clashes between police and students continue almost nightly on the Boulevard St Michel, close to the heart of the French capital.

Top: A CGT trade union leader urges striking Citroën employees to return to work.
Above: Reverberations of May: helmeted students, protesting about the death by drowning of a youth fleeing from police officers, occupy the Sorbonne and defend it against the riot police.

A government announcement is issued stating that any non-French nationals found to have taken part in the May demonstrations will be deported. A huge protest demo is called by all the groups who have been participating in what are already being called the Events of May: Trotskyists, Maoists, the March 22 Movement ... The next day, the groups themselves are banned and all demonstrations ruled illegal until after the elections are over.

11th Kitakyushu, Japan Blood on the Tracks

Railway workers in Japan ask the Zengakuren students at Kyushu and Kitakyushu universities for their help in stopping a freight train, loaded with ammunition for the Vietnam War, travelling from Kitakyushu to the US Forces ammunition depot at Yamada. The students and workers rally with their banners outside Kitakyushu station and then charge through on to the tracks, sitting down in the path of the train and forcing it to stop. Protesters swarm up into the engine's cab to talk to the driver and his mate and explain what they are doing. It is nine hours before the Japanese riot police succeed in clearing the protesters off the track and sending the deathly cargo forward to its destination: the villagers of Vietnam.

20th Dagenham, UK Equal Pay for Equal Work

At the Ford Motor Company's plant in Dagenham, on the eastern outskirts of London, the women sewing-machinists are talking about a strike. Questions of women's inequality are in the air: it is fifty years since British women first won the vote and there is a lot of discussion in the press asking whether it has made any difference to the situation of women in general.

The workforce at Ford's is completely sex-segregated. The men work on the track, with the metal: they are paid according to how their work is graded, in five grades of skill, from the lowest – unskilled labourer – up to those who are classed as the most highly skilled engineers. The women work in the canteen and in the sewing-machine section. They don't have grades, they aren't rated as having skills at all: they come all together, in a class below the lowest, unskilled men's grade; they are just women.

'It isn't about pay,' says Rosie Boland, one of the most determined of the Ford women strikers. 'It's about *recognition*.'

The sewing-machinists are upholsterers: they make the cars' seats. Their work is fiddly and detailed. It takes concentration and a lot of manual dexterity and it is a strain on the back and the eyes. It *is* skilled work, the women argue. Yet they are paid less than any young lad pushing a broom.

Their strike brings the whole factory to a standstill. The Ford women, militant, articulate and brave, go on TV to argue their case in the face of more hostility than support from a lot of the male workforce. But their husbands are backing them.

'And most of them help with the housework, too – at weekends,' Rosie Boland says. 'Not like the women up north. It's a different world. They're completely at their men's bidding up there and they'll never get their rights.'

The strike ends with a compromise, negotiated by the (male) union leaders with the (male) bosses. The women aren't that happy about it but they are glad they took the stand they did. It is the beginning of a nationwide campaign for equality of pay between men and women: a first step on the road to recognition.

Women strikers at Ford's Dagenham factory voice their feelings on the dispute to the news media.

Labour MP Audrey Wise will be one of the speakers at the Trafalgar Square rally for equal pay the following year, part of the campaign that has grown out of the Dagenham women's strike. The first, seminal British women's liberation groups will help to organize the event, held on a Sunday afternoon in the pouring rain.

'Of course the discussion centred on equal pay,' Wise remembers later. 'But as with everything to do with women, it can never stay on wages. There's no boundaries, ever. I could imagine the conversations going on in those women's houses: "I'm going to London, how can we afford it? What about the dinner? Who will look after the children?" Whereas a man would simply say, "I'm going on a demonstration." I looked out from the platform at all these thousands of women tipping back their umbrellas to see you speak. They were drinking in every word. I thought of all the Sunday dinners gone uncooked.'

22nd   Karlovy Vary, Czechoslovakia   Memories of Underdevelopment

A stunning new Cuban film opens at the Karlovy Vary (Karlsbad) film festival: *Memories of Underdevelopment*, directed by Tomás Gutiérrez Alea. Its hero is an 'apolitical intellectual', a Cuban landowner whose property has been nationalized by the revolutionary government and whose wife runs off to Miami. The hero, however, decides to stay. 'I know what will happen there. I don't know what will happen here.'

Throughout the film, fragments from his past – from Cuba's past – well up, as memories. Tightly packed crowd shots home in on faces of extraordinarily expressive significance. There are close-ups in which Alea's camera is so close that the image goes to grain, or even to dots, as though through a longing to enter right inside the skin. Conscious and unconscious elements of the Cuban experience jostle against each other, seen reflected through the hero's wondering mind.

June 1968

25th Solna, Sweden Bleak Visions

Swedish Film-maker Ingmar Bergman is asked about his political attitudes.

He replies: 'I've a strong impression that our world is about to go under. Our political systems are deeply compromised and have no further use. Our social behaviour patterns – interior and exterior – have proved a fiasco. The tragic thing is, we neither can nor want to, nor have the strength to alter course. It's too late for revolutions, and deep down inside ourselves we no longer even believe in their positive effects. Just around the corner an insect world is waiting for us – and one day it's going to roll in over our ultra-individualized existence. Otherwise, I'm a respectable social democrat.'

26th Czechoslovakia *Two Thousand Words*

An Extraordinary Congress has been called for September 9 and local elections of Congress delegates are taking place inside all the Party organizations. Dubcek and his colleagues are travelling the country, speaking at Party meetings, urging support for their Action Programme of basic reforms.

The Congress will be vital. It alone can elect a new Central Committee, effectively the supreme governing authority.

Meanwhile the Warsaw Pact troop manoeuvres that began in Czechoslovakia at the beginning of June show no sign of ending. Rumours of armoured columns sighted in country districts darken the summer air.

A manifesto, signed by seventy leading Czechoslovak citizens, is published in four different newspapers. The government disowns it – in moderate terms – but Prague Radio reports a huge volume of support. The manifesto's only title is *Two Thousand Words*. It ends:

'People have recently had fears that the progress of democratization had stopped. This feeling is partly a manifestation of tiredness due to the agitated events and is partly due to the fact that the season of surprising revelations, resignations from high places, and intoxicating speeches of unprecedented verbal boldness is past.

'However, the struggle of forces has merely become less obvious to a certain extent. The fight is now being waged for the substance and for the working of the laws, for the extent of practical steps. Under apparently boring headlines a very hard struggle is going on.

'The recent great apprehension springs from the possibility that foreign forces may interfere with our internal development. Being faced with all these superior forces, the only thing we can do is to hold our own decently and not to start anything. We can assure the government that we will give it our backing, if necessary, even with weapons, as long as the government does what we gave it the mandate to do: and we can assure our allies that we will observe our treaties of friendship, alliance, and trade.

'This spring, just as after the great war, we have been given a great chance again. Once again we have the possibility of taking into our hands our common cause, which for all practical purposes we call socialism, and giving it a shape which will better correspond with our former good reputation and with the relatively good opinion which we once had of ourselves. This spring has just ended and will never come back again. In the winter we shall know everything.'

1968
July

'It takes balls to say NO.'

National Guardsmen confront protesters in Berkeley, California, in the summer of 1968.

Popular misconceptions notwithstanding, the history of the United States is littered with examples of volcanic militancy. The expressions of dissent, however, were usually economic. The record of American working-class struggles during the late nineteenth and the first half of the twentieth centuries for better working conditions and rights is unsurpassed to this day. The same can be said of the degree of violence inflicted on American workers by armed gangs hired by private capitalists as well as by uniformed men in the pay of the state.

But, despite its militancy, the American working class, alone in the West, failed to create a political party to defend its interests. Social democracy proved to be still-born in the United

States. Political dissent was confined to a small, if vocal minority of intellectuals and politically conscious worker-activists. The New Deal saw the size of this layer double and quadruple during the Second World War, but with the advent of the Cold War came McCarthyism, a home-grown demagogy designed to wipe out radical dissent in American cultural and academic life.

Those hauled up before Senator Joseph McCarthy's House Un-American Activities Committee were presumed guilty and had to prove their innocence by naming 'Communist sympathizers'. As a consequence, dissenters in the late forties, fifties and early sixties had to pay a heavy price in terms of their careers. The freedom to express dissident views was never formally curtailed, but publishers' advances, research grants and subsidies were usually made available only to those who wished to study 'non-controversial subjects'. Thus while it was perfectly possible in the early sixties to procure a lucrative subsidy to interview Cuban exiles in Miami to 'obtain the truth about Castro's Cuba' it was impossible to get backing for a project which entailed travelling to Cuba to study the mass literacy and health programmes of the revolutionary government. The CIA was engaged in a covert subsidy of individuals and magazines throughout the world to help the pursuit of 'safe studies'.

This sickness had become so widespread it led Senator Fulbright to state publicly that certain foreign policy truths were considered 'unspeakable' by the US establishment. All this changed in 1967–8, the direct result of US defeats in Vietnam. The Cold War fog was dispelled by the stormy breezes emanating from the Indo-Chinese peninsula.

While the students were the first to breathe the new air and challenge their government on the streets of US cities, there was, from the establishment's point of view, a far more disturbing development, unprecedented in American history. American soldiers in the battlefields of Vietnam began to say no.

The GIs Against the War movement traumatized the Pentagon and the White House. These were not lily-livered rich kids but real soldiers. Many of them had suffered combat injuries, and some of their key leaders were war heroes who had been awarded the highest honours for courage in the field. The military establishment attempted to crush the soldiers through imprisonment and courts martial, but this had the opposite effect.

Opposite: Uncle Sam has had enough. A poster urges the US government to withdraw from Vietnam.
Above: Burning draft cards – a powerful symbol of opposition to an immoral war.

The GI protest movement grew dramatically and war veterans planned throughout 1968 for their 1969 March on Washington. Thousands of them came, in their uniforms and wheelchairs, to tell the government that they would not be a party to genocide and murder. On the steps of Capitol Hill, the GIs sang: 'Ho, Ho, Ho Chi Minh, the NLF is gonna win.' It was their finest hour and they relished the apoplectic faces observing this from the safety of the Pentagon. Protest on this scale and from this quarter would have been remarkable in any country. In the United States, where ideology plays such a major part, it was unthinkable. The dissident GIs sparked off a wave throughout US bases in Western Europe and there were many desertions. Under Olof Palme, Sweden publicly opposed the war. Palme himself had marched at the head of a torch-lit procession to the US Embassy, and Sweden offered US deserters rights of asylum. The White House raged and ranted, but was powerless. GI resistance to Vietnam has been underestimated by historians, but it played a decisive role in bringing the war to an end.

1st Sweden Dodging the Draft

High·summer, and Europe is filled with young Americans, bringing with them their music, their grass, their enthusiasms and their hatred of the Vietnam War. Country Joe, Jimi Hendrix, Jefferson Airplane float out across the Arno and the Seine and the talk is all of the call-up and dodging the draft.

The number of American GI deserters is growing, and there are even starting to be reports of GIs killed in battle while fighting for the NLF – the other side.

Terry Whitmore, a twenty-one-year-old black GI who has been awarded the Purple Heart and Bronze Star for bravery in action, goes AWOL while recuperating in a Japanese hospital. He contacts the anti-war organization Beheiren, who give him shelter and smuggle him to Stockholm. He tells his story.

A GI in South Vietnam briefly escapes the madness of war with an ingenious hookah.

'My unit of fighting men was composed of young men, around the ages of eighteen to twenty-one. My Commanding Officer was out for revenge after losing a brother in the conflict. After his arrival, within a period of two weeks the young men were turned into a mob of blood-hungry animals. There was no time to think, for every day was filled with fearsome fighting and at night the sky was filled with rockets and missiles, searching out the enemy on both sides.

'Then came Con Thien. During this time, Con Thien was the most feared spot known to US Marines. Marines often referred to it as the God-forsaken hill.

'My company was on patrol when we ran into a large force of NVA. My platoon was cut off from the rest of the company in a perfect ambush. The men were sent tumbling to the ground. Only two of us were able to get up. I could hear the cries of my Commanding Officer calling out my name. Without thinking of the danger, I rushed out in the open to his side. The enemy had a clear view of me and could have taken my life very easily, but he didn't. Why?

'I managed to get my Commanding Officer to safety but the cries and pleas of other wounded men pinned down filled my ears. Three buddies and myself stood over one of the wounded when a vast enemy attack cut across us. Again, I was in perfect range for the enemy. All three men were hit. All three were white. I was not. I was not hit. Why?

'But I didn't have time to think; I had to get the rest of the men back to safety. A buddy helped me to pick up another badly wounded man. We had run about five feet when the enemy cut my buddy down. Again I was not hit. Why?

'Still no time to think, for the cries of the rest were getting louder. I started back into the action. There were six more to get out. The enemy had them well pinned down. My buddies and I managed to get behind a large rock to focus the enemy's attention on us, while the others got out. At this time a mortar round fell no more than four feet from me, picking me up and slamming me into the rocks. I was unable

Top: Some got away: American defectors from the aircraft carrier _Intrepid_ learn Swedish after seeking political asylum in Sweden, whose government opposes the US presence in Vietnam.
Above: Some didn't: soldiers of 173rd Airborne Division tough out the long fight for Hill 875.

to move. The US jets were given the signal to bomb despite the fact that two of us were still down and wounded. For forty-five minutes or so powerful bombs were dropped no more than thirty yards from us.

'While I laid praying I said to myself if I made it out of this one I would NEVER come back to another one. And thank God I did make it out. After about three or four hours a company of men came down to get us. I was rescued and transferred to hospital.

'While in the hospital at Cam Ranh Bay, President Johnson awarded me the Purple Heart and Bronze Star for my actions in battle. I was treated like a real hero, but deep down inside me the big question WHY was still there.

'Why didn't the enemy shoot me when he had so many chances? Why? Why did he shoot my white buddies and let me go? Was it because he knows that the black man has as hard a time as he does? Did he know I was being forced to fight him, and did he know that when I got home, I would still be fighting a war?

'To My Fellow American Servicemen:

'Some of you may label me a coward or some kind of "ist". Well I'm not any "ist" and I'm not a coward. It takes more guts and balls to say no. NO! I've been there ONCE and I had to DESERT to keep from going back and listen to me, fellows, I know what it's like. WAR IS HELL.

'Ask yourself. Why are we fighting in the Nams? Vietnam is having a family problem between the North and the South. When we had a family problem (the Civil War) Vietnam didn't come and interfere because it wasn't their business. Just like this, it's none of our business what Vietnam does. If you had a friend that got into a fight with his brother, would you fight his battle? I wouldn't and you're crazy if you would.

'Some of you have nothing to do with the war. But I know you have some relatives or buddies that do, that are right now laying in some mud hole or yelling for help. He's a long way off, you can't help him, but you can bring him home. I know that it is hard to take individual actions. But you can form groups and help the fellows in the Nams: bring them home.

'And for those of you that are engaged in activity on the battlefields, I would advise you to do likewise and follow me and hundreds of others, and remember it takes guts TO GO but it takes balls to say NO. Anybody can have guts but only a man has balls.'

Berkeley, California, USA Having a Good Day

Telegraph Avenue is thronged with cheering crowds, claiming the street as their own, after six days of violent clashes with the California police, who had been trying to stop them demonstrating there.

The trouble had started on June 28 when the police fired tear-gas to break up a rally that students and peace campaigners had called to demonstrate their support for the left-wing organizations banned in France, two weeks before, for their arrested French comrades and for the United States's own political prisoners, in particular the Oakland Black Panther leader Huey Newton.

As the crowd fled the gas, the police ran after them, wielding batons and grabbing people to arrest. The demonstrators began throwing up protective barricades to defend themselves from the attack, using wooden pallets and building material from a construction site and anything else they could get their hands on, but they were finally driven out.

The next day a larger crowd returns to Telegraph Avenue and the street fighting is sharper still. Then, on June 30, Mayor Wallace Johnson and Police Chief Beale declare a day and night curfew around the whole area, taking the opportunity to harass and arrest anybody they don't like the look of who is out on the streets.

The demonstrators change their tactics and march on City Hall instead, demanding that the City Council grants them a permit to rally on Telegraph Avenue on July 4, Independence Day. Finally, on the eve of the rally, the permit to hold an assembly on the streets comes through. The next day, the music blares joyfully out over Telegraph Avenue, drowning out the speeches, as the singing, dancing demonstrators celebrate California-style.

10th San Diego, USA Death Threats

The Ku Klux Klan issue a death threat to the renowned seventy-year-old philosopher Herbert Marcuse, Professor of Philosophy at the University of California's San Diego campus. It is highly unlikely that the Klan have read any of Marcuse's books

(*Eros and Civilization, One-Dimensional Man, Counterrevolution and Revolt*) but his name has begun to feature in the press as one of the intellectual inspirations behind the student revolt.

Marcuse is inclined to treat the death threat as a joke, until he finds out that his phone has been mysteriously cut off …

Who was Herbert Marcuse?

And if you want biographies,
do not look for the legend:
'Mr So-and-So and his times'
but for those whose title page might be inscribed,
'A fighter against his times'.

Nietzsche, *The Use and Abuse of History*

Herbert Marcuse was among the few professors respected by the student generation of 1968. Born in Berlin in 1898, Marcuse came of age during the revolutionary turmoil that followed the First World War in Germany. After the sailors' revolt in Kiel, the soldiers began to mutiny and soon Workers' and Soldiers' Councils were formed everywhere.

Marcuse was elected a delegate to the Berlin Soldiers' Council from a working-class suburb. He attended political meetings addressed by the revolutionaries of the Spartakusbund, Rosa Luxemburg and Karl Liebknecht, but even at a young age he realized that the intransigent radicalism expressed by the Spartacists was way ahead of the consciousness of the majority of politicized German workers. He had become a socialist and a Marxist but did not believe that Berlin, let alone Germany as a whole, was ripe for an insurrection on the model of Petrograd in 1917. The crushing of the Berlin uprising in 1919 and the murder of Luxemburg and Liebknecht vindicated his position, but left him sad and bewildered.

A Marxist thinker of great originality, Marcuse became associated with the Frankfurt Institute of Social Research. Together with his colleagues Theodor Adorno and Max Horkheimer, he emigrated to the United States in 1934, after Hitler's assumption of power the previous year. It was here that the Frankfurt Institute was kept going in exile.

During the Second World War, Marcuse worked for the American Office of Strategic Service, and later at Harvard and Brandeis Universities. Unlike most of his academic colleagues, he was excited by the student revolt but at the same time sober enough to realize, alone among his peers on the Left at that time, that the ruling class's response to the upheavals of '68 could lead to the birth of extremely reactionary and vengeful regimes.

Despite the May Events in France, Marcuse, based in the United States, remained extremely sceptical of the industrial working class as an agency of social change. He suggested that the future lay with the 'new' workers: highly qualified salaried employees, technicians, specialists. While supporting the need for change as demanded by the students, he argued that the majority of the population in the United States and Western Europe was not politically conscious of the need for revolution. For this reason he criticized orthodox Leninist practices and predicted that the model and method of the 1917 October Revolution in Russia was outdated.

He was a libertarian socialist critic of those on the Left who refused to provide an alternative with arguments such as 'What is necessary is to destroy; afterwards we will see what comes.' Marcuse countered this by insisting that 'our goals, our values, our *own* morality, must be visible already in our actions. The new human beings we want to create – we must already strive to be these human beings right here and now.'

The following words, addressed to a large gathering of radicals in December 1968, retain a certain value to this day:

'To the degree to which the pseudo-democratic process, with the semi-monopoly of the conservative mass media [and today, we could add, the dumbing-down nature of most television programming], creates and constantly reproduces the same society and a largely immune majority, to that degree must political education and preparation go beyond traditional liberal forms.

'Political activity and political education must go beyond teaching and listening, must go beyond discussion and writing. The Left must find the adequate means of breaking the conformist and corrupted universe of political language and political behaviour. The Left must break out of the language and behaviour pattern of the corrupt political universe. It requires finding a language and organizing actions that are not part and parcel of the familiar political behaviour.'

17th London, UK Bottoms Up

Yoko Ono's new film opens in London. Entitled *Number 5*, it is a successor to *Number 4 (Bottoms)*.

'It is conceptually much more advanced,' Yoko explains. 'In *Bottoms* there was far more obvious movement. In this it is much more settled.'

The film took three minutes to shoot but lasts for an hour and a half. It depicts John Lennon in his garden.

'We call it our smile movie because John smiles in it and sometimes says, "Don't worry, love."'

'Originally, I wanted to make a movie of everybody in the world smiling, but then I realized this was impossible, so I just let John represent everybody and send out vibrations.

'I think people in 500 years' time will watch it and just feel the vibrations.'

Japan, Narita No to Giant US War Planes

Narita: a flat plain 30 miles outside Tokyo where, for generations, the rice fields have been farmed by the same 300 families. Now the land is threatened by a huge new international airport extension - big enough, the American President has said, to take the new SST planes, which can carry an entire army unit. The Narita airport is a key element in the expansion of the US military presence in Japan.

The Narita farmers have linked up with student and anti-war protesters to fight the new development. For the last year they have been resisting the Airport Company every inch of the way, tearing down the perimeter fence as it is erected and preventing the surveyors from measuring the site. There have been dramatic clashes with the riot police over every stage of the process so far. A close relationship has developed between the farmers and the anti-war protesters who have rallied to their support: the outsiders have been invited to the farmers' families' homes as guests.

The Company's surveyors have returned to take the last measurements on a sweltering summer day. The farmers and their allies have thrown up barricades against the heavily armed riot police that confront them.

The stand-off lasts ten hours, like some epic of the Samurai tradition. On the one side, armed only with sickles and sharpened bamboo poles, the lean, leather-faced farmers and their idealistic young supporters in their white headbands and shabby clothes. On the other, the armoured police ranks with their clubs and metal shields, waiting to do the bidding of their absent masters, the men of power in Tokyo and Washington.

Then comes the first clash, accompanied by screams and yells and the frantic rhythmic whistling of the Zengakuren.

The second clash is more determined. With the third, the barricades are taken, the defenders sent scattering into the fields. The Company surveyors take their last measurement inside a circle of police.

The protesters regroup at the farmhouses. Together, they take a pledge that the struggle will go on.

Czechoslovakia The Warsaw Letter

Soviet troops are still rumoured to be in Czechoslovakia, weeks after the Warsaw Pact troop manoeuvres were supposed to have ceased.

Clashes between protesters and Japanese riot police over Narita airport continued into the 1970s.

'When *will* the last foreign troops leave?' asks the Prague newspaper *Mlada Fronta*, echoing a stream of letters and articles in the Czechoslovak press. 'If everything is all right, what prevents our officials from publishing a precise report? Unclear and contradictory information only plays into the hands of those who disseminate alarming reports. The citizens of this country have the right to be informed truthfully.'

The month draws on, hot, sultry, tense. The rumours are that Marshal Yakubovsky is back on Czechoslovak soil and has ordered the Soviet troop convoy to move by night only. People are beginning to think that the presence of troops may be kept up right until the crucial Party Congress meeting on September 9.

Pravda, the official Soviet organ, has pilloried the 'Two Thousand Words' manifesto as a counter-revolutionary call to armed secession, into the West German and NATO embrace.

'The Czechoslovak people are not worried by the presence of friendly Soviet troops,' says Soviet Foreign Minister Kosygin. 'It is only the press which is worried.'

But, worryingly, the Soviet Union, East Germany, Poland, Hungary and Bulgaria are holding an emergency summit meeting in Warsaw to discuss 'The Situation in Czechoslovakia'. The letter that they send to the Central Committee of the Communist Party of Czechoslovakia setting out the results of their deliberations adopts a very tough tone.

'We are deeply disturbed by the events in your country,' it begins.

In effect, the Warsaw letter calls for the use of security forces against the leaders of dissent in Czechoslovakia; for Party control over all mass media and the abolition of the freedom of the press; for the banning of all opposition organisations and of all oppositional tendencies within the Party.

'We cannot agree to expose Czechoslovakia to the danger of being torn away from the Socialist community. This is no longer only your concern. This is a common concern of all Communist and workers' parties and of States united by alliance, cooperation and friendship.

'The peoples of our countries paid the price of tremendous sacrifices for the victory over Hitlerite fascism, for their freedom and independence, for the possibility of marching forward along the road of progress and socialism.

'The boundaries of the socialist world shifted to the centre of Europe, to the Elbe and the Sumava mountains. We shall never consent to see threatened these historical conquests of socialism and the independence and security of all our nations. We shall never allow imperialism to make a breach in the socialist system, by peaceful or non-peaceful means, from the inside or the outside, and change the alignment of forces in Europe in favour of imperialism.'

Alexander Dubcek goes on TV and radio to broadcast to the Czechoslovak nation. He will stand firm, he declares. He appeals for the help of the whole country, for calm deliberation in this moment of responsibility. It is the sort of performance a man gives when he knows that the day has come to stand up and be counted.

Alexander Dubcek, leader of the Czechoslovak Communist Party, realizes that he has the people behind him.

The following morning impromptu meetings bring the country to a temporary standstill as workers gather to decide what to do. Overwhelmingly, they vote to send messages of support. Telegrams, letters, resolutions pour in to Dubcek's office.

At the Hotel Alcron, in Prague, the thirty staff knock off work for a meeting. The reception-desk manager takes the chair. The chef is present in his white topper, along with the man who stokes the boilers, the chambermaids, the waiters and the kitchen staff.

'What should we do?' The decision to send a message of support to the government is unanimous. The letter is painstakingly drafted. One by one, the signatures are carefully inscribed at the end.

'All over the country people are holding meetings like this now,' a chambermaid tells one of the guests.

The Warsaw letter is addressed to the Central Committee of the Czech Communist Party – a body on which the old guard still retains a majority. A Central Committee meeting will now have to be convened to reply to it.

Dubcek has been trying to avoid convening the Central Committee before the special Party Congress, on September 9, can meet to elect a new one. Already, the local party elections for delegates to the Congress that have been taking place have shown a massive wave of support for the reformers.

In an adroit backstage manoeuvre, Dubcek manages to get sixty of the newly elected Congress delegates mandated as having Central Committee voting rights, and sweeps them into the meeting with him.

The newly enlarged Central Committee sends a staunch reply to the Warsaw letter, reassuring its neighbours that it will never think of threatening the safety of the socialist nations or of altering the balance of power in Europe. Nevertheless:

'The overwhelming majority of the people of all classes and sectors of our society favour the abolition of censorship and are for freedom of expression. The Czech Communist Party is trying to show that it is capable of a different political leadership than the discredited bureaucratic-police method.'

19th Moscow, USSR Offers that can't be refused

The Soviet Politburo issues a formal invitation to the entire Praesidium of the Czechoslovak Communist Party to meet in Moscow next week to discuss the situation in Czechoslovakia. In the circumstances, it is impossible not to imagine the aircraft that would carry them exploding into flames.

Dubcek is urged on all sides not to leave the country at this moment of crisis.

Instead, he invites the Soviet Politburo to come to Czechoslovakia to talk.

Meanwhile, *Pravda* reports that a secret arms cache of American weapons has been discovered near the West German border, and hints at a CIA/Pentagon plot to arm 'Sudeten revenge seekers and supporters of the old (capitalist) order'.

26th Cierna nad Tisou, Czechoslovakia A People United

The location of the crisis talks is finally decided. They will take place at Cierna nad Tisou, a tiny Slovak town hard by the Russian border.

On the eve of the talks *Literarni Listy* publishes a Manifesto to the Czechoslovakian Praesidium:

'THE MANIFESTO

'Dear Comrades,

'We are writing to you on the eve of your meeting with the Politburo of the Communist Party of the Soviet Union in which you will influence the fate of our entire nation. There have been many times in the history of the human race when a few men have decided the fate of millions. This is another of them. It is difficult for you, and we want to make it easier for you by our support.

'The history of our country in the last few centuries is the history of restriction. Except on two brief occasions we have had to create our nation illegally. Several times we have stood on the brink of catastrophe. For this reason our two nations (Czechs and Slovaks) applauded the democracy that the liberation of 1918 brought us so splendidly.

'It was not total democracy because it did not bring social security to working people. But it was just the working class which in the days of Munich showed its determination to save democracy against disaster. And so enthusiastically our nations applauded socialism which the 1945 liberation brought us. This was not true socialism because it did not give its working people creative freedom. We were looking for it very hard and began to find it last January.

'So the moment came when our country was – after centuries – a cradle of hopes. Now the moment has come when we can prove to the world that socialism is not only a temporary solution for underdeveloped countries but the only way for the whole of civilization.

'We thought that this fact would gain the sympathy, above all, of the whole socialist world. Instead, we were accused of treachery. We have been given ultimata from comrades who proved more and more in every speech that they don't know what has been happening here. We are accused unjustly of violating laws, we are suspected of ideas which we have not had. The threat of unjust punishment hangs

over us: if some punishment exists it will also befall our judges, devalue our work, and above all tragically contaminate socialism all over the world for many years. Comrades, it is your historic task to stop this danger. It is your task to show the Russian Communist leaders that the democratization of socialism in our country must in the end correspond to the interests of all progressive movements in all continents.

'Everything we fight for could be summed up in four words. Socialism. Alliance. Sovereignty. Freedom. In socialism and alliance is a guarantee for our friends that we shall not allow anything to happen which could threaten the real interests of our nations, on whose behalf we have for more than twenty years fought honourably for the same things.

'Our sovereignty is our guarantee that the mistakes of the past few years will not be repeated. Explain to your partners that the extreme voices that can be heard from time to time in our discussions are the very products of a bureaucratic system which limited creative thinking for so long that many people were driven into a secret and mute opposition. Give them many examples and assure them that the authority of the party as well as the position of socialism are right now stronger in our country than at any time in the past.

'Tell them that we need freedom, peace and plenty of time to become more confident and better partners than before. Tell them in the name of the people, who have now ceased to be merely a notion on paper and who have become again (as Stalin said) history creating strength.

'Comrades – it is possible that not all of you are of the same opinion. Some of you, in spite of taking an active part in the fight in January, are criticized for mistakes made before January. This is the lot of politicians and the last seven months have proved that there will be no retribution.

'It would be a tragedy if any personal feelings of yours prevailed above the responsibility you have to this nation. Don't forget that you are part of it. Act, explain and together stick to the way we have already trodden and from which they

Opposite and above: Citizens of Prague and Brno flock to sign the 'Manifesto' petitions in support of the Dubcek leadership on the eve of the crucial Cierna nad Tisou talks with the Soviet Politburo.

shall not take us alive. We shall in the next few days, hour after hour, follow your negotiations. We shall be awaiting news of you. You must think of us. You are writing a page in Czechoslovak history. Write it with care but above all with courage. It will be our tragedy if we lose our last chance. We believe in you.'

At this crucial hour the peoples of Czechoslovakia rally behind their Communist leadership as never before. By mid-morning the queues in Prague are stretching all the way along Narodni Trida and down Na Prikope as people wait to buy their copies of the Manifesto, and to add their signatures to the list in its support.

Thoughtful-looking men with berets and briefcases, old women in battered shoes, young people, soldiers, housewives, wait patiently, defiantly in the sunshine, totally convinced of what they have to do.

Rickety tables have been set up, like improvised ballot stations, in the streets. The people crowd to put their names down on the paper. Some add their addresses.

'It gave our delegation a mandate of confidence such as few Czechoslovak delegations have ever had for foreign negotiations,' says Josef Smrkovsky, Chairman of the National Assembly and one of the participants in the Cierna talks. 'The signatures on the Manifesto were almost like a national plebiscite. Very few were missing. The whole country took part. And when we got to Cierna, a delegation arrived from one of the small districts, Trencin or Zilina, bringing us all the sheets they had collected of the Manifesto petition…. It had been signed by all the citizens of the district, including those who were sick, whom they had gone round and visited. There were over 20,000 signatures. Nobody was missing. Such a consensus and awareness by people of what they wanted can hardly have existed before in our history.'

29th Cierna nad Tisou, Czechoslovakia The Godfathers Arrive

The talks begin at Cierna nad Tisou. It is a tiny place, little more than a sprawling railway depot with a long, wooden-built street attached, scarcely developed since the 1930s. Six hundred yards away lies the Russian border. Beyond it, the horizon stretches away eastward, towards the steppe. The delegations are staying in their two sets of sleeping cars, side by side, the Czechoslovakian ones on their small-gauge rails, the Russians on their large ones. Every evening, the Soviet sleeping cars are shunted back across the border, to spend the night on Soviet soil. Unbeknownst to the Czechoslovakians, Ulbricht, the East German leader, Gomulka from Poland and Zhivkov from Bulgaria are also waiting there, near the border town of Uzhgorod.

The talks are held in the Railwaymen's Club by Platform One, decorated for the occasion with new red carpets, curtains and chandeliers. The temperature is in the eighties. All the top leaders are there: on the Soviet side, Brezhnev, Kosygin, Podgorny, Suslov and the rest; for the Czechoslovakians, Dubcek, Svoboda, Cernik, Smrkovsky and the others – some of whom (Bilak, Kolder, Svestka) seem rather to be putting the Soviet case.

Brezhnev outlines the Politburo's demands, developed in the Warsaw letter: a clamp-down on press freedom; the banning of political groups; absolute adherence to the alliances of the Warsaw Pact; a stress on the 'leading role of the party'; the special Fourteenth Congress should not take place. He depicts a Czechoslovakia fallen prey to semi-fascist, revanchist factions, on the verge of defecting from the Warsaw Pact. The Czechoslovakians try to reassure him that, on the contrary, the Communist Party of Czechoslovakia has never stood higher in the people's eyes.

'Come to us, Comrade Brezhnev,' says Smrkovsky. 'Come to Prague, to Ostrava, to Brno, to Pilsen, to Bratislava, choose where you want to go. We'll go with you. You'll see how our people support the Communist Party and the socialist alliance. Four hundred thousand people took part in our May Day in Prague, a hundred thousand in Brno. There are a few, tiny, extremist groups, attended by fifty or a hundred people, but they are a result of the bureaucratic errors of the past. You have been misinformed. Come and see for yourself. What you have here is a collection of tittle-tattle, trivialities which can in no way decide the course of our country.'

The Soviet delegation raises the question of the 'American' arms cache, found near the border. The Czechoslovakians produce the evidence of their chemistry labs, who have analysed the guns: their markings have been clumsily obliterated, and the dye that has been used to stain them is of East German origin. There are even photographs of the haversacks used to transport them, clearly showing the 'nommer' label of the well-known Moscow department store, GUM.

The atmosphere is tense, extremely nasty. On the second day, when the Ukrainian Secretary Shelest produces a string of accusations of attempts to get

Dubcek's stare at USSR leader Brezhnev (with document) during the tense summit meeting on the future of the Czechoslovak Communist Party symbolizes his country's refusal to be bullied.

Transcarpathian Russia, in his fiefdom, to secede from the USSR, Dubcek stands up and announces that if the meeting is to continue like this, the Czechoslovak side will pack up and go home.

The talks break down. Dubcek retires to his sleeping car. He is suffering from stomach pains and on the verge of tears. The others walk up and down the platform. Finally, Brezhnev, Kosygin, Suslov and others come to Dubcek's car. Shelest had exaggerated. There must be grounds to talk. Dubcek is visibly at his limit. After two hours some sort of reconciliation is reached.

The talks are delayed again on Wednesday morning. It is said that Comrade Brezhnev has stomach pains. There are rumours that the Soviet Ambassador in Prague, Chervonenko, was supposed to have arranged for some right-wing provocation to have taken place in Prague during the talks, and that when none occurred 'he got his face slapped'. There are other rumours that consultations are going on with the other leaders in Uzhgorod – where Ulbricht has been putting most of the hard-line pressure on.

The delegations go for a stroll around Cierna. The Czechoslovakians are greeted everywhere with encouragement, which they answer with wan smiles.

The air is full of threat. At midday Dubcek tells his delegation that the talks are over. A communiqué has been drafted, in the usual terms. A further meeting of the six core Warsaw Pact countries in Bratislava at the weekend will lead to the signing of a more formal pledge.

Now it is time to go home. The Soviet leadership will soon see whether the Czechoslovakians do as they have been told.

1968
August

'We don't want to live
on our knees.'

**The human faces of socialism: Dubcek's supporters in
Wenceslaus Square.**

History has not been kind to Czechoslovakia. For centuries the Czech lands were part of the Austro-Hungarian Empire. The first Czechoslovakian Republic, which arose from the ashes of that empire in 1918 under President Tomás Masaryk, was the only democracy east of Switzerland. It was destroyed by German fascism in 1938 with the collusion of France and Britain. As a result, the Red Army's entry into Prague in 1945 was welcomed by a majority of the population. Czechoslovakia had had a Communist Party with a mass base and a strong influence within the intelligentsia before the Nazi occupation; Czechoslovak communists had played a staunch role in the Resistance during the Second World War. Their popularity offered Moscow a unique opportunity to permit at least a limited democracy here. Instead, as elsewhere in Eastern Europe, a hated Stalinist structure was imposed upon a people whose eyes had been filled with hope as they had cheered the entry of Soviet tanks.

By 1948 the new system was in place: a dictatorship by the bureaucracy. The Party exercised a monopoly of information and power. The Politburo was accountable only to Moscow. Conformism was rewarded in every field. A stagnating command economy and a stultifying

intellectual climate led a group of intellectuals inside and outside the Communist Party to search for new ideas that could synthesize real socialism and democracy. Czech Communists quietly studied Antonio Gramsci and Rosa Luxemburg, both of whom had been unorthodox thinkers in their time. Their non-communist colleagues began to revive the social-democratic ideas of the late Tomás Masaryk. These ideas spread. The Writers' Congress in the summer of 1967 and the student protests in the autumn were the first signs of a new Czechoslovakia struggling to emerge from its Stalinist cocoon.

By the end of 1967 the reformers in the Party had understood that Novotny, the old Stalinist State and Party boss, would have to be replaced. They encouraged a freer debate of the country's problems in the state-controlled media. The results were electric, both within and outside the Party. The debate outgrew the bounds set by the reformers. Newly elected First Secretary Dubcek and his colleagues were both nervous and excited. They thought that they could initiate 'socialism with a human face' by economic reforms, freedom of speech and press, equality for the Slovaks and pluralism. They accepted the need for a multi-party system.

Alarm was growing in the ruling circles of the Soviet bloc. Intoxicated by free debate, the Czechoslovaks were thinking what Stalinism had considered unthinkable: of abandoning the Party's monopoly of power and information. This is what scared the grey men in Moscow most. For if they were seen to succeed, there could be no holding back the demands from below in other countries.

On August 21, 1968, Soviet tanks entered Prague to crush 'socialism with a human face'. It was to prove a turning point for the communist world and for the prospects for socialism

Above: Czech students protest in the streets against the Soviet invasion.
Left: Cartoons in the Czech press after the invasion.

everywhere. Dubcek and his colleagues had tried to establish a 'third way' – a system that was neither capitalist nor based on a Stalinist monopoly of power. Their failure both frightened and demoralized others like him. It was not until the emergence of Mikhail Gorbachev as the General Secretary of the Communist Party of the Soviet Union in 1985 that reform communism found a new leader, but by that time the moment for a 'third way' had passed. The push towards a post-capitalist order, genuinely popular in many parts of the world in 1968, had dissipated by then. The United States had recovered from its military and political setbacks and had rearmed massively with new-era Cruise and Pershing missiles during the early eighties resurgence of the Cold War. The world capitalist system was far stronger and more bullish, both politically and economically, than it had been two decades before. What Russia got as a result was not a reformed, democratic, humanized socialism but mafia-capitalism on the Al Capone model.

The muted response to the invasion from the West was unsurprising. The USA, West Germany and Britain were moderate in their opposition, as if pleased that firm action had been taken to crush what might have developed into a popular model for socialism in the West. The West Germans expressed their gratitude in the most dramatic fashion by rewarding Brezhnev with massive aid and trade, as well as making a significant new opening towards East Germany.

Before August 21, 1968, the course of development that the 'post-capitalist' countries might take was still an open question. After that date, their fate seemed sealed into the stagnating Brezhnevite mould that would prolong the privileges of the bureaucratic élite for a few more decades, while guaranteeing the death of all popular support.

21st Prague, Czechoslovakia The Murder of Socialism

The dog days of August. Czechoslovakia is tense and uneasy, calling for reassurances that do not come. The vagueness and secrecy that surround the Praesidium's report back from the Cierna talks has left the people full of misgivings.

The leadership are still trying to negotiate a way forward to democratization. The Soviet demand for press censorship is the hardest circle to square.

'There will be no return to censorship, but the time for self-censorship may be here,' the editors have been told.

Meanwhile Comrade Brezhnev has been telephoning Alexander Dubcek. The Soviet leader wants to know what is going on, and why the accords reached at Cierna are not being implemented.

'We are trying to implement them democratically,' says Dubcek, close to despair.

The Praesidium has been meeting at the Central Committee building since 2.30p.m. the previous day, discussing the vexed question of the 14th Party Congress, the key milestone in the process of reforming both Party and State. A vote is taken: the reformers have the majority. Despite Cierna, the Congress will go ahead, after all.

It is now after 11.30p.m. The Congress arrangements are still being discussed. Cernik is called to the telephone in the next-door room. He comes back pale-faced, looking completely crushed. He sits down at the table and motions to the speaker that he should stop.

There is a short silence, and then Cernik says, 'I have just been informed that troops of the Warsaw Pact have crossed our frontiers from all directions, from the north, the east, the south from Hungary, and that by six in the morning our country will be occupied.'

The effect is absolutely crushing. Dubcek breaks down, unable to talk. The meetings starts discussing, disjointedly at first, what they can do, what attitude to take, what lead they should give, as the Praesidium, to the public.

Radio Prague is instructed that there will soon be an important announcement from the Praesidium. A communiqué is drawn up, condemning the invasion as an infringement of the Warsaw Treaty and international law. They go round the table, taking the vote, for or against. Dubcek, Cernik, Smrkovsky are for; the Soviet faction – Kolder, Bilak and others – are against. The communiqué is passed, by seven votes to four.

The announcement is despatched to the radio station. The leadership at the Central Committee building gather round their radio set to hear it broadcast.

The music stops.

The announcer says, 'We are announcing the resolution of the Party Praesidium...' Silence. Prague Radio has gone off the air.

The phone rings again, from another radio centre. It seems that the Communications Minister, Hoffman, has taken the Soviet side and refused to put the message out, saying it's a fake. The Praesidium members repeat their instructions:

'Broadcast it through all channels and keep doing so until you are stopped.'

The communiqué is picked up in Vienna almost immediately and, from there, broadcast on around the world.

Outside, the sky is beginning to lighten. It is nearly 5a.m. A Soviet tank drives along the right bank of the Vltava River, halts in front of the main entrance and

Soviet tanks enter Prague on 21 August 1968.

turns its guns on the Central Committee building. Armoured troop carriers converge around it. Paratroopers jump out and cover the corners of the building. Others jump out of cars, readying their automatics, and burst into the building.

The leadership, with their small band of staff and supporters, are assembled in Dubcek's room, on the first floor. A KGB Colonel, a small man, twice-decorated Hero of the Soviet Union, is asking questions, wanting to know where other people are. There is a sound of shouting from the street outside. A large crowd of young people come round the corner towards the Central Committee building, carrying the Czechoslovak flag. Their way is blocked by a line of Soviet troops, armed with automatics. Behind them, armoured cars and tanks.

The protesters march towards the troops, singing the national anthem, 'Where is My Homeland?' When they are barely ten paces away, orders are shouted out. The troops raise their rifles and fire a volley into the air – all save one soldier, at the far end of the line, who fires his volley into the crowd, straight into the chest and neck of a young student, who falls over backwards, dead. He lies on the cobblestones, a pool of blood around his head

Smrkovsky, watching from the first-floor window, leaps to the phone and rings Chervonenko, the Soviet ambassador.

'*You* are responsible for the blood that has been spilt!' he screams, but before Chervonenko can reply a Soviet guard has ripped the telephone from Smrkovsky's hand and smashed it to pieces. Dubcek is phoning, too. Another soldier rushes up

The morning of the invasion: flag-waving protesters circle Wenceslaus Square in a truck before a Soviet tank opens fire on them.

and tears the flex out of the wall, leaving Dubcek standing there with the receiver in his hand and the long flex dangling, unable to speak.

The Czechoslovak leadership is herded down the stairs, through dark corridors, not knowing whether they are to go before some revolutionary tribunal, or to the cellars. Many fought against the Nazis and have some experience of cellars.

They are led out into a tiny courtyard and shoved into armoured cars. They are separated, driven to the airport in twos and threes, separated again and flown off in different directions. Eventually, shaken, disoriented and utterly exhausted, they will be reunited in Moscow and presented with a document to sign.

As the leadership is driven off under armed guard, Czechoslovak television is still broadcasting live images of the invasion to the rest of the world: of Czechs and Slovaks besieging the Soviet tanks, demanding to know of their fresh-faced young drivers, 'Why? Why?' Many of the Soviet troops are embarrassed to find themselves occupying a friendly country which is at peace; they had thought that the Germans were attacking. 'SHAME TO THE OCCUPIERS' is the slogan painted up in Russian letters on walls, roads and war memorials. Within the next week, Moscow will find it necessary to send over two hundred special police to deal with the disaffection in its own invading force.

August 1968

Half a million troops have rolled across the borders. Endless convoys of army trucks pour through the Czechoslovak countryside, aeroplanes and helicopters buzz overhead. A huge angry crowd fills Wenceslaus Square, dispersing only after frantic appeals from a loudspeaker on top of a civilian car. Red, white and blue flags are flying everywhere, from trucks and cars. A group of boys tour Wenceslaus Square in a truck, shouting slogans and waving a large Czechoslovak flag. They round a corner and a tank opens fire on them. Most are killed. Later, the bloodstained flag is paraded through the square again, to heartfelt cries of 'DUBCEK, DUBCEK!'

Posters appear everywhere, pictures of Dubcek and Svoboda, and also fake traffic signs reading: 'MOSCOW: 2500 MILES', 'NO ENTRY FOR TANKS', 'IVAN, GO HOME, NATASHA IS MISSING YOU'. As fast as the Soviet troops tear them down, they magically reappear, fourfold.

There is heavy artillery fighting outside the Radio building, where a tank is set on fire, its smoke billowing up into the twilight. At night, with the curfew, Soviet armoured cars roar through the streets, shooting at anything that moves in the darkness. The façade of the National Museum has been shot to pieces. There are rumours that the Soviet troops, still thinking they have reached Berlin, have mistaken it for the Reichstag building. Others say that the Soviet commanders mistook it for Prague Radio.

In a move that completely baffles the occupying forces, all the street signs and house numbers are taken down. The city of Kafka becomes a blank and nameless maze. Arresting officers have no idea where to look for the people on their list.

Clandestine radio stations advise the citizens to back all those resisting the invasion.

Unbelievably, clandestine radio stations are still broadcasting everywhere, operating from tiny flats, factory cellars, the back of lorries. As soon as one transmitter is seized, another begins to operate. A Soviet train is dispatched for Prague carrying special radio-jamming equipment. The clandestine radio stations put out special appeals for it to be sabotaged at all costs. Railway workers all along the line do their bit: tracks are switched, signals changed, lines disrupted and dug up. The equipment never reaches Prague.

Even as the Party leadership is being forced off under armed guard to Moscow, Central Committee leaders are broadcasting calls on the clandestine radio stations. They call for calm and responsibility in the face of the harsh reality of the situation. Militarily, the balance of forces is clear to everyone: the relationship of Czechoslovakia to its surrounding neighbours is that of a pea to a mountain range. The only possible solution is through political negotiation. They beg the Czechoslovak people to avoid the loss of more young lives. Meanwhile, the special 14th Party Congress will go ahead straight away, at a clandestine location, to take stock of the new situation and give a national lead.

Despite the troops, despite the transport problems, the uncertainty and the danger, over twelve hundred of the elected Congress delegates go to secret destinations

'We will not surrender': defiance in Wenceslaus Square on 22 August 1968.

in Prague, where they are given factory overalls to change into and then led on, in groups of three and four, to a large electronics factory in the Vysocany district.

Half the delegates are smuggled in with the night shift. The other half join them in the factory's large assembly hall when the day shift clocks on at 6a.m. Lookouts are posted on the factory roof and the workers carry on with normal production, as noisily as possible. Nevertheless, to avoid attracting any attention from outside, the delegates don't clap or cheer but raise their arms in a silent forest of approval when they agree with the speeches. And the Chair announces, as the Congress begins:

'Comrades, before we start, allow me to make a technical comment. The organizers wish to point out that, should it become necessary to leave, there are two emergency exits by which you can reach the dining room and the kitchen and then scatter through the factory....'

Yet, despite taking place beneath the very guns of the occupying army, the 14th Party Congress is the most democratic gathering that the Communist Party of Czechoslovakia has ever held. For once, nothing has been decided in advance. It is a real working Congress, striving to reach results. Everybody can speak from the heart. The business includes an analysis of the developments of the last few years, a discussion of the present situation and the election of a new Central Committee. The Congress agrees to issue a one-hour strike call for the following day in protest against the occupation, to be signalled by blaring horns, sounding sirens and the deafening clang of church bells.

It ends with the drafting of a letter to Dubcek, still being held incommunicado in the Soviet Union:

'Dear Comrade Dubcek,

'The 14th Party Congress, which met today, sends you warm comradely greetings. We wish to express our thanks for all the work you have done for the Party and the Republic. The chanted cries of "Dubcek, Dubcek" from the lips of our young people as they carried a bloodstained Czechoslovak flag around Prague yesterday and sang the national anthem and the 'Internationale', bear witness that your name has become the symbol of our sovereignty.

A demoralized Soviet soldier wonders why he's in Prague.

'We protest against your illegal imprisonment, as well as against the imprisonment of the other comrades. The Congress has re-elected you to the new Central Committee, and we continue to see in you our chief representative. We firmly believe that the Czechs and Slovaks will again be masters in their own house and that you will return to our midst.

signed: The 14th Party Congress of the Communist Party of Czechoslovakia'

But Dubcek, in Moscow, is a broken man.

'If you don't sign now, you'll sign in a week. If not in a week, then in a fortnight and if not in a fortnight, then in a month,' the Czechoslovak delegation is told.

They are being kept in the Kremlin, twenty or thirty people all together. Dubcek has been ill with heart disease induced by stress. His head is bandaged from where, he says, he slipped in the bathroom and knocked himself out on the basin.

'A terrible thing has happened,' Brezhnev says, and he tells them about the secret 14th Party Congress, about the strike call, about the stand the country has taken. Their task is to overturn the decisions of the Congress, censor the press, reform the government under Soviet demands and agree to the stationing of Warsaw Pact troops along the Czech border with West Germany.

The occupying troops will be withdrawn once this 'normalization' has occurred.

All of the Czechoslovakians have, at one time or another, broken down in tears at the choice that confronts them: to drown their nation in bloodshed, or to bring a halt to the democratization process and return to the old, repressive ways.

26th **Czechoslovakia** Let History Judge

'In the end we signed,' says Josef Smrkovsky, the National Assembly Chairman, afterwards. 'Each of us had to state: I'll sign, or I won't sign. We all hesitated. I hesitated for a long time, should I, shouldn't I?

'I'd find it hard to say today who resisted most or who was more ready to sign, because we all resisted more or less. Nobody wanted to do it. I was aware what a serious step it was, and I said in my speech after our return that I wasn't sure whether I should have done it or not.

'I did it, I stand by that of course. But I said in that speech that history will judge one day whether we were right, or whether we were guilty of treachery. I don't know. But under the circumstances then I did it by my own decision. Though I hesitated very long.'

The Czechoslovak leadership fly home that night. There is not much talking on the plane. The next day, the clandestine Czech Free Radio broadcasts the Czechoslovak Army's appeal:

'We anxiously awaited the results of the negotiations in Moscow. We were under no illusions. Now we appeal to you all: support the standpoint of Comrade Dubcek, which at the present time is the only way out. Maintain calm and prudence. We do not fetter your thoughts. Your actions, however, must be thoughtfully considered. Hence we call upon you: for Dubcek.'

A demonstration five thousand strong gathers in Wenceslaus Square. Again, it is mainly the young. They march twenty-five abreast to the National Assembly building, chanting 'WE WANT THE FULL TRUTH' and 'WE DON'T WANT TO LIVE ON OUR KNEES.'

Dubcek makes a tearful broadcast to the nation that evening:

'I have signed this agreement for our country in order to avoid more bloodshed. In today's reality all we can do is face the question of how to find a way out. The issue is the gradual withdrawal of troops.... We have agreed that the troops will immediately be located at reserve places.... The final goal of our action is the complete withdrawal of troops.... We will have to take ...' His voice breaks. 'Some temporary measures which will reduce the degree of democracy which we have, but I *beg* you to realize the times we are living in.... I have heard about the distrust in the results of the Moscow talks and the promised withdrawal of troops. I *must* warn you against this point of view. It is easy to bandy such words about. But we must weigh them against further loss of life, which is already great enough.'

The Czech and Slovak people heed his words, in the bitter knowledge of the Manifesto that so many of them have signed:

'The moment came when our country was – after centuries – a cradle of hopes. The moment when we could have proved to the world that socialism is not only a temporary solution for underdeveloped countries but the only way for the whole of civilization.

'We thought that this fact would gain the sympathy, above all, of the whole socialist world. Instead, we were treated to accusations of treachery....'

Within the next year the entire Dubcek faction in the Czechoslovak leadership will have been purged and replaced by those more loyal to Moscow.

The initial response to the invasion of Czechoslovakia among young students and radicals around the world who have been campaigning against the war in

Students throughout Western Europe march on Soviet Embassies in solidarity with the Czechs. Here, Swedish students try to storm the embassy in Stockholm.

Vietnam is one of stunned shock and horror. There are immediate and passionate protest demonstrations outside Soviet embassies all over the world, supported in many countries by the local Communist Parties (although in France, a small group of ultra-left *cinéastes* did welcome the invasion on the grounds that it would 'put an end to the petit-bourgeois films of Milos Forman'; later they admitted that this was a mistake). In London, Maurice Hatton is filming *Praise Marx and Pass the Ammunition*, with John Thaw in the leading role. He films the demonstration outside the Soviet Embassy in Kensington.

In Moscow itself, a small protest in Red Square on August 25 is violently broken up by the police. Seven people are arrested and their banners, reading 'HANDS OFF CZECHOSLOVAKIA', 'SHAME ON THE OCCUPIERS' and 'FOR YOUR FREEDOM AND OURS' are hurriedly bundled away. One protester, Viktor Fainberg, has several teeth knocked out by the police and is later incarcerated in a mental hospital – a particularly ominous form of detention in Brezhnev's Russia. Five others, including Larissa Daniel (imprisoned writer Yuli Daniel's wife) and Pavel Litvinov (grandson of the former Soviet Foreign Minister) are charged with 'group actions that grossly violate public order' – a charge more aptly levelled at the invasion itself.

There is an eruption of spontaneous protests all across East Germany on August 22 and 23, although Ulbricht's regime has been one of the most hard-line backers of military intervention in Czechoslovakia. In Erfurt and Gotha several hundred young protesters take to the streets, chanting *'DUBCEK JA, ULBRICHT NEIN!'* There are protests in Dresden, Frankfurt an der Oder and Jüterbog, as well as East Berlin. Over a hundred protesters are reported arrested altogether, most of them aged between fourteen and twenty-one, and many of them the children of Party members.

The Communist world is split by the invasion. China and Rumania are strong in their denunciation of the Soviet tanks, and most of the European Communist Parties oppose the move. In Yugoslavia, Tito organizes a giant public rally in support of Czechoslovakia's right to self-determination. For Castro's Cuba, however, the

A Soviet tank and truck burn on the streets after a student onslaught with Molotov cocktails.

invasion is a grim coming of age upon the world stage. Castro agonizes in public, questioning, in a seven-hour speech to a huge audience in Havana, whether the Soviet tanks would not have been better used in helping the Vietnamese to fight the Americans. His depiction of the old Novotny leadership in Czechoslovakia is vicious.

'We all know that the leadership that ruled Czechoslovakia for twenty years was a leadership saturated in many errors – dogmatism, bureaucratism and many things that could hardly be put forward as a model of really revolutionary leadership,' Castro declares. 'They sold us arms for a high price which they had taken as war booty from the Nazis. In many cases they sold us industrial tools of a very backward technological level. There was also an abandonment of communist ideals – of internationalism, of revolutionary vigilance and of all those beautiful aspirations which go to make up the communist ideal of a society without egoisms, and in which man ceases to be a miserable slave of poverty.'

Ultimately, however, he accepts the Soviet excuses that the democratization of Czechoslovakia represents a capitalist threat to the entire bloc:

'We have no doubt at all that the Czechoslovak regime was moving towards capitalism and inexorably towards imperialism. The imperialist world received this situation with extraordinary satisfaction. It encouraged it by all means and there is no doubt that it was rubbing its hands thinking of the disaster which this would constitute for the socialist world. This defines our position. One cannot claim that there was not a violation of the sovereignty of the Czech state. That would be a fiction and a lie. But the essential thing is whether the socialist camp could or could not permit the development of a political situation which would lead to the detachment of a socialist country and its falling into the arms of imperialism....'

This was to be the end of Cuba's unruly internationalist independence. From now on, the country would become increasingly bureaucratized, decaying slowly into the Brezhnev model of a stagnant command economy. The Vietnamese Communists, too, after delaying any statement for as long as possible, bow to the *realpolitik* of their Soviet allies' move and give a muted endorsement of the invasion.

Condemnation from the governments of the United States and Western Europe is extremely mild, however, and within weeks of the invasion fresh loans and trade treaties are being offered to the Brezhnev government from Washington and Bonn, as if in reward for crushing the possibility of a popular, democratic socialist model from emerging within central Europe.

Chicago, USA The Year of the Pig

The President of the United States of America will not be attending his own party's Convention this year. The security risks are too great. Instead, Lyndon Baines Johnson will settle down to watch the show on TV, in Texas, along with most of the rest of the country.

For Mayor Daley of Chicago, machine-politician, friend of big business and vicious opponent of his city's black constituency, this is the chance to show how America should be run.

The black residents have been evacuated from a cordon sanitaire of five blocks from the ready-built slums that surround the Amphitheatre where the Convention is to be held. But the gamy smell of the nearby stockyards where much of the pig and cattle population of America comes to be slaughtered before being dispatched as carcasses, north, south, east and west, still lingers over the proceedings.

Board fences have been erected around the Amphitheatre, to stop the delegates catching sight of the slums, with rows of barbed wire stretched along the top of them to prevent the remaining residents from climbing up to see the delegates. Ten thousand police have been deployed around the city, as well as an extra five thousand National Guards. Mace and tear-gas have been stockpiled in vast quantities. And now the water reservoirs, filter plants and pumping stations are under guard, too, and the manhole covers have all been tarred over, since the Yippies threatened to put LSD in the city's water supplies.

In fact the Yippies are mainly joking. An attempt to fuse the new protest politics with the hippie underground, sometimes rationalized as the Youth International Party, the Yippies are a mobile group of punks and publicists calling for a four-day rock 'n' roll orgy in a city park to protest against the Democrats' Convention in Chicago – Czechago, as the Yippies dub it, drawing the comparison between Mayor Daley's riot squads and the occupying forces in Prague. Their mission:

'To create:

1. The blending of pot and politics into a potlitical grass leaves movement – a cross-fertilisation of hippie and New left philosophies.

2. A connecting link to tie as much of the underground as is willing into a gigantic national get-together.

3. A model of an alternative society.

4. A statement in revolutionary action-theatre terms about LBJ, electoral politics and the state of the nation.'

Or, in the words of one Yippie activist:

'To freak out the Democrats so much that they disrupt their own Convention.'

There are plans for bands, street-theatre groups, a Free Shop, for giving things away, and workshops on draft resistance, commune development, guerrilla theatre and underground media. The Yippie Presidential Candidate, a pig, will be running on the slogan 'VOTE PIG IN '68'. Other slogans include: 'FUCK ON THE BEACHES', 'DEMAND THE POLITICS OF ECSTASY', 'ACID FOR ALL' and, above all, 'ABANDON THE CREEPING MEATBALL.'

Sunday night in Lincoln Park: five thousand hippies, yippies, anti-war protesters and assorted citizens of Chicago are dancing to MC5, chanting peace mantras with Allen Ginsberg or watching a guerrilla theatre group's play on LBJ and Humphrey – or Hump-Free – when Mayor Daley's police arrive.

Jerry Rubin, in *Scenarios of the Revolution,* describes the scene thus:

'Creatures from the Smoky Lagoon, grotesque, massive machines like tanks lit with powerful lights, entered the park and shot tear gas that made you vomit.

'Pigs with masks – looking like sinister spacemen – led the way, ghouls in hell, turning the park into a swimming pool of gas.

'Yippies faced the Big Machine until the last minute. Then we split into the streets, shouting joyously, "The streets belong to the people!"

'Yippies set fires in garbage cans, knocked them into the streets, set off fire alarms, disrupted traffic, created chaos in a hundred different directions.

'Police cars zoomed after us. We'd hit the ground, lying low, not making a sound until the cars passed by.

'You found a group of friends you could trust, and that became your revolutionary action cell. The streets provided the weapons. A tree's branch became a club. Rocks everywhere.

'Citizens opened their doors to give us sanctuary from club-wielding porkers.

'White working-class kids helped the yippies build barricades.

'Black bus drivers on strike joined yippies in the streets throwing rocks at scabbing white bus drivers.

'Reporters stood around taking notes and snapping pictures. They thought they were standing on the 38th parallel or something.

'Whack! A pig cracked one right across the head.

'Crack! Another photographer goes down, blood staining his white shirt.

'Crack!

'"Hey, I work for the Associated Press."

'"Oh, you do, motherfucker. Take that!"'

So begins four days and nights of ferocious police violence, broadcast live to thirty million watching Americans by cameramen who have to wear gas masks in order to breathe in the chemical fug, and who themselves often have to duck and run to escape from the indiscriminate clubbings and beatings of Mayor Daley's men. Michigan Avenue becomes a war zone, where photographers and reporters are just as likely to be clubbed senseless as demonstrators or innocent passers-by – or even more likely.

'Some of us here have begun to feel that we are targets,' says Hugh Downes, of NBC's *Today* show. 'Wearing a reporter's badge in Chicago this week is like being a Jew under Hitler.'

News reporters are going on air battered, bandaged and bleeding. The Chicago police seem to feel a particular red-neck hatred at the very sight of a free press,

Chicago police after confiscating Pigasus the Pig, Yippie Presidential Candidate outside the Democratic Party Convention. © Fred W. McDarrah

intent on filming a country at war with itself. 'THE WHOLE WORLD'S WATCHING,' the protesters chant, as the police begin to advance upon them, batons held aloft. But the presence of the cameras does nothing to restrain the police brutality. The world watches as a demonstrator being pinned down by police is beaten over the face and head with a revolver butt, as a maddened cop repeatedly drives his motorbike at full speed into a crowd with nowhere to run to, even pursuing them down into a pedestrian subway.

Mayor Daley's security within the barbed-wire-fenced Amphitheatre of the Democratic Convention is almost as tight as that outside. The delegates are herded about like sheep; no one is allowed to move from one level of the hall to another and armed security guards roam everywhere, making spot checks on the delegates' passes. One delegate from New York is punched by a policeman for refusing to submit to yet another verification of his right to attend his Party's Convention – an incident that brings helmeted cops on to the Convention floor. Delegate after delegate rises to denounce the Gestapo tactics being put into practice on the streets outside, while Daley's delegation attempts to drown them out with a storm of boos and jeers and shaking fists.

Within this atmosphere, the Convention itself and the entire American political system is revealed as an empty farce, and the political business being conducted there as a bad joke. Everyone knows that the Party machine has given Grey Man Humphrey the nomination months ago. Everyone knows that he will lose.

1968
September

'Why not women, too?'

The beginnings of a movement: women unite.

September 1968 sees one of the first public protests of a movement that, of all those that erupted in this year, will leave perhaps the most lasting changes on the world: the women's liberation movement. The zany, high-spirited disruption of the Miss America beauty competition in Atlantic City brought the utopian protest politics of radical students into the living rooms of Middle America. The high points in the battle for women's rights have always arisen on the crest of a wave of wider social struggles. The appeals of Mary Wollstonecraft and Olympe de Gouge for the 'Rights of Women' grew out of the ferment during the French Revolution over the 'Rights of Man'. The European revolutions of 1848 saw utopian socialist feminist groups calling for free crèches and medicine, and public housing with communal facilities.

'Why should a woman be under the power of her husband? She should be able to act freely,

as he does. No more slavery, no more masters, it's time we defended our rights,' argued a letter in *La Voix des Femmes*, a Paris newspaper of 1848 run by a group of seamstresses, school teachers and midwives. The nineteenth-century women's rights movement in America grew directly out of the campaign for the abolition of slavery, and the suffrage campaigns in Britain and Germany in the early twentieth century had as their background a great wave of industrial protest and revolt.

The women's liberation groups that sprang into being amid the ferment of 1968 were no exception. Even their name proclaimed an immediate solidarity and identification with the other struggles of the time, with the National Liberation Fronts of Vietnam and Algeria, and with the aspirations of the black liberation movement. The young women with their beautiful long hair and hippie beads, sitting round cross-legged on the floor in flats and squats and occupied universities in New York, Toronto, London and Berlin, and talking so ardently about the nuclear family as the key site of the oppression of women, draw immediately upon the collective utopian visions of the radical 1968 movements to describe the new life they are arguing for: a world run for the people, and not for the super-profits of a tiny ruling clique; a world where the free development of all is premised upon the free development of each.

In such a world the positive role of the nuclear family – to provide love and support and a warm, caring home for children and the very old – could be fulfilled far better and more freely if it were organized in a more collective way and did not depend upon the unpaid labour of an isolated woman in each individual housing unit. The tasks that were then assigned as 'women's work' should be the responsibility of the whole community. The women's liberation movement called for a massive extension of imaginative and well-run nurseries and crèches, free for all, and for flexible, well-built public housing cooperatives, as well as for women's right 'to act freely, as men do', for equal rights at work, and for free abortion and contraception on demand. But that world did not come. Instead, women have found themselves battling for freedom in a situation

Above: Early days: a picket pauses in her protest against the Miss America beauty pageant.
Left: The United States' best-loved icon comes into her own.

of growing inequality and social atomization that has served to divide women against each other again, in ways that can be just as fiercely competitive as the Miss America contest. Without the support of free, good-quality childcare, socialized housework and transformed work practices, women are having to pay for their independence themselves.

The changes in women's lives since the sixties have not all been wrought by the pressure of the women's movement. Broader economic changes may account for the massive increase of women in paid labour – servicing the expanding white-collar and commercial sector in the West; while, in Asia, the super-growth rates of the 'tiger economies' are largely based on the super-exploitation of very young women – and for the increase in independence that a wage packet brings. But, since 1968, all these developments have been inflected to some degree by women's own demands for recognition, independence and an equal voice in the world.

The protesters in Atlantic City gaily tossed away into a big dustbin all the symbols of women's docility and subservience that they could find: shorthand notebooks, to represent women's subservient, men-pleasing role in the office; scouring pads for their hours of silent labour in the home; false eyelashes and underwired bras. In doing so, they opened a door for women that has never yet been shut.

7th   Atlantic City, USA   Zapping Miss America

Every year at about this time, in the seaside town of Atlantic City, New Jersey, a row of nervous, smiling young women in swimming costumes and high-heeled shoes line up before a bunch of middle-aged men to be ranked in order of desirability. The girls have been preparing for this day for months with diets, skin care, hair treatments and depilation. Their eyebrows are plucked, their legs are waxed, their armpits shaved. Hours have gone into applying their make-up and dressing their hair. Now they wait in trepidation to find out whether their efforts will be crowned with the ultimate accolade: the title 'Miss America'.

But this year it is different. Outside the Atlantic City Convention Hall, a women's guerrilla theatre group is putting on quite a different show.

These women have been meeting for a few months now in one another's apartments in New York. Most of them have come from the New Left or the anti-war movement. All of them have felt a need to start exploring more deeply their own role as women within the movement, and to question some of the assumptions about what that means.

It feels strange, at first, to be meeting just 'as women'. None of them is quite sure what they are setting out to do. The atmosphere is different, somehow – lighter – with no men there. There are suddenly no rules about what they can or cannot say. Tentatively, the women begin to talk about the hidden experiences that they have in common. They start to look for the patterns in what they share. After a while they get on to the question of what they each find themselves doing to themselves every day, in order to please men, and soon they are falling about laughing at the ridiculousness of it all. The talk moves on to the annual Miss America beauty contest, which they regard as the ultimate, tacky symbol of women competing with each other for men's approval.

The Politics of Housework

It seemed perfectly reasonable. We both had careers, so why shouldn't we share the housework? I suggested it to my mate and he agreed – most men are too hip to turn you down flat. So ensued a dialogue that's been going on for several years:

He says, 'I don't mind sharing the housework, but I don't do it very well. We should each do the things we're best at.'

MEANING unfortunately I'm no good at things like washing dishes or cooking. What I do best is a little light carpentry, changing light bulbs, moving the furniture (how often do you move the furniture?)

ALSO MEANING I don't like the dull stupid boring jobs so you should do them.

He says, 'I don't mind sharing the housework, but you'll have to show me how to do it.'

MEANING I ask a lot of questions and you'll have to show me everything every time I do it because I don't remember so good. Also don't try to sit down and read while I'M doing my jobs because I'm going to annoy hell out of you until it's easier to do them yourself.

He says, 'We used to be so happy!' (said whenever it is his turn to do something.)

MEANING I used to be so happy.

He says, 'I hate it more than you. You don't mind it so much.'

MEANING housework is garbage work. It's degrading and humiliating for someone of *my* intelligence to do it. But not for someone of *your* intelligence....

He says, 'Women's liberation isn't really a political movement.

MEANING the revolution is coming too close to home.

Pat Mainardi
Redstockings Group
New York, 1968

Doing it for ourselves – the birth-pangs of the women's liberation movement.

'We should zap it,' one woman says.

'Almost all of us had been active in the civil rights movement, the student movement, or some other wing of the New Left, but not one of us had ever organized a demonstration on her own before,' writes Robin Morgan, one of the group. 'I can still remember the feverish excitement I felt: dickering with the company that chartered buses, wangling a permit from the mayor of Atlantic City, sleeping about three hours a night for days preceding the demonstration, borrowing a bullhorn for our marshals to use. The acid taste of coffee from paper containers and of cigarettes from crumpled packs was in my mouth; my eyes were bloodshot and my glasses kept slipping down my nose; my feet hurt and my neck ached and my voice had gone hoarse – and I was deliriously happy.

'Each work-meeting with the other organizers of the protest was an excitement fix: whether we were lettering posters or writing leaflets or deciding who would deal with which reporters, we were affirming our mutual feelings of outrage, hope and readiness to conquer the world. We also all felt, well, grown up; we were doing this one for ourselves, not for our men, and we were consequently getting to do those things the men never let us do, like talking to the press or dealing with the mayor's office. We fought a lot and laughed a lot and felt extremely nervous.'

In an October 1968 piece collected in her *Going Too Far*, Morgan explained: 'The Miss America pageant was chosen as a target for a number of reasons. It is, of course, patently degrading to women (in propagating the Mindless Sex Object Image). It has always been a lily-white, racist contest (there has never been a black finalist). The winner tours Vietnam, entertaining the troops as a Murder Mascot. The whole gimmick is one commercial shill-game to sell the sponsor's products. Where else could one find such a perfect combination of American values – racism, militarism, capitalism – all packaged in one "ideal" symbol, a woman? This was, of course, the basic reason why the protesters disrupted the pageant – the contestants epitomize the role all women are forced to play in this society, one way or the other: apolitical, unoffending, passive, delicate (but drudgery-delighted) *things*.

'About 200 women descended on this tacky town and staged an all-day demonstration on the boardwalk in front of the Atlantic City Convention Hall, singing, chanting and performing guerrilla theatre nonstop throughout the day. The demonstrators flung dishcloths, steno pads, girdles and pointy, up-lift bras into a Freedom Trash Can. (This last was translated by the male-controlled media into the totally invented act of "bra-burning", a non-event upon which they have fixated ever since.)

'At night, an "inside squad" of about 20 brave sisters disrupted the live telecast of the pageant itself by keening the eerie Berber yell (from the *Battle of Algiers*), shouting "Freedom for Women!" and hanging a huge banner reading WOMEN'S LIBERATION from the balcony rail – all of which stopped the nationwide show for 10 blood-curdling seconds.'

8th Oakland, USA Prisoners of War

Huey Newton, one of the founder members of the Black Panther Party, has been held in a cell measuring four and a half feet wide by six feet long at the Alameda County Jail in Oakland for the past eleven months, awaiting trial for an incident that had taken place on October 28, 1967.

According to Huey, he had driven down to get some food in West Oakland with an old school friend, Gene McKinney, late that night, when a police car pulled up behind him.

Here we go again, more harassment, is Huey's initial reaction, but he has been stopped so many times before that this time he is ready for them. He always keeps his law book to hand between the bucket seats of his car, because he knows that, once he begins to read out the actual law to the police officers, they will have to let him go. He wonders what the excuse will be this time: he has obeyed all the traffic regulations.

The police officer gets out, comes up to the car window and sticks his head in to within six inches of Huey's face.

'Well, well, well, what do we have here? The great, *great* Huey P. Newton.'

A poster showing an armed Bobby Seale and Huey Newton.

Angry blacks demand freedom for Huey Newton.

Huey makes no reply. He simply looks the policeman in the eye.

The cop checks his driving licence and registration. Another police car pulls behind them and a second cop gets out.

Huey and Gene are told to get out of the car and lean their hands on top of it while they are searched. One cop pulls Huey's shirt-tail out, pat-searches his legs and feels his buttocks and genitals, too. 'He was both disgusting and thorough,' Huey will say later.

'Come on back to the patrol car, I want to talk to you,' the cop says, taking Huey's left arm and marching him forcibly back to the second police car. Huey opens the law book he has been holding.

'You have no reasonable case to arrest me,' he begins.

The cop is standing to his left, slightly behind him.

'You can take that book and shove it up your ass, nigger,' he says, stepping forward and shoving a punch into Huey's face.

Huey stumbles back four or five feet, falls down on one knee, starts to rise and sees the officer draw his service revolver, point it at him and fire.

'My stomach seemed to explode, as if someone had poured a pot of boiling soup all over me, and the world went hazy.'

More shots are fired, a rapid volley, but Huey has no idea where they are coming from. They seem to be all around him. He is vaguely aware of being on his hands and knees on the ground, disoriented, with everything spinning. After that, nothing.

When he comes to, Huey is shackled to a hospital bed in a room full of cops, threatening him with the gas chamber, with 'accidental' gunshot wounds, threatening to pull the catheter tubes out of his nose and abdomen. He is to be charged with the murder of one of the police officers who arrested him and the wounding of the other. At the trial, there is no evidence whatsoever to prove that Huey Newton ever carried or fired a gun. The likeliest scenario seems to be that the two policemen actually hit each other in the process of shooting Newton. Nevertheless, he is convicted of manslaughter and sentenced to two to fifteen years.

A blitzkrieg of state repression will decimate the new Black American leadership over the next few years: beatings, shootings, imprisonment; many of the best people will disappear in a hail of bullets. But wider support for the movement is growing rapidly, both in the black communities and among liberal and radical whites. In September, Eldridge Cleaver is invited to deliver a course of lectures to the students at Berkeley University – to the outrage of the Californian Right. Ronald Reagan, ex-Hollywood ham and current Governor of California, leads the campaign to get the lectures banned with his customary glazed eyes and broad, reassuring smile.

'If Eldridge Cleaver is allowed to teach our children they may come home some night and slit our throats,' he intones.

Cleaver replies, 'I have never liked Ronald Reagan. Even back in the days of his bad movies – bullshit flicks that never turned me on to any glow – I felt about him the way I felt about such nonviolent cowboys as Roy Rogers and Gene Autry: that they were never going to cause any action or allow anything to happen. They were just there, occupying space and wasting my time, my money and my sanity. There was a sort of unreality in their style. One knew that movies were into a make-believe bag, but the unreality exposed on the screen by the flat souls of such pabulum-fed actors as Reagan reflected to me – black ghetto nigger me – a sickening mixed bag of humorless laughter and perfect Colgate teeth.

'But what happened was that Ronnie landed a TV show. Equipped with opulent sponsors and some slick script writers, the mediocrity of his grade-B spirit was glossed over and concealed by the make-up of a rhetoric fashioned by a committee of crew-cut wordmongers. With all this going for him, it was natural for him to turn to politics when Hollywood's keenest make-up artists began to find it increasingly difficult to deal with the wrinkles that were slowly turning his face into a replica of well-furrowed, depleted, single-crop soil.

'He was in the best of all states to get into his thing. California had demonstrated its ability to relate to the politics of the absurd by electing to office such blobs of political putty as Richard Nixon and Max Rafferty. And having picked the proper place, he could not have chosen a better style. Ronnie used a pat formula that said: pick the toughest problems confronting people and launch blistering attacks upon all sincere efforts to come to grips with these problems; offer as an alternative a conglomeration of simple-minded clichés and catch-phrases that go back to the *Mayflower*; sing the 'Star-Spangled Banner' and smile broadly, effusively, as you wave the flag at the people; use a fighting "I'm fed up" form of delivery. And finally, always remember that, when nothing else works, there is the tried and proven gambit of demagogic politicians, especially in California – viciously attacking the perennial whipping boys of the American Dream: subversion concealed in the words of textbooks, the "decadence of universities" and the misguided students being duped by a handful of professors who are under the subtle influence of the Communist Conspiracy'.

Eldrige Cleaver challenges Ronald Reagan to a public debate as he addresses several thousand students at UCLA.

'Well, it worked. Mickey Mouse is governor and Donald Duck is a candidate for the US Senate. That is what we have to worry about. And deal with.

'It has been said that the people get the rulers they deserve. I do not believe, however, that America has the rulers it deserves. The State of California, emphatically, could not deserve the rulers it has. Yet we have them, and this is an election year: the nightmare election year of the American Dream.

'Everything is out in the open this year. Nobody is trying very hard to conceal anything. As usual, the key issue in the election is what to do about the niggers - only this time, the question is being rewritten to read, what to do *with* the niggers. From the point of view of the niggers themselves, the question has also been rewritten and now reads, what are we going to *do* about this shit?'

Mexican students marching to the Presidential Palace. Attacked by riot police, they fought back, triggering off a movement for democracy.

22nd Mexico City, Mexico Zapata's Children

Preparations for the Olympic Games, which this year are to be held in Mexico City, are well under way, and two thousand athletes have already arrived here and have begun their training. The University's largest sports stadium has been decked out for the occasion and thousands of millions of pesos have been spent on new arenas and running tracks, housing for the foreign teams and vast amounts of publicity – despite the fact that the Mexican government can never find such sums to spend on its own impoverished population.

The ruling party – the PRI – has governed Mexico since 1910, when it was swept to power by the insurgent peasant supporters of Emiliano Zapata and Pancho Villa, in the hope that it would destroy the old oligarchy of the big ranch owners. It has now ossified into an oligarchy itself, with only the occasional spurt of populist rhetoric as a memento of its revolutionary past.

With even more brazen hypocrisy than usual, the PRI, under President Díaz Ordaz, is now trying to flaunt Mexico's credentials as a dynamic and successful 'one-party democracy' during the Olympic Games, while simultaneously stamping out any attempt by the Mexican people to raise their desperately low standard of living, or to protest against the repressive policies of the regime.

The treatment of the Mexican students, currently occupying most of the country's schools and universities, is a case in point.

The flashpoint for the occupations was a peaceful demonstration, back in July, on the anniversary of the Cuban revolution. The demonstrators, several hundred of them, carried pictures of Castro and, above all, Che Guevara. The Mexican riot police – the much-hated *granaderos* – launched a vicious attack on the unarmed young demonstrators, clubbing many of them to the ground. The next day thousands of students gathered to protest against the *granaderos'* behaviour. Some school students retreated into their school building and barricaded the doors as protection against the police; the doors were blown apart with a bazooka, the *granaderos* charged in, and several school students were killed. After this, more and more students feel that they cannot stand idly by while such outrages take place; more school and college buildings are occupied, as they protest and defend them. Government thugs machine-gun the façades of the occupied buildings, break into some and beat up any students they can grab.

The images of the student revolt of May and June in France are reverberating through everybody's heads. The students strive to make the same links their French comrades did, to widen their protest into a social revolt. They throw the occupied buildings open to everyone, they hold teach-ins, they set up Action Brigades to go leafletting in the streets and factories, demanding the release of the political prisoners and the resignation of the security forces' chiefs.

The *granaderos*, for their part, see foreign agitators everywhere, and above all, French agitators – young veterans of the May events. Mexicans with foreign surnames feature prominently on the lists of 'principle agitators' and the police go so far as to record Mexican names like Emilio, Antonio and Maria Antonieta as Émile, Antoine and Marie Antoinette, with duly Frenchified last names.

Article 145 of the Mexican Penal Code permits the police to arrest anyone, Mexican or foreigner, at any time, for the faintest suspicion of committing the ill-defined crime of 'social dissolution'. Being young is the most suspicious sign of all. Many young tourists, in Mexico for the Olympic Games, are snatched at random from the street and thrown into gaol, facing a prison sentence of five years and a fine of 50,000 pesos – under Article 145; Mika Seeger, daughter of folk singer Pete Seeger, is one of them.

Yet the repression continues to backfire, driving wider and wider layers to protest against the government's brutal overreaction. On August 27, a huge anti-government demonstration of between 300,000 and 400,000 people marches from the Museum of Anthropology in Chapultepec Park along the flowered Paseo de la Reforma, up Avenida Juárez to the Zócalo, Mexico City's constitutional square. Joining the students now are large numbers of their parents and grandparents, brothers and sisters. There are contingents of railway workers, oil workers, electricians, taxi drivers and pushcart peddlers, and small groups of peasants, come in from the outlying villages.

The demonstrators carry the portraits of their national heroes, Emiliano Zapata, Benito Juárez, Miguel Hidalgo – and of the sweet face of the imprisoned railway workers' leader, Demitrio Vallejo. There are placards showing the five Olympic rings as five smoking bombs, and others showing a *granadero* racing along with his police club held aloft like an Olympic torch. The legends read: 'MEXICO: GOLD MEDAL FOR REPRESSION' and 'WE ARE NOT THE AGITATORS. HUNGER AND HOPELESSNESS ARE THE AGITATORS.'

As the rally ends, the students plant their flags and banners in the square, announcing that they will camp there until the political prisoner are free. There is a festive atmosphere in the square that night, with the smell of corn-meal tortillas roasting in the smoke of the camp-fires, with guitars and talk and singing. At four in the morning, when the students lie asleep on the ground, four thousand paratroopers, infantry men and *granaderos* charge through the camp, indiscriminately

A student is arrested as army units move in to occupy the National University.

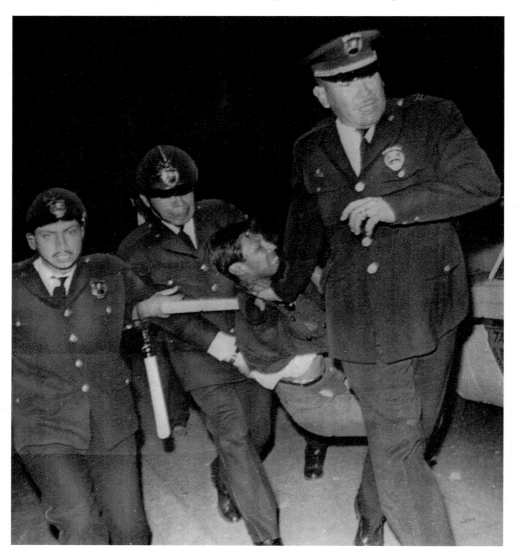

clubbing and kicking and dragging demonstrators off under arrest. As the terrified students flee for the side-streets, eight armoured cars, with cannons levelled and sirens wailing, charge down towards them.

The only refuge from the government security forces is now inside the occupied schools and colleges. By the beginning of September they are barricaded more strongly than ever, and fortified with rocks and bottles as weapons against attacks by the mob of *granaderos*.

The Olympic Games are due to start on October 12. The government has the choice of defusing the situation, by pulling back the riot police and freeing at least some of the detainees – or of escalating it.

They choose the latter.

On the night of September 18, troops invade and occupy the main University buildings at bayonet point, fighting off three attempts by the students to retake it.

Soldiers point their guns at a workers' apartment building in readiness for an insurrection.

There are scores of arrests. It is the start of a major offensive against the protesters, the brutality of which will shock the world.

The technical school – Vocational School 7 – in the Plaza de las Tres Culturas has been the site of one of the most militant and determined student occupations all summer. (The Plaza, in the Ciudad Tlatelolco quarter near the heart of the city, is the site of the last and most heroic resistance of the Aztec civilization to Cortés's invading Spanish troops.) Local residents have an excellent view of what takes place on the night of September 22. One recalls:

'At 6 o'clock, looking out of the kitchen window, I could see that the entire barrio was ringed with *granaderos* and army troops. Including only those I could see, I think there were more troops out there than I've ever seen together in one place in all my experience. But the school was incredibly well fortified – although the students had no arms, or if they had them they never used them.

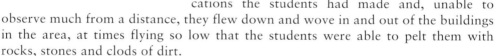

'The students had made a barricade out of at least ten buses and siphoned out the gasoline, and gone from house to house collecting bottles and rags as well. Next, they helped the people in the low-rent, ISSSTE buildings to do the same. Basically, it was a trap to draw the *granaderos* into a building from which they would not emerge on their own feet.

'At 6.30 the soldiers and *granaderos* began to close in on the area, from Calle Almacenes, from the Reforma, from Manuel González and San Juan de Letrán. Thousands and thousands of them. Helicopters were circling overhead to see the fortifications the students had made and, unable to observe much from a distance, they flew down and wove in and out of the buildings in the area, at times flying so low that the students were able to pelt them with rocks, stones and clods of dirt.

'Sometime close to 6.30, a group of *granaderos* was sent out to overturn one of the buses that formed the barricade, thus opening a space through which the troops could pass. I think this took the students by surprise, because it was all done very quickly. *Granaderos* entered, shooting tear-gas grenades ahead of them. But relatively few of the students were in the school itself. Those who were there were on the roof, and very well prepared, with wet handkerchiefs over their noses and mouths. From that height they rained stones, Molotov cocktails and the police's own tear-gas grenades down upon the *granaderos* in the courtyard below.

'At this point, seeing the *granaderos* enter the building, a shout went up from the windows of the surrounding blocks of flats – or rather, a thousand shouts: *"ABAJO ASESINOS!" "MUERA DIAZ ORDAZ, ASESINO!"* From the top of the same blocks of flats, more students were hidden, with

'A government of hordes of thieves and days of misery': a pun on Diaz Ordaz.

'People Unite! Don't let them rule you with tanks and speeches.'

'Visitor: want to see Mexico? Visit our prisons.'

supplies of stones, bricks and bottles that they had collected from all over the area, enough for a long siege. In this way the battle became generalized. The army and the *granaderos* turned their attention from the school, which was virtually impenetrable, and began to attack the people of the ISSSTE buildings. For two hours the battle between these people – civilian population and the national army – was waged....

'And all this time the chant was kept up. *"ABAJO ASESINOS!"*, *"MUERA DIAZ ORDAZ!"* At 9 o'clock the *granaderos* and soldiers began to retreat. It should be remembered that there were never more than a hundred students involved in this struggle. All the rest were plain common people. Women, children and old people as much as the men. When the *granaderos* began shooting their tear-gas grenades into the windows of the ISSSTE buildings, setting fire to some of the rooms, it was certain that the people would fight until they had driven off the troops.

'At 9.30 the people assaulted the Ministry of Foreign Relations, which ... is directly across from Vocational School Number 7. Even after the people had set the Ministry on fire, the police forces came closer, but did not dare to cross the ruin to reach the building.

'All this time the school was silent, but from the tower blocks the chant was kept up: *"ABAJO ASESINOS!"* By now it was almost dawn and with the daylight thousands of people came streaming into the barrio from all directions, on foot, in buses, in cars. They brought food and gasoline and sometimes even money, or just expressions of their solidarity with the people of Tlatelolco.

'I think the people of Mexico will not support a situation in which the Army is used against ordinary people in this way. At any rate, the Mexicans have had a revolution, and they will know how to fight.'

The police forces withdraw for the time being. They will be back.

A militarized Olympics.

1968
October

'The gentlemen
of the government
are dead. For that,
they kill us.'

José Revueltas

A mural by José Orozco depicts the 1911 revolution in Mexico led by
Emiliano Zapata and Pancho Villa.

'Get rid of Cueto and his Ordaz. Long live the students!' A sticker of protest against the Mexican Chief of Police and the President. Ordaz is pronounced like 'hordas', hordes.

The October 2 massacre of the student protesters in Mexico City on the eve of the Olympic Games there leaves a smear of blood across the Western world. For decades Mexico has been a *de facto* one-party state, in which the leaders of the ruling PRI (Institutional Revolutionary Party) can boast that they could teach the Russian Communists a few tricks on how to stay in power. Like the Communist Party of the Soviet Union, the PRI has had a radical past. It can claim linear descent from Pancho Villa and Emiliano Zapata, the peasant Generals who inaugurated the 1910 Mexican revolution.

Zapata's popularity was due to his uncompromising stance against the landowners. In November 1911 he announced his plan:

'Be it known that the lands, woods and waters, which have been usurped by the owners of haciendas through tyranny and venal justice, will be restored immediately to the pueblos or citizens who have the corresponding titles to such properties, of which they were despoiled through the bad faith of our oppressors. They shall maintain such possession at all costs through force of arms.'

Zapata, like Che Guevara many years after him, was ambushed and assassinated by those in authority who feared him. He became a legend. One result may be that Mexico is one of the few countries of Latin America where the Indians can be seen to smile.

It is also a country which gave birth to a vibrant artistic tradition, where images speak to the populace from the walls. A country that produced the greatest muralist of the twentieth century: Diego Rivera. The Mexican painters, who included Frida Kahlo (married to Rivera), Siqueiros and Orozco, were, in the main, identified with various sections of the Mexican Left. They spoke to and for the people. They were encouraged and provided with state subsidies during the regime of Lazaro Cardenas in the thirties.

By 1968 the PRI has become mummified. Corruption seeps out of its every pore and it acts only for the moneyed élite. However, it still permits a certain amount of press and cultural freedom (unlike its Soviet counterpart) and, provided its monopoly of power is not challenged, it can turn a blind eye to literary denunciations of its record in office.

The only Mexican politician who remains popular in 1968 is Lazaro Cardenas, who, in the thirties and forties, initiated land reforms and labour reorganization on a massive scale and introduced tariffs which favoured indigenous capital. Cardenas was the only Mexican leader to dismantle the political power of the hacienda owners and redistribute their lands to hungry peasants. Before he became President in 1934, 17 million acres of land had been redistributed. During his six years in office 34 million acres were transferred from landowners to village communities under communal forms of tenure. Still alive in 1968, he lives on a farm in northern Mexico. Earlier this year, the Yaqui, a warrior tribe, ask to see him. The chiefs, in full plumage reserved for special events, welcome him with affection. They have not seen him for thirty years.

'Do you remember, Tata Lazaro?' they ask him. 'You gave us back the lands. You gave us hospitals and schools. You remember? We want you to know, the rich have taken back the lands. The hospitals have been turned into barracks. The schools are cantinas.'

Cardenas listens with a sad look in his eyes. He knows that his successors have reversed his reforms. In his heart he loathes the new PRI and its current leader, Díaz Ordaz. He knows that today the Mexico Which Has is riding roughshod over the Mexico Which Has Not.

The complacent and self-confident leaders of the PRI are excited that the 1968 Olympic Games are being held in Mexico City. The Games will bring them prestige and money. But their joy is tempered with impatience at the rising temperature in the universities and the unconscionable demands for the release of political prisoners. They are determined that the protesters will not spoil their moment of glory and that the Games will go ahead as planned.

They are determined, but so are the students, whose banners include giant portraits of Zapata and Che Guevara. These are students with a historical memory. They remember Zapata. They remember Cardenas and Che, who was killed the previous year. They will not let the Olympics take place without their demands being understood. But they are unarmed. Their enemy is the Mexican State as represented by armed men under the control of the PRI. The power of this state will be deployed before the eyes of the world.

On the evening of October 2, on the direct orders of President Ordaz, troops open fire on a crowd of 10,000 people listening to speeches in the Plaza de las Tres Culturas. Over sixty people are murdered in cold blood and hundreds more are injured.

The writer José Revueltas declares: 'The gentleman of the government are dead. For that, they kill us.'

2nd | **Mexico City, Mexico** The Night of the Massacre

Some 10,000 people are in the Plaza de las Tres Culturas this evening, listening to the student speakers explain, through the microphones on one of the balconies of the surrounding blocks of flats, that they refuse to back down on their demands for civil liberty, despite the armed troops and *granaderos* of the Díaz Ordaz regime.

There had been plans for a demonstration this evening, but now the young speaker on the balcony is trying to call it off.

'There are twenty-two truckloads of troops, fourteen jeeps with machine-guns and many tanks at the campus,' he explains, his voice echoing from the tall buildings that surround the Plaza. 'The committee does not believe in sterile bloodshed. We ask you to go home when this meeting is over.'

There is some mild hissing and booing from the crowd, but they are in good humour. Many of them are residents of the housing estate who had joined in the battle with the *granaderos* the week before: old people, women, men and children, as well as the students' parents and their younger brothers and sisters. Students are circulating through the crowd, distributing leaflets.

The helicopter circling overhead is joined by a second one. Suddenly there is a ripple of uneasiness from the rear of the crowd. One of the helicopters shoots off four green flares into the darkening sky.

'Don't move, don't yield to the provocation,' the student speaker is shouting, but the crowd panics, stampeding towards the centre of the square, away from the soldiers. A tremendous commotion breaks out on the balcony as secret service agents seize the student by the neck. There are more agent on the balcony above, where the other student leaders are. From the back of the crowd comes the deafening rattle of machine-gun fire.

The troops pour in from all sides of the square, opening fire indiscriminately into the fleeing, screaming mass of people. Bullets are coming from all directions, shattering all the glass in every window of the apartment buildings, blasting showers of rubble from the walls. One of the apartment blocks is blazing, and the lights have all gone off. Then it begins to rain, a torrential downpour on the people running, slipping, screaming, alive and dead, trying to find shelter from the massacre.

María Elena, a student at the University of Mexico, recalls:

'I had gone with my fifteen-year-old brother to the meeting that day. He was a student at one of the Vocational Schools, not very political, but he was just starting to get involved. We were close to the south end of the plaza when the shooting started, near where the Aztec ruins are. We saw the green fireworks and what was happening on the balcony and then behind us came the rattling and cracking of the machine-guns and all in an instant we were caught up in a crowd, running in terror.

'I heard my brother shout, "Don't let go of me." We gripped each other's hands. We were running towards the right, pushing toward the garden where the ruins are. Many people were already there trying to hide from the terrible spraying of bullets coming from all directions. The whine of missiles cut through the other sounds, and showers of chips flew from the stones of the ruins under the impact of the bullets.

'I still had firm hold of my brother's hand, although people had got between us and I tried to pull him closer. Students caught between us had fallen, some had been killed, some wounded. At my side was a girl who had been hit in the face with an expanding bullet – what horror. The whole left side of her face had been blown

Mexican soldiers killed 25 students in the Tlatelolco district of Mexico City on 3 October. Roland Ranetsberger, the photographer, was arrested but he slipped the film to a woman who escaped.

off. You could see her teeth and palate, and also that she herself was not yet aware of what had happened.

'The yelling, the screams of pain, the sobbing, the pleading, and the continual deafening sound of the guns made the Plaza de las Tres Culturas into an inferno. I dragged at my brother's arm.

'"Julio, what's the matter?" I pulled at him again. His eyes were very sad and half closed and I caught the words, "It's that ..."

'I couldn't think of anything. The tremendous packing together of people made it difficult to hear. Later I thought that if I had realized Julio was dying, I would have done something crazy right then and there. Little by little people made room for us so that I could get closer to my brother.

'"Julio, answer me."

'"He must be wounded," a woman told me. "Loosen his belt."

'Gradually, and then all at once, I began to grasp the possible reality. When I loosened his belt, my hand sank into a wound. Now, close together, I was able to lift my head and look around. My first impression was the number of people lying in the Plaza. The living and the dead were intermingled. My second impression was that my little brother was riddled with bullets. He had been hit in the stomach, in the neck and in the leg. He was dying, there in the square.'

Over fifty people lie dead in the Plaza de las Tres Culturas. Several hundred more are badly wounded. The next day the President of the International Olympic Committee, Mr Brundage, states, 'We have been assured by the Mexican authorities that nothing will interfere with the peaceful entrance of the Olympic flame into the Stadium on October 12. We have full confidence that the Mexican people, universally known for their sportsmanship and great hospitality, will join participants and spectators in celebrating the Games, a veritable oasis in a troubled world.'

Elsewhere the reaction to the slaughter is one of horrified shock and anger and an immediate campaign to boycott the Games is begun. In Nicaragua, students protesters stone the Mexican Embassy and carry away its crest, saying that they will keep it until Mexico has representatives worthy of its people. In Amsterdam, students seize the Mexican General Consulate in protest at the massacre, and raise the red flag over it in solidarity with their fallen comrades. Students in Santiago, Chile, demonstrate outside the US Consulate, as the biggest friend of Díaz Ordaz's government, defending themselves with sticks and stones against the Chilean riot police. Thousands of students demonstrate in Milan, La Spezia, Florence and Rome; in Paris, Grenoble and London.

'If the Games are to be stopped every time the politicians violate the laws of humanity, there will never be any international contests,' comments Brundage.

On October 6 the Olympic torch is carried ashore at Veracruz by relays of Mexican swimmers. Enormous crowds of protesters line the waterfront, crying out in grief and anger until they are beaten back by the paratroopers' rifle butts. Meanwhile Black American athletes are planning their own protest at the Games.

5th Derry, Northern Ireland, UK   Orange Laws and Orange Orders

The civil rights marchers assembled in Derry this afternoon come mainly from the working-class Catholic streets, one of the poorest parts of Britain, where unemployment stands at twenty-seven per cent. Under Northern Ireland's 'special' property-based electoral system, many of the families here will have no vote in the municipal elections, because they are not ratepayers. Local magnate Sir Basil McFarlane, on the other hand, will have twenty-six votes to cast. The result is a Tory–Unionist-run City Corporation of unmatchable arrogance and complacency. Despite Derry's dire housing crisis, only fifteen new houses have been built by the Corporation in the last three years. In February this year, local tenants got together to form the Derry Housing Action Committee. Denied the vote, they concentrated on a campaign of civil disobedience, mindful of the black civil rights campaigns in the United States a few years before. In their efforts to get the slum housing improved, they have demonstrated at corporation meetings, organized rent strikes, picketed bad landlords' homes and helped a family of four to block one of Derry's main streets with the caravan that was all they had to live in.

As the campaign goes on it begins to draw in wider layers and take up broader issues: the systematic discrimination between the religions in Northern Ireland in housing, jobs and politics. But although it is largely Catholic, the movement is very clear that it is about civil rights, not religion; nor, necessarily, about republicanism.

The march for civil rights has attracted over a thousand people altogether, more than the organizers had been expecting – and this despite a last-minute ban by the Northern Ireland Home Affairs Minister, William Craig. There is some trepidation but a good, lively spirit, too, as they set off down the road.

The first march for civil rights in Derry, Northern Ireland, October 1968.

In Duke Street two double lines of the Royal Ulster Constabulary police bar the way, their batons drawn. The marchers halt to discus what to do. One man calls for them all to go home now:

'We've made our point by coming here today ...'

But the general mood is more determined.

'What about the Mexican students?' someone calls.

'What about in Vietnam?'

The crowd is boxed in, with little room for manoeuvre anyway. Police whistles blow. Within seconds Duke Street is a battleground, echoing to the thud of clubs against bodies, the screams of the women watching from the houses, and the shouts of demonstrators. People try to take shelter in shop doorways but the police seem intent not so much to disperse the frightened marchers as to systematically bludgeon them to the ground.

An eighteen-year-old cub reporter, Martin Cowley, vainly displaying his press credentials, is repeatedly beaten to the ground by District Inspector Ross McGimpsie. Another man is grabbed by two policemen and flung, bodily, over a wall by them, breaking a leg as he lands. Water cannons are brought up, to drive the fleeing marchers back into the arms of the police.

The marchers are driven back into the Catholic areas, and there they throw up barricades against the police, with local residents rushing to help them – the children, especially. Molotov cocktails, bricks and stones are stockpiled by the barricades. Houses are turned into casualty centres as the injured are carried home. Over twenty people are in hospital.

One of the marchers, Anne Kerr, who was in Chicago for the Democratic Convention in August, tells reporters: 'These police are in exactly the same league as the riot police of Chicago. The methods used by the Metropolitan Police in Grosvenor Square [London] last March were like a Buckingham Palace garden party compared to those used in Londonderry today.'

William Craig, the hard-line Unionist Home Affairs Minister for the province, springs to the defence of his men, denying that there has been any unnecessary brutality. To allegations that the RUC have been deliberately clubbing demonstrators' testicles, he replies, 'The code of instruction in baton drill lays it down that the police must aim at the legs in order to minimize the injury to a demonstrator.'

The following day, a Sunday, the clashes continue, with police again confronting crowds trying to move up Duke Street towards the city gates. They are driven back with baton charges and there are running battles with the police as barricades are thrown up again and water cannons brought out. As dusk falls, there are a reported ninety-six casualties in Londonderry's Altnagelvin Hospital. Calls are raised for Craig to resign and a picket is mounted outside his house in Belfast with placards reading 'CRAIG THE BULLY' and 'GIVE LONDONDERRY A FAIR CORPORATION', but the Minister remains unrepentant.

The following Wednesday, October 9, a huge civil rights demonstration sets out from Queen's University, Belfast, and holds a sit-down protest outside Belfast City Hall. Leading Ulster Unionist Ian Paisley organizes a counter-demonstration. A crowd of about a thousand of his supporters gather near the City Hall, separated from the student sit-in by about 100 yards and two lines of RUC. The Paisleyites sing 'The Derry Walls' and other Orange songs and taunt the students with Union Jacks. There is a tense stand-off as darkness falls and a chill autumn wind blows down Linenhall Street. A desperate student leader with a megaphone calls for the civil rights protesters to disperse:

'If there is bloodshed in Belfast tonight there will be a return to violence and pogrom all over Northern Ireland. We have made our point. Let us now go home with a little dignity.'

Commenting on the five days of protests, the *Guardian* newspaper's special correspondent in Northern Ireland writes of the high unemployment in the province, especially in the Catholic areas where many have no hope of a steady job; of the gerrymandering of local election boundaries; the local government franchise tied to property qualifications; and the allocation of council houses by Unionist councillors on a crony basis:

'If these genuine and deeply-felt grievances are perpetually bottled up there will, in time, be an explosion. If redress does not come from Westminster or, less plausibly, from Stormont [seat of the Unionist-dominated Northern Ireland parliament] something very unpleasant is going to happen.

'Some feel that the Unionists in Ulster have out-Marxed Karl Marx himself, by diverting the electorate from thoughts of jobs, food, education and homes with thoughts of religion, which may have made them a little mad. Unionist leaders still beat the Orange drum, probe old sectarian wounds, incite the [Protestant] majority against the [Catholic] minority, reap the harvest of bigotry and so retain their hold on power and influence. So strong is it that not only Catholics but liberal Protestants who decline to join the Orange clubs become second-class citizens.'

12th San Francisco, USA 'That bastard Johnson'

A 15,000-strong demonstration in San Francisco against the war in Vietnam is electrified by the presence of over five hundred serving GIs, marching against the war – despite a strong Military Police force trying to stop them. At the rally in the Civic Centre, one Vietnam veteran describes to the crowd how his camp was shelled by the NLF, and two of his friends killed.

'When Burns stumbled out of that bunker into the arms of Larry Craig, he didn't mumble "those bastard Vietcong", he didn't mumble "those bastard communists". He mumbled only one thing, over and over: "That bastard Johnson, that bastard Johnson ..."'

13th Nablus, Israeli-occupied Palestine The Palestinian Diaspora

Hundreds of Arab schoolgirls march through the streets of Nablus in protest against the occupation of their town by the Israelis. The Palestinians are still reeling from the effects of the 1967 War and the emergence of the 'New Israel' with its aggressively expansionist policy. The schoolgirls carry banners reading: 'WE SHALL NOT SURRENDER', 'WE SHALL NOT EMIGRATE', 'WE SHALL NOT YIELD TO THE OCCUPIERS'.

Armed Israeli police blocking the entrance to the Military Governor's residence disperse the demonstration, firing live ammunition over the girls' heads and hosing them with a cannon firing water containing red dye. Later they will be easy to identify in house-to-house searches.

An old Palestinian woman, Fadwa Tuqan, describes how she struggled to find a new identity as a poetess of her people: 'Poetry became the sole preoccupation, awake or asleep, of my spirit and mind. My absorption in my new world taught me the taste of happiness. I was immersed in the act of creating myself, building myself anew....' Her poem 'Face Lost in the Wilderness' explores this experience:

> And my life continues –
> the wind merges me with my people
> on the terrible road of rocks and thorns.
> But behind the river, dark forest of spears
> sway and swell; the roaring storm
> unravels mystery, giving to dragon silence
> the power of words.
> A rush and din, flame and sparks
> lighting the road –
> one group after another
> falls, embracing in one lofty death.
> The night, no matter how long, will continue
> to give birth to star after star
> and my life continues,
> my life continues.

Victorious American athletes at the Mexico Olympics give the clenched fist salute in solidarity with the struggles of Black Americans and Mexican students.

A hush falls over the huge crowd at the Olympic Stadium in Mexico City as the two Black American winners of the men's 200-metre events, gold medallist Tommie Smith and bronze medallist John Carlos, raise their fists in the Black Power salute during the playing of the American national anthem. The protest is silent, dignified and moving, bringing to mind the conditions in which innumerable Black Americans have died and in which millions more continue to live, before the eyes of the watching world.

'We are black, and we are proud to be black in white America,' Carlos tells a crowded international press conference later. 'Black Americans understand the nature of our demonstration. We are not a show horse, doing a performance ...'

The next day the two athletes are expelled from the US team, accused of 'mixing politics with sport'.

'They have violated the standards of sportsmanship and good manners which are so highly regarded in the United States,' the US team managers say, 'and are therefore suspended from the team forthwith and ordered to remove themselves

Sport: A Prison of Measured Time
Sabotage the Mexico Olympics!

Few self-perpetuating maxims have received as little criticism as the notion that sport is a non-political activity. It has, so far as I know, never been mooted that the whole business might be totally undesirable.

There are at least four grounds on which sport is generally objectionable.

1. It encourages the 'competitive spirit'.

2. As at present organised, it encourages the crudest forms of nationalism.

3. The emphasis on physical fitness is essentially militarist.

4. The idea of 'mens sana in corpore sano' (with its overtones that the beautiful are good) is fascist.

But, in society now, there is a more important objection: sport now serves as a major opiate of the people.

At best, it offers the working class a spurious 'escape route' from its toils. The complacence and general reactionariness of top sportsmen is hardly surprising when it is remembered that they are mostly working class lads who have 'made it'. In the old days those who made it got a pub or a sports outfitters. A step up, anyway. [The Northern Ireland footballer] George Best's boutique is only a change in style, not kind....

Yet the few successes are used to justify the system. At its crudest, the headlines when Lee Trevino won this year's American Golf Open brimmed with the joys of rags to riches....

Another area where sports are used to suggest that all is well with the system, the Olympics, has just at last come under attack. The Project for Human Rights, most associated with the proposed boycott of the US Olympic team by black athletes, but with other strings to its bow including the re-instatement of Muhammad Ali, points out that the alleged and vaunted 'integration' in the sports arena is phoney.

For a black athlete, there are even fewer who make it. But many thousands waste their precious youth in attempts to hit the big time. And many hundreds of thousands, by associating themselves with black stars, castrate themselves politically.

It will be a courageous act for a black runner to face the storm of execration which will greet him if he stays out of the Olympic team, or otherwise disrupts the Mexican Games. It may turn out too much to ask – and the white press will claim the movement is a paper tiger.

But they will be wrong: the impact of the proposals has already reached far beyond the surface ripples; not only the American sporting establishment, but the whole caboodle could come crashing down if the message isn't heeded that the people can't be fooled all the time.

It would be ironic, but should not be surprising, if 'non-political' sports, because they have been so little considered, become a revolutionary flashpoint.

Gordon Peters, *Black Dwarf*, 1968

from the Olympic village ... A repetition of such incidents by other members of the US team would warrant the imposition of the severest penalties.'

The team managers' threat backfires the next day, however, when three more Black American athletes – Lee Evans, Larry James and Ron Freeman – mount the rostrum to receive gold, silver and bronze in the men's 400-metre race and, as the national anthem is played, raise their fists in the Black Power salute.

20th Rio de Janeiro, Brazil Che's Legacy

The USA's General Westmoreland is in Rio de Janeiro, addressing a conference of Latin American generals on the lessons of the Vietnam War. All the latest 'counter-insurgency' tactics are discussed, including the prophylactic use of air power against unarmed villagers to ensure that they won't, in future, even think of offering food or shelter to the young guerrilla fighters coming their way.

'Guevara's revolutionary thesis – "Create two, three, many Vietnams" – represents a real danger,' Westmoreland says. The generals agree. Che's spirit is now revered in Bolivia, where many peasant homes have a shrine to San Ernesto. There are several guerrilla bands operating in Colombia and in Uruguay, where the famed Tupamaros have kidnapped a much-loathed figure of the local oligarchy, the landowner and telephone company boss Pereyra, this summer. The Tupamaros take their name from the eighteenth-century South American Indian chief Tupac Amaru, who organized a two-year rebellion against the Spanish colonists. They release Pereyra a few days later (having kept him in a farmhouse, on a diet of classical music and the works of Che Guevara); but not before their student supporters have smashed every Coca-Cola sign the length of Montevideo's main avenue.

In Guatemala the guerrillas are still fighting, despite a murderous land and air onslaught, aided by US 'advisers', on the peasant villages in the mountainous western part of the country, where the guerrillas have their main support. The same is true in Venezuela, where hundreds of specially trained counter-insurgency troops, supported by US Green Berets, have clashed with guerrillas.

The French left-wing newspaper salutes the Mexican students.

Worse still, the Latin American armies themselves cannot always be counted upon. Young middle-class Peruvian officers, sent up into the mountains from Lima, are so appalled by the living conditions of the peasantry whose land expropriation movement they have been sent to crush, that they organize a leftist coup, take over the oil wells and hand the national press over to the workers' and peasants' organizations to run.

In the Portuguese colonies of Mozambique, Angola and Guinea, too, young Portuguese officers who have been reading Fanon, Mao and Guevara as part of their counter-insurgency training are starting to suffer from the same contamination: in 1975 they will use what they have learnt from 'the enemy' in a popular uprising against their own oligarchy at home.

And even as Westmoreland speaks, the voices of young protesters can be heard outside. Despite the threat of arrest and torture by the Brazilian military regime, several thousand kids are dodging the armed troops through the traffic outside, shouting, 'GO HOME, WESTMORE-LAND. VIETNAM WILL WIN.'

October 1968

22nd | **Berkeley, California, USA** The Struggle Continues

Black Panther leader Eldridge Cleaver delivers his first lecture at the Berkeley campus, part of the University of California, despite concerted opposition from the State Governor, Ronald Reagan, and others, but the University authorities refuse to grant the students who attend it academic credits for the course. Police arrest 121 students during a sit-in protest against the decision, and drag them off to be charged. The students retaliate by occupying one of the main University halls and barricading the doors, demanding an amnesty for their arrested comrades. Just before dawn, the barricaded doors are battered open and a large force of California police charge into the hall, drag down the red and black flags that bedeck the walls and march the students off into waiting vans.

26-27th | **London, UK** Marching in the Streets

The London School of Economics is occupied by its students to provide a sanctuary for protesters on the huge anti-Vietnam War demonstration the next day and a space for political discussion. Eight doctors and nurses will be there for the demo, as well as lawyers who have set up the October 27 Legal Defence Committee. Five thousand people crowd into the LSE over the weekend, despite the authorities' attempts to close it. Student-run seminars on 'The Sociology of Revolution', 'Colonial Revolution' and 'Combatting Bourgeois Culture' draw large attendances.

Students occupy the London School of Economics in solidarity with the 27 October demonstration.

October 27 sees the biggest-ever demonstration through the streets of London against the Vietnam War: nearly 100,000 people march along Whitehall, fifty abreast, their arms linked, chanting: 'HO, HO, HO CHI MINH, THE NLF IS GOING TO WIN!'

For weeks beforehand, the British press has been whipping up hysteria as to how much violence there is going to be on the day. In the event, only a breakaway group of the sub-Maoist Britain–Vietnam Solidarity Front leaves the march for a confrontation with the police outside the US Embassy in Grosvenor Square. The rest of the march goes on to Hyde Park.

'We always said that if the police left us alone we would march to Hyde Park, hold our meeting and disperse. We were left alone, and that is exactly what happened,' says a Vietnam Solidarity Campaign speaker.

Among the huge crowd is Mick Jagger, who afterwards writes the song 'Street Fighting Man.' British record companies refuse to release it as a single and the BBC bans the song. Jagger sends the lyrics to the radical newspaper *Black Dwarf*.

Left: Mick Jagger's hand-written lyrics of his song 'Street Fighting Man' as published in *Black Dwarf*.
Below: Nearly 100,000 people march in London on 27 October to demonstrate their support of the Vietnamese resistance to the United States.

Czechs mark the 50th anniversary of their independence outside the castle in Hradcany chanting 'Long live Dubcek!'

28th Prague, Czechoslovakia The Tears of Dubcek

It is Czechoslovakia's national day and fifty years since the founding of the country by Tomás Masaryk in 1918. Thousands march through Prague to the gates of Hradcany Castle, carrying flags and chanting slogans against the occupying troops: 'MOSCOW – MUNICH', 'HITLER – BREZHNEV', 'OCCUPYING ARMY, GET OFF OUR BACKS'. In the evening, the demonstrators pour down through the streets to the Prague National Theatre, cheering the Czechoslovak leaders as they arrive for a special performance of Smetana's patriotic opera *Libuse*. The street is so full of people that Dubcek and Svoboda's cars cannot get through and they have to walk the last 100 yards through wildly cheering crowds of their supporters. Both have tears in their eyes.

Until now, Czechoslovak opposition to the occupying troops has largely taken the form of passive resistance since the Dubcek leadership's return from Moscow on August 26. Requests for food and lodgings for the occupying troops meet with polite obfuscation and insuperable although mysterious difficulties. Russian lorries are observed having to wait an absurdly long time at rural level crossings, although as soon as a car with Czechoslovak numbers plates drives up, the barriers rise. At the Brno Trade Fair the local workers declare themselves baffled by the workings of Russian nuts and bolts and Russian troops have to be called in to erect the Soviet stalls and take them down again. Large portraits of Dubcek, Svoboda, Cernik and Smrkovsky in every other factory, shop and office are another sign of protest. For the most part, the people of Czechoslovakia respect the leadership's call to avoid giving the occupying forces any excuse for armed repression and bloodshed.

1968
November

Pakistani lessons:
how to overthrow
a dictatorship!

Students in West Pakistan beat back a police charge.

187

Following the massacres in Mexico, the defeat in Czechoslovakia and the stalemate in France and Germany, it seems as if the momentum of the worldwide upsurge of young people that has shaken five continents is on the decline. The upheavals of November come from an unexpected quarter.

Students in Asia have always played an active part in politics. Especially in those countries where political parties and trade unions were outlawed, the students have seen themselves as the only oppositional force with a ready-made point of assembly: the school and the university. Students in Japan, Korea, Indonesia, South Vietnam and Thailand have tested their strength against their rulers. Despite the brutality inflicted on them – mass arrests, vile tortures, cold-blooded murders – they have always regrouped to fight again.

In the second week of November news of massive student demonstrations in West Pakistan starts to seep through to the West. A country virtually unknown to the rest of the world begins to capture the headlines, as though Pakistani students have timed their protests to dispel the growing gloom in Europe with the brilliant sun of revolt.

Pakistan is a strange confection. Carved out of the Indian subcontinent as a homeland for the Muslim minority in 1947, it consists of two parts – West and East – supposedly united by religion, but in fact separated by language, culture, tradition and a thousand miles of Indian territory. The Bengali majority of the population (sixty per cent) lives in East Pakistan – soon to become Bangladesh. Virtually the entire civilian and military élite belong to the Punjabi province of West Pakistan. The Bengali majority have begun to feel more and more alienated from the very concept of a Pakistan which denies them their democratic and economic rights.

The movement which erupts in 1968 will be the only time in its history that the entire country is united, East and West, against the US-backed military dictatorship of Field Marshal Ayub Khan. These are truly days of hope; and if the politicians had been capable of rising to the occasion the country's future might have turned out differently.

It is police brutality that triggers off the student uprising that spreads to every city in the country. The demand is simple: restoration of democracy. Despite the fact that the students are baton-charged, tear-gassed and shot dead, they refuse to be defeated. The marches on the streets grow in number. The students' courage and determination impress the workers in the big towns and the unemployed, as well as the professional petty-bourgeoisie: lawyers, doctors, architects and the like. These social layers now begin to join the struggle. The government closes the schools and universities to deny the students a meeting-point, but the mobilizations continue to grow in size and intensity. As their spirits rise higher, students defiantly sing the poems of Habib Jalib and Faiz Ahmed Faiz, both of whom are banned from appearing on television. One such poem is Faiz's 'Today Come to the Market-place in Fetters':

> The tear-stained eye, the stormy spirit, are not enough
> The accusation of illicit love is not enough,
> Today come in fetters to the market-place
> Come waving hands, come exulting, come dancing,
> Come with dust on the head, come with blood on the dress.

Women students in Dhaka (then East Pakistan) march bare-footed and silent in solidarity with students who have died in the struggle.

> All the city of the beloved is gazing, come;
> There the governor waits and there the populace,
> The arrow of calumny, too as well as the stone of abuse,
> The unhappy daybreak too, as well as the wretched day.
> Who is their intimate, besides us?
> In the city of the beloved who now is pure
> Who is worthy of the executioner's hand?
> Fasten-on the burden of the heart, lift the heart's sad load, come;
> Let us once again go to be murdered – friends, come.

The railway workers stop the trains. Factory workers cripple industry. Bus drivers and rickshaw-scooter drivers paralyse city transport. Prostitutes refuse to service police officers and army officers, and lawyers in their black robes march in dignified processions to endorse the student demands for democracy. The people have lost their fear and, once that stage is reached, even the most powerful regimes are powerless.

Those politicians and cabinet ministers who have stayed loyal to the dictator are greeted wherever they go by thousands of demonstrators waving spoons of every age and size. In northern India the spoon has long been a symbol for a toady and a stooge. The origins of the abuse are disputed, but one version says the spoon became a dirty word in the early days of colonialism. Native aristocrats who entertained the British stopped eating with their fingers and began to use spoons, knives and forks. They became known in popular parlance as the '*chamchas*' or spoons of the British. The revolt against the dictatorship and its spoons which begins in November 1968 will end the following March with the fall of Ayub Khan. A dictatorship will be toppled. The Pakistani uprising will prove to be the most successful of all the upheavals of 1968.

1st Beijing, China How to be a Good Communist

> 'Comrades, you should always bear your own responsibilities. If you've got to shit, shit! If you've got to fart, fart! Don't hold things down in your bowels, and you'll feel easier.' (down-to-earth advice from an early Chinese edition of *The Thoughts of Chairman Mao*)

At the Twelfth Plenum of the Central Committee, Liu Shaoqi, President of the People's Republic of China and the man previously regarded as Mao Zedong's most likely successor, is denounced by Mao's supporters as a 'traitor, renegade and scab' and expelled from the Chinese Communist Party, of which he was a founder member. Liu is the author of *How to be a Good Communist,* a handbook which has acquired the status of a catechism for Asian communists who are desirous of repeating China's success.

The downfall of Liu Shaoqi marks Mao Zedong's final triumph over his critics in the Party and the beginning of the end of the Cultural Revolution, the process of tumultuous civil strife that Mao had unleashed upon the country in 1966 in order to re-establish his control.

Mao Zedong had been the undisputed leader of the new People's Republic of China, proclaimed from the terrace of the Forbidden City overlooking Tiananmen Square when the victorious Chinese Communist Party finally entered Beijing in October 1949. It was a position built up through years of epic struggle, during the Long March and the war against the Japanese occupation. During the fifties the new regime had pushed through a wave of reforms, destroying the feudal past for ever. A spirit of hope had swept the country; the whole of Asia rejoiced.

Mao's pre-eminence within the Chinese Communist Party had been based upon the real successes achieved by the revolution, but it was a party built on the Stalinist model: inner-party debate was discouraged, the leadership ruled supreme and the Supreme Leader was Mao Zedong. It was only after a series of disastrous policy decisions initiated by Mao that an alternative faction within the Party had begun to make itself felt.

Chief among the disasters was the 'Great Leap Forward' of 1957–9, Mao's scheme to industrialize China at a stroke: three years of hard work and sacrifice would lead to a thousand years of happiness. Instead, the Great Leap Forward's reorganization of agriculture, and its mobilization of millions of peasants to create the 600,000 backyard steel-smelting furnaces that were supposed to triple China's industrial production, caused a massive economic crisis and a dreadful famine in which millions died.

Liu Shaoqi, Mao's second in command – a veteran Party *apparatchik* whose education had begun at the University for Toilers of the East in Moscow, in 1922 – had toured his native Hunan province in 1962 and made a bitterly critical speech about the devastation wrought by the Great Leap Forward and the sufferings of the peasants, claiming that the famine was seventy per cent man-made. Mao himself blamed lower-level Party cadres for misinterpreting his policy, but meanwhile Liu and three other leaders – Zhou Enlai, Deng Xiaoping and Chen Yen – had taken it upon themselves to embark on a new economic policy of stabilization and retrenchment that included the restoration of some peasant initiatives in agriculture. Real control over the Party seemed to be slipping out of the Great Helmsman's hands.

In January 1965 Mao had told his American Boswell, Edgar Snow, that Liu must

Mao's legions in the Chinese Army demonstrate their support for the 'Great Helmsman'.

go. Mao's faction alleged that 'Persons in power taking the capitalist road had formed a bourgeois headquarters inside the Central Committee which pursued a revisionist political and organisational line – and had agents in all provinces, municipalities and autonomous regions, as well as all central departments. In order to be rid of them, it would be necessary to carry out a great cultural and political revolution, in which one class would overthrow another.' This doctrine was further formulated at a special Political Bureau meeting on May 16, 1966 which set up the Cultural Revolution Group that would soon become the *de facto* supreme body of the Chinese Communist Party.

The mass campaign of the Cultural Revolution began the next week at Beijing University with an attack on the University President, Lu Ping, by a philosophy don in her fifties, Nie Yuanzi, who was to become one of the Cultural Revolution's most fanatical ideologues. Nie's group pasted up a 'big-character' poster against Lu Ping declaring, in the exemplary language of the moment: 'Let us unite and hold high the glorious red banner of Mao Zedong Thought, to resolutely, thoroughly, totally and completely wipe out all monsters, demons and counter-revolutionary revisionists of the Krushchev type!'

Chinese miners support Mao and denounce his enemies as 'lackeys and lick-spittles of counter-revolution'. Their tired faces show little enthusiasm.

At the same time, the Cultural Revolution Group and Mao's faction within China's People's Liberation Army began organizing University and Middle School students into units of Red Guards, charged with the glorious task of carrying forward the revolution. A thousand million copies of *The Thoughts of Chairman Mao* – the 'Little Red Book' – were distributed, and the cult of Mao's personality was elevated to a new religion: the Red Guards were to be his 'little Red generals' in the fight against the counter-revolutionary demons and monsters who had burrowed their way into leading positions in every walk of life.

Armed with their copies of the Little Red Book, the Red Guards were allowed to travel free on China's railways. It was a moment of unheard-of adventure and excitement for millions of provincial teenagers, many of whom were filled with genuine idealism and enthusiasm for the tasks they had been set. They poured into Beijing to attend the giant rallies, over a million strong, in Tiananmen Square, at which their adored Leader addressed them from the terrace above the archway to the Forbidden City, the very spot from which he had proclaimed the establishment of the People's Republic of China less than two decades before.

The tragedy was that the only goal that Mao offered for all this energy and excitement was the denunciation of 'enemies' and, where none existed, they had to be found. Teachers were beaten up, doctors were tortured. Leading intellectual, political and military figures of the Party, veterans of the Long March and years of selfless struggle, were paraded through the streets with dunce's hats on their heads and tried in kangaroo courts before mass rallies. Old buildings, statues, works of art, even graveyards were destroyed in a frenzy of hostility to the ancient civilization of the country. All knowledge beyond the Thoughts contained in the Little Red Book was held to be a crime. Soon rival Red Guard groups were denouncing each other as revisionists and 'Capitalist Roaders': traitors to the glorious red banner of Mao Zedong, whose smiling, fatherly face looked down at them from every wall.

By 1967 fierce fighting had broken out between rival Red Guard factions at Nanchang, Nanjing, Xinjiang, Yunnan, Guangxi and Guangdong. People's Liberation Army units, sent in to restore the peace, often found themselves caught up in the factional confusion, unsure which loyal supporters of Mao Zedong Thought they were supposed to be fighting for. In the huge industrial centre of Wuhan, PLA troops were fighting on both sides of what was rapidly turning into a local civil war. By the summer of 1967 Red Guards were looting PLA depots and holding up shipments of Chinese and Soviet military equipment destined for the Vietnamese, to use for themselves. By the spring of 1968 the struggle had spread to the Army, with Red Guards fighting under the slogan, 'Drag the Capitalist Roaders out of the PLA'.

Mao's wife, Jiang Qing, and Lin Biao, the People's Liberation Army leader and Mao's new second in command, were tireless factional organizers, pulling strings from the top while assiduously building the cult of Mao. Huge demonstrations were organized against the country's foremost Capitalist Roader, President Liu Shaoqi, and his number two, Deng Xiaoping, and vicious caricatures of them were paraded through Beijing. By the summer of 1968 both of them were under house arrest in Beijing's élite residential quarter of Zhongnanhai, within the Imperial City. By this stage it was becoming clear that the Cultural Revolution had got completely out of control. Red Guard groups were beginning to develop a political autonomy of their own and some were beginning to challenge the authority and the cult of Mao himself, while Party committees had virtually collapsed at national, provincial and district level. The invasion of Czechoslovakia in August 1968 also served to concentrate Chinese minds on the question of a Soviet threat, in conditions of such domestic instability.

At the end of August 1968 renewed directives were issued to the People's Liberation Army to clamp down on the still smouldering local conflicts, whatever the price. There were more heavy casualties while these were being put into effect; but, with PLA armoured cars patrolling the streets of many cities, the 'Great Proletarian Cultural Revolution' finally came to an end. A few months later Mao will take the extreme step of closing down all the country's Middle Schools and sending the students out to the countryside to work in the fields, thus ensuring the final demise of the Red Guards.

The Twelfth Plenum of the Central Committee of the Chinese Communist Party that meets in October 1968 is thus a completely different body from that which would have met a few years before. It is now packed with loyal adherents of Mao and its principal task is to consider the report on the number-one Capitalist Roader.

Liu Shaoqi is duly charged with being a renegade, traitor and scab, a lackey of imperialism, modern revisionism and the Kuomintang, and sent to prison in Beijing, where his treatment is such that, within a year, he will have to be transported on a stretcher to his next jail, sick with pneumonia and diabetes. Liu will die in a prison cell in November 1969, with only his jailer present. Some of his supporters, such as Deng Xiaoping, will be publicly humiliated.

Tens of thousands of innocent Chinese citizens have died in the course of the Cultural Revolution. Nevertheless, Mao's purge has taken a very different course from that of Stalin in the thirties. The most common punishment for Mao's opponents within the Party has been exile, not death; and indeed, many of the Capitalist Roaders, including Deng Xiaoping himself, will survive to lead their country along that very highway in the 1980s.

3rd Athens, Greece A Subversive Funeral

The spell of fear that has held Greece in thrall since the Colonels' coup in April 1967 is shattered by the crowds, hundreds of thousands strong, who turn out to line the streets for the funeral of George Papandreou, ex-Prime Minister and opposition leader who would certainly have been in power had the 1967 elections been allowed to go ahead.

Papandreou has been held under house arrest since the NATO-backed coup, despite the rapid deterioration in his health. His doctors have only been allowed to visit him in the presence of military guards, his son Andreas (who will found the social democratic party PASOK in 1974, and rule Greece in the eighties) is now in exile abroad and Papandreou's closest friends and colleagues are in prison or exiled to the Greek islands, incommunicado. But if his dying has been lonely, his death is the occasion for a great coming together of the people of Athens, the first since the coup of the previous year.

'Sit up, old man, and see us,' cry voices from the enormous crowd as the flower-bedecked coffin is carried through the sunlit streets. The spectators sing the national anthem as it passes by and chant, unstoppably: '*OCHI, OCHI, OCHI!*' 'NO, NO, NO!' – their own answer to the rigged referendum, held on September 29, which the military junta has been using as a fig-leaf before its NATO allies.

The referendum had asked the Greek people to ratify the Colonels' new constitution, in which the rights of the people to free assembly and trade unionization were sharply limited, and that of the police to make arbitrary arrests was greatly enlarged. The country's police forces, unreformed since the Civil War save for Papandreou's attempts before the coup, played an active role in ensuring that the government got the 'Yes' vote it wanted. According to the electoral rules, each voter was supposed to be given a 'Yes' ballot paper and a 'No' one, to go behind a screen and put the desired answer into an envelope, and then post the envelope into the official ballot-box. In several villages, however, there were no screens at all, and in many districts either selected villagers or the police chiefs themselves were there to record names if anyone was foolish enough to pick up a 'No' ballot paper or, worse still, to go behind the screen.

Terrified by months of pro-regime propaganda and by horrific stories of the possible consequences if they were seen to vote 'No', many country people simply picked up the 'Yes' ballot paper and stuffed it into the envelope before the watchful eyes of the police, in order to ensure that they could get out of the polling station and safely back home. In these areas it was only the very brave or the very angry who dared to vote against.

Now the defiant chants of 'NO, NO, NO!' from the gigantic crowd as the coffin is carried through Constitutional Square mark the beginning of the end of the fearful, traumatized silence with which the Greek people have so far supported those brave enough to stand up to the Colonels' rule.

Nixon acknowledges the large crowds that have gathered in Philadelphia to celebrate his election.

5th | USA | It's Nixon

As widely predicted, the shifty and ghoulish, ultra-ambitious Republican Richard Nixon defeats the damaged Democrat Hubert Humphrey in the US Presidential election. Humphrey, as the incumbent Vice-President, is perceived by anti-War voters as having Vietnamese blood on his hands.

Once in office, Nixon will exhibit a paranoid obsession with the anti-Vietnam War movement and a penchant for secret bombing raids on small neutral countries like Laos and Cambodia. His attempts to save face in Vietnam will prolong the war by many more years as his 'advisor', Henry Kissinger, enters into innumerable secret peace talks in an effort to persuade Hanoi to accept some variant of the pro-US South Vietnamese military clique's continuing rule over at least part of the country.

Meanwhile, to pacify US public opinion and prevent a complete breakdown of discipline in the armed forces, Nixon will be compelled to withdraw increasing numbers of US ground troops. In June 1973 Congress will block all American military action in Vietnam. On May 1, 1975 Saigon will be renamed Ho Chi Minh City.

7-8th | Rawalpindi, Pakistan | A Hot Winter in Pakistan

'We must understand that democracy cannot work in a hot climate like Pakistan. To have democracy we must have a cold climate like Britain.'
General Ayub Khan, after seizing power in October 1958

At the Soviet Embassy in Islamabad, an official reception to mark the anniversary of the 1917 Revolution is under way. The Ambassador and Field Marshal Ayub Khan, watched by 'spoons' on both sides, are toasting each other's health.

Elsewhere, a tiny event has taken place the previous day. Twenty-five miles north of the town of Peshawar is the Landi Kotal shopping centre. It is in the 'tribal areas', and so smuggled goods from all over the world are available there. Bourgeois ladies in search of cheap trousseaus for their daughters mix easily here with arms salesmen and drug-peddlers. Seventy students are returning to Rawalpindi after a shopping trip in Landi Kotal. On the way back, swaggering, overbearing local police officers confiscate their goods, worth Rs5000, and bring charges against them. This tiny act of repression triggers off the most successful of student uprisings.

The only political leader challenging the dictatorship in the West is Zulfikar Ali Bhutto, a disaffected former Cabinet Minister in the Ayub regime. This same day Bhutto is on his way to address the students at the Polytechnic, a few miles outside Rawalpindi. The Landi Kotal affair has angered the students. An all-night meeting on November 6 at the hostel of Gordon College convened by a student leader, Raja Anwar, has decided to call a students' General Assembly on the morning of November 7. Three thousand students attend and denounce Ayub Khan. They vote by a huge majority to march out into the streets and welcome Bhutto. On their way they stop at the Secretariat (headquarters of the bureaucracy), debag the Deputy Commissioner and spank his bare bottom in public.

Students in Rawalpindi march to support Bhutto.

Bhutto has been stopped by the police from reaching the Polytechnic and the students respond by pelting them with radishes. Angry words are exchanged and the police, who normally baton-charge and tear-gas the students before escalating the conflict, now dispense with these formalities and, without warning, open fire. One bullet hits Abdul Hamid, a Polytechnic student. The seventeen-year-old youth dies on the spot. Enraged, the students fight back with paving stones and bricks, setting a few police vans on fire. Hissam-ul-Haq, leader of the Students' Action Committee, declares: 'For the last ten years, Ayub, his family and a coterie of sycophants have looted our country. Under his dictatorship, twenty families have come to control eighty per cent of our national wealth. That's why we're angry, you motherfuckers!'

Bhutto has been sent on to the Intercontinental Hotel in the heart of Rawalpindi. Students follow him here and form a guard of honour for him. The police tear-gas them and the stench reaches the interior of the hotel. While some students begin to stone the hotel, a tiny commando group leads an attack from the back and stones American diplomats sunbathing by the swimming pool. The students are driven out of the hotel, but clashes continue on the streets for the rest of the night. Tension grows in the city as news of Abdul Hamid's death spreads like a prairie fire. He was a boy from a poor family and there is great anger in the poor quarters of the city. Ten years of bitterness and frustration explode on the streets of Rawalpindi, the military capital of the country.

A large public meeting demands an end to the American presence in Asia.

The next day Ayub Khan welcomes Nixon's election victory and declares himself 'an old friend and admirer'. (This praise is reciprocated when Lyndon B. Johnson says, on November 9, 'Pakistan is a model of dynamic development under the wise and constructive leadership of President Ayub.') Pakistan begins to implode. On November 8 tens of thousands of students take to the streets, shouting 'Death to Ayub Khan', 'Down with the dog Ayub' and waving spoons at government cars and army officers. By late afternoon the entire city is involved.

The revolt spreads throughout the country. It is when people banish fear from their hearts and are prepared to die for their cause that even the most powerful dictatorships begin to totter and then fall. 'Mass support for our actions was so total that if there had been a well-disciplined revolutionary organization we would have taken the city and the radio and railway stations,' declares student leader Raja Anwar on November 8.

As the revolt spreads, the Urdu poetry of Habib Jalib and Faiz Ahmed Faiz travels throughout Pakistan. One such poem is Faiz's 'Speak':

> Speak, for your two lips are free;
> Speak, your tongue is still your own;
> This straight body still is yours ...
> Speak, your life is still your own.
>
> See how in the blacksmith's forge
> Flames leap high and steel grows red,
> Padlocks opening wide their jaws,
> Every chain's embrace outspread!
>
> Time enough in this brief hour
> Until body and tongue lie dead;
> Speak, for truth is living yet ...
> Speak whatever must be said.

11th Lisbon, Portugal A Decaying System

Hundreds of students stage a protest over the death of their comrade Daniel Texeira, at the hands of the PIDE – the hated secret police who deal with all dissenters under Portugal's fascist regime.

The old dictator, Salazar, has now been replaced by a more up-to-date version, Caetano, after a stroke in September. Caetano and his modernizing cronies favour turning the rickety Portuguese economy towards Europe. For decades, Portugal has relied on the increasing exploitation of its colonies to prop up the oligarchy at home. Yet despite the profits sweated from forced labour in the sugar plantations of Guinea-Bissau, the diamond mines of Angola and the cotton fields of Mozambique, Portugal people remain the poorest in Europe, with illiteracy and infant mortality rates of 'Third World' proportions and a fifth of Lisbon's population living in shanty dwellings while many villages still lack electricity. Meanwhile over half the government's budget is being spent on the armed forces who are fighting to defend Portugal's colonies from increasingly successful guerrilla movements – the PAIGC in Guinea, FRELIMO in Mozambique and, in Angola, the MPLA.

Now the authoritarian Portuguese regime, which has survived intact for over forty years, is being undermined from every direction at once. The students are refusing to kowtow to the antiquated university structures. A high proportion of Portuguese immigrant workers in France have been caught up in the May events, and news filters back from brothers, uncles and cousins slaving in the Citroën and Renault factories there who have come into contact with an explosive new mixture of revolutionary ideas. Finally, the junior and middle-ranking officers of the Portuguese Army, whose job it is to lead so many expeditions in the field against the rebels in Africa, are becoming infected by the 'know-your-enemy' training manuals that they are having to read – the works of revolutionaries such as Amilcar Cabral and Che Guevara. The result will be the formation of the Armed Forces Movement in 1973, which will challenge the role of the Portuguese Army in sustaining both the disastrous wars in Africa and the repressive, dictatorial regime at home. On April 25, 1974 the Armed Forces Movement will lead a coup against the Caetano regime which will unleash a tumultuous upheaval in Portuguese society over the next year that only just stops short of socialist revolution: the high point of the European upheavals which started in 1968, yet also the moment of their ultimate defeat.

17th Northern Ireland, UK Civil Rights versus Unionist Violence

The mood of 1968 has gripped the Six Counties of Northern Ireland, where, for over four decades, electoral chicanery and anti-Catholic discrimination in housing and jobs have helped the Orange Order and Unionism to preserve a stranglehold and prevent the province's democratization. The failure of successive British governments, Labour and Conservative, to treat the cancer will have grim consequences.

The dark autumn nights see growing tension on Northern Ireland's streets. On November 17 a huge civil rights demonstration called by the Derry Citizens' Action Committee, some 10,000 strong, crosses the Craigavon Bridge over the River Foyle to hold a rally within the city walls. Two days later a large crowd of Paisleyites attack another Citizens' Action Committee meeting from the side-streets, letting fly with volleys of bottles and stones over the Royal Ulster Constabulary's heads. The

John Hume, a civil rights leader, speaking at a dockers' march in Derry.

CAC supporters struggle to reach the side-streets and the RUC lay into the crowd with truncheons and water cannons as the fighting gets worse.

Two weeks before, the British Labour Prime Minister Harold Wilson had taken a tough line with the Unionist leaders of Northern Ireland, warning O'Neill, Craig and Faulkner (respectively Prime Minister, Home Affairs Minister and Minister of Commerce in Northern Ireland) that if they did not meet the civil rights campaigners' demands for 'one-man, one-vote', the British government might intervene over their heads. Since then, however, Craig has refused to concede a thing. Instead of democracy, the citizens of Derry are being offered a 'Development Commission' which will draw up a new plan for the allocation of council houses. A British government statement warns threateningly: 'Any who now continue to disturb the peace and dislocate the life of the country will be exposed as trouble-makers and treated as such.' The civil rights campaigners stick by their demands.

The following week another civil rights demonstration in Armagh is broken up by a thousand Paisley supporters, many wearing crash helmets and armed with spade handles, cudgels and chair-legs. Arriving by the coachload from Belfast and other parts of the province, they establish themselves at 2a.m. on one of the streets that the march is due to take the next morning and refuse to budge. The civil rights march is rerouted, but clashes erupt around the town between the two groups, while the RUC distinguish themselves by punching and kicking a BBC TV crew from the *Panorama* programme in their efforts to 'keep the peace'.

29th | **Madrid, Spain** *Franco, Asesino!*

Spanish riot police advance through the pouring rain towards the Science Faculty building at Madrid University, their grey and white shields raised in readiness. A huge red banner, over thirty feet wide, hangs from an upstairs window of the building that the students have been occupying in defence of their right to organize a free student union at the University. What the Francoist police hate most is the students' lack of deference, their refusal to bow the knee to the Generalissimo. A few weeks earlier the high-spirited young protesters had burnt Franco's portrait on a bonfire outside the Philosophy Faculty, amid cheers of '*Libertad, libertad!*' and 'Franco, assassin!' as the flames licked higher.

The ageing fascist regime is still deadly. Strikers have been shot dead in Catalonia and repression continues in the Basque country, where police use torture to extract confessions. Nearly two hundred students are dragged away from the Madrid University occupation, and ten are handed to a military tribunal, charged with 'terrorist' activity. But the movement cannot be crushed. The next day three-quarters of Madrid's students are on strike, protesting against the police invasion.

1968
December

'There are no innocent bystanders.'

Dr S. I. Hayakawa, President of San Francisco State College

A San Francisco State College student lies bleeding after Governor Reagan declares war.

Italy is supposed to have been one of the success stories of postwar European capitalism: between 1958 and 1967, its GNP grows by 5.6 per cent per year, and per capita income increases over twice as fast as in Britain. It is an economic dynamism (second only to Japan) that is based on the exploitation of a large reserve army of labour in the rural South. Politics, however, remain dominated by competing factions within the right-wing Christian Democrats, fully backed by NATO, the Vatican and a supine Socialist Party – all determined to prevent Italy's giant Communist Party from ever getting close to power.

The paranoid style of Italian politics will be graphically depicted in Francesco Rosi's remarkably prescient film, *Illustrious Corpses* (1976), which (long before former Christian Democratic Prime Minister Giulio Andreotti is indicted for being on the Mafia payroll) will portray a ruling élite that thinks nothing of using murder to preserve its power. Another path-breaking Italian film of the period, Elio Petri's *The Working Class Goes to Heaven,* is a direct attempt

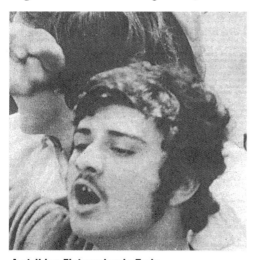

A striking Fiat worker in Turin.

to understand the degree of alienation felt by workers under capitalism. A lathe-operator works as an industrial robot who will lose his job for siding with militant students. The film graphically portrays how his life is affected by speed-up, union indifference, unsafe working conditions and low pay. Petri insists that this is not the problem of a single worker but of an entire social mileu.

The economic buoyancy of the sixties brings a broadening avalanche of factory struggles and working-class militancy which, in some ways, leaves a deeper imprint on Italian society than even its French counterpart of May. It is the combination of student militancy in Milan, Turin and Rome with the raw anger of freshly recruited workers from the South that fuels the explosion which will shake Italy between 1968 and 1970 and create a severe crisis of legitimacy for both the Christian Democrats and the Communist Party. The latter, desperate to be part of the governmental apparatus, is now confronted by forces to its left which cannot be safely ignored: it is simultaneously challenged from within by the Manifesto grouping, which systematically criticizes the Party leadership from the Left, and, from without, by the *mélange* of Maoists, Anarchists and Trotskyists who dominate campus politics.

Unlike the French Communist Party, the PCI cannot insulate itself from the mass movement, for the simple reason that the movement itself is reflected within the Party's own structures. The PCI leaders reject the ultra-leftism of the radicals but adopt a relatively open attitude, and debate publicly with the left inside its own ranks. This openness is never permitted to affect the PCI's own stance *vis-à-vis* the Italian government, however. In fact, its moderate wing openly berates the Christian Democrats for their failure to permit the PCI to take its rightful place in society and thus prevent the excesses of the ultra-radicals.

The tumultuous wave of factory struggles in the *autunno caldo* ('Hot Autumn') of 1969 frighten the Italian State and its backers, as well as the PCI. The latter will move quickly to block the trend towards rank-and-file democracy and workers committees by channelling everything through narrow trade-union structures. The State, for its part, embarks on a series of provocations to split the mass movement. Secret agencies funded by NATO and the infamous P2 organization of the far Right use bombs (imputed to far-Left groups) to foster anarchy and fear.

A layer of frustrated activists lose patience with the established structures and turn to sporadic acts of violence and terrorism which culminate in the kidnapping and execution of the liberal Christian Democratic leader, Aldo Moro, by the Red Brigades. This 'terrorist wing' of the students' movement is strongest in Germany, Italy and Japan. It is the angry and embittered (though unjustifiable) response of a layer who felt betrayed by their parents, who had welcomed or tolerated the fascist regimes.

The consequences of the radicalization in Italy can be observed to this day. It is one of history's sweeter ironies that the Left-Centre coalition government in Italy nearly three decades after 1968 is dominated by the old PCI, dressed in new clothes but dependent for its political life on the Refounded Communist Party, an indirect heir of the struggles that shook the country in the late sixties and seventies. Its leader, Fausto Bertonotti, is a skilful political operator attempting to develop a new strategy for the radical Left in Italy. In a country that is fairly equally divided between Right and Left and where the 'post-fascists' represent a sizeable force, the Refounded Communists have sought to pursue a policy that eschews sectarianism while resisting opportunism and the blandishments of office and the politics of patronage.

A mass demonstration by Italian workers in support of a sliding scale of wages.

1st San Francisco, USA Reagan Plans his Future

Governor Ronald Reagan's hard-line new appointee as President of San Francisco State College, Dr S. I. Hayakawa, declares total war on the students who have been on strike since November 6.

San Francisco State College, with a student body of some 26,000, principally drawn from the working classes, is one of the largest ethnically mixed colleges in the United States. Local student leaders have been inconspicuously using student funds to address broader social and political issues since the middle of the decade. In 1965 they had established an experimental college where students could design their own courses and hire their own teachers: a microcosm of the society they wanted to create in the world outside.

By November 1968 the campus is rife with different radical factions. The Black Students Union (BSU) is a student front of the Black Panthers, the Chicano activists have created the Third World Liberation Front (TWLF) and a group of Maoists dominate the local SDS. All are agreed that San Francisco State College needs a Black Studies Programme. The faculty, backed by Governor Reagan, vetoes the idea. On November 6 the BSU, supported by other groups, call a strike on the issue. The College President, Robert Smith, who favours a compromise, is unceremoniously sacked by Reagan.

Reagan and the hawks on the Faculty Board are set on defeating these uppity niggers and their Chicano and white friends. On December 1 Hayakawa declares a 'state of emergency' and orders students to return to their classes by the following day. The BSU and TWLF mount pickets on the campus to persuade their fellow students not to attend. An overwhelming majority of students continue to back the strike. Leo McClackley, chairman of the academic Senate, speaks out against Hayakawa's decision and calls for a negotiated settlement, declaring that 'Professors would not teach under the shadow of violence.'

It is all strangely analogous to the bigger war going on in Vietnam. The hawks want more bombs. The doves want a negotiated settlement. Hayakawa is a bomber. He now decides to embark on a policy of naked repression. The police are invited on to the campus, where, in a symbolic show of strength, they parade their hardware outside the Library.

Throughout December there are constant skirmishes, marches and demonstrations around the campus. The city as a whole is divided, but shows a surprising degree of support for the college students. Just before the Christmas break the TWLF call for a Third World community day March to the campus. The response is impressive: Blacks, Chicanos, Latinos and representatives of the Chinese, Filipino and Japanese communities announce their intentions to join the march. Hayakawa panics and closes the College. The students march to the City Hall, to be joined by several thousand supporters, including striking oil workers.

Ultimately, the student strike is crushed by repression and mass arrests – 450 students are charged with a series of offences.

Nevertheless, it has reforged an interracial unity on the streets of California where thousands of students (ninety per cent of whom were white) have fought together. In the months that lie ahead divisions will arise, encouraged by police provocateurs who seek to fan racial tensions. But the memory of those December days will not fade.

A black student activist is arrested after being clubbed by police at San Francisco State College.

2nd | **Italy** They Still Kill the Old Way

Sparks from the student conflagration in the spring have ignited the smouldering discontent in Italian factories into outright rebellion. In Turin, young workers from the local Fiat factory – many of them migrants fresh from the South of the country – took over the microphone at a student assembly in November to speak out about their conditions. Continuous assembly-line speed-ups over the last few years have heightened social tensions in the factories even more than they have increased productivity. Sixty thousand southerners have poured into Turin in the past year alone, filling the jobs in the expanding car industry, but the local government has had no plans for housing them.

When spontaneous strikes break out at the Fiat Mirafiori assembly-line plants, students go to the factory gates to meet the workers at the change of every shift, go with them to the local cafés and help them write new leaflets about the latest developments. The students duplicate 50,000 copies of the material and hand them out at the factory gates.

The social rebellion that is taking place against bad working conditions, bad housing, poor transport and services and the rising cost of living is becoming general. There are huge strikes in November in support of social security reforms and for greater workers' control over social security pension funds. At the end of November

A crowd of 50,000 trade unionists march in Rome against unemployment.

school students win the right to hold discussion meetings in their school assembly halls, after weeks of turbulent protest.

The temperature in the countryside is just as high. Agricultural workers have been striking against the grinding rural poverty of the South, where the police, hand in hand with the big landowners, have been particularly savage in their attacks on workers' picket lines and protests. On December 2, Sicilian police fire on a crowd of agricultural workers in dispute with a local landowner over pay. Two fall dead, six more are badly injured. Outrage at the killings sparks a wave of protests which sweeps the country. Twenty thousand people follow the two coffins through the pouring rain as they are buried amid the bare-branched almond trees in the little town of Avola. On the same day a protest demonstration, 30,000 strong, marches through the streets of Rome, while in Genoa, Florence, Naples and Milan crowds storm the prefecture, the provincial government and the local police headquarters.

The following day over a million people come out on strike all over Italy in protest against the Sicilian slayings. Factories, shops, banks, offices, cinemas and schools are closed and all transport comes to a halt. A mass rally of 50,000 people gathers in the Piazza of St John's Lateran in Rome to protest against low pay and unemployment. The protests will continue, gathering in intensity, into the Italian 'Hot Autumn' of 1969.

12th | Rio de Janeiro, Brazil | A State of Siege

Colonel Arthur da Costa e Silva, the military-backed President of Brazil, closes down the Congress that 'elected' him and declares a state of siege. Emergency powers are announced. These give the Colonel the right to suspend the Constitution, replace all elected governors or mayors with his own appointees, impose censorship and suspend habeas corpus wherever he thinks that the crimes committed are 'of a political nature'. The President can also fire public employees without any legal processes and annul the mandates and political rights of legislators. These measures are accompanied by a further clamp-down, with mass arrests of student activists, dissident politicians, inquisitive newspaper columnists, trade union leaders and two former Brazilian Presidents, Kubitcshek and Quadros.

The impetus for closing down Congress has come from two powerful speeches made by Opposition Deputy Marcio Moreira Alves, who has called for a boycott of the annual military parade and urged Brazilian mothers not to permit their daughters to date military men. Costa e Silva responds by declaring: 'The entire nation understands that the military does not accept criticism and abuse covered by cowardly Congressional immunities.' The Army wants Alves tried by a military court, his head on a platter, but angry Congress Deputies reaffirm his immunity by 216 votes to 141. Costa e Silva suspends the legislature.

Brazil is the recipient of more US aid than any other Latin American country and it is widely assumed that the new changes have been approved by Washington. The *New York Times* of December 16, 1968 asserted that 'Brazilians appeared indifferent to the new order laid down by President Arthur da Costa e Silva over the weekend', and went on to inform its readers that the weather was lovely and hot, 'the beaches are crowded, and business seems to go on as usual'.

The *Guardian* in London is not so sanguine. Its Latin American correspondent, Richard Gott, warns that Brazilian students, inspired by France and Mexico, are in a state of ferment and 'it is doubtful whether a divided Army can contain the situation'. Though he is not unduly optimistic about the uprising: 'The most likely outcome of the present crisis is a new strong man who will repress insurrection savagely wherever it is to be found.'

The Brazilian film director, Glauber Rocha, whose films *Black God and White Devil* and *Land in Ecstasy*, with their stunning imagery and allegorical power, have brought the Brazilia *cinema novo* exploding on to screens throughout Europe, is preparing the last part of his trilogy. He explains his cinema to a European critic:

'While *Black God and White Devil* evoked the years before 1940, *Antonio-das-Mortes* is set very clearly in the late sixties. Now. There is a certain élite group that thinks Brazil is on the path of development because of the construction of motorways, electrical plants, hospitals, schools, etc., which are a sign of progress.

'Well, in my new film, I wanted to show that today, parallel with this movement of "progress" and in this supposedly modern atmosphere, there still exists a savage condition, a medieval system of domination and oppression in which the landlords are just the same as the old lords used to be.

'I also wanted to show something which is very important to me: the expression of popular culture in a violent mythology... It strikes me that our political confusion is to a large extent the result of ignorance, prejudice and a moral hysteria that defines the bourgeois élite that dominates the country.

'The real Brazil is Indian, black (there are still the remnants of African religion), mystical, violent, barbarous and sentimental. For these reasons a revolutionary programme has to based on the real structures of our country. It has to break with prejudice and the subjective racism that characterises the bourgeoisie, but has been overcome by the masses through a wide-ranging religious and racial mix. In my film, and for this reason, I make St George a black saint. *Antonio-das-Mortes* is about a forgotten people which has been kept aloof from the squabbles of the élite and which attempts to solve its own problems and contradictions on its own through orgiastic behaviour. What does that mean? A permanent state of madness in which imaginative improvisation takes the place of ignorance, where irresponsibility and a sense of humour and mockery alleviate the lack of established values, and where aggressiveness tends to conceal a social complex of underdevelopment....'

13th East Pakistan Bangladesh: The Birth of a Nation

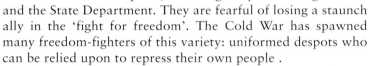

Fires continue to rage in West Pakistan. Unable to appear in public, the military dictator, Field Marshal Ayub Khan, visits the Bengali province of East Pakistan, a thousand miles away. The ruling élite has always treated Bengal as a satrapy, and his arrival is greeted by a general strike in Dhaka and Chittagong. Tens of thousands of students march in the streets and demand a full restoration of democracy. The police are ordered to open fire, and dozens of students are injured, many seriously, although there are no deaths on this day. Seven student activists are arrested.

The only supporters Ayub has left are outside the country; most of them are leader-writers in the British and American press, encouraged by the Foreign Office

General Yahya Khan succeeded Ayub Khan in March 1969.

and the State Department. They are fearful of losing a staunch ally in the 'fight for freedom'. The Cold War has spawned many freedom-fighters of this variety: uniformed despots who can be relied upon to repress their own people .

The Student Action Committee (SAC) in East Pakistan unites all the different factions of the student movement: revolutionaries and reformers, moderates and extremists, Maoists and nationalists. The SAC Eleven Point Programme is radical in tone. It demands immediate general elections, pledges itself to extensive nationalization of the large industries and commits itself to an anti-imperialist foreign policy. The SAC offers a lead to the country, calling for a general strike throughout Pakistan for January 17, 1969. It is the first and last time that a co-ordinated action of this sort will be possible in both West and East Pakistan. The whole country is paralysed.

In the months to come, many of these militants will be killed. After the fall of the dictator the Bengali nationalists of the Awami League will win an overwhelming majority in the general election, but Ayub's successors will crush them, provoking the bloody civil war that gives birth to Bangladesh in December 1971. It is the failure of the students and workers in West Pakistan (and the politicians who had jumped on to their bandwagon) to prevent the Pakistan Army from embarking on the bloody repression in the East that seals Pakistan's fate. It is irrevocably split, making a mockery of the Partition of India that Muslim leaders had considered so vital in August 1947.

From November 1968 to December 1969 the Bengali students and workers of East Pakistan were prepared to make common cause with their counterparts in West Pakistan. The struggles of 1968 created a new mood of hope, but the idealism was confiscated by cynical politicians with disastrous results, whose consequences are only too visible in the nineties.

19th London, UK A Call to Revolt

A young red-haired woman is hunched in front of the gas fire in a basement room in Hackney, scribbling furiously, surrounded by a sea of notes. *Black Dwarf* is putting out a special women's issue. It will have something on equal pay and contraception, a piece by a single mother and a long editorial by a man who has read Wilhelm Reich. But some of the women involved want a different sort of piece, something that will explore their inside feelings. Sheila Rowbotham offers to have a go.

Upstairs, the communal house is full of people, discussing, arguing, cooking, rolling joints at the kitchen table, falling in and out of love. Downstairs in the basement, Sheila is writing this:

'WOMEN: A CALL TO REVOLT.

Revolutions are made about little things.

Little things which happen to you all the time, every day, wherever you go, all your life.

The particular pummels you gently into passivity.

So we don't know how to find one another or ourselves.

We are perhaps the most divided of all oppressed groups.

Early Women's Liberation poster.

Divided in our real situations and in our understanding and consciousness of our condition.

We are in different classes.

Thus we devour and use one another.

Our "emancipation" has often been merely the struggle of the privileged to improve and consolidate its superiority – the women of the working class remain the exploited of the exploited, oppressed as workers and oppressed as women.

We are with families and without them.

Hence we distrust one another.

The woman with a home and children is suspicious of the woman with no ties, seeing her as a potential threat to her territorial security.

The single woman feels the married woman is subtly critical because she is not fulfilling her "role" as homemaker, her "function" as child bearer.

She feels she is accused of being unable to be a woman.

We walk and talk and think as living contradictions.

Most of us find the process too painful and not surprisingly settle for limited liberated areas. We give up struggling on every front and ease into a niche of acceptance.

Marxists have quite rightly always stressed that the subordination of women is part of the total mutual devouring process called capitalism. No one group can be liberated except through a transformation of the whole structure of social relationships.

But this has been twisted into a rather glib justification for inactivity and quietism.

Wait until the revolution, we'll dole you out your equality then. (Oh no you won't, power never concedes – remember?)

There are infinite practical possibilities, which could be made to happen under capitalism but would be more feasible under socialism and would help illustrate what it's about. For example, the campaign for equal pay and economic independence is crucial.

As for the family, why simply nursery schools, why not creches at the workplace of both the mother and father, with time off from work to play with the children, who would get to know both parents, too. Or numerous street and flat co-operatives for looking after children, for baby sitting and visiting the old. If adolescents, either young workers or people at school, didn't want to live at home, why couldn't they go to stay in flats which they ran themselves. These would provide another means of looking after old people.

Certainly these would mean a real liberation for many women. But subordination is not an affair of economics or institutions only. Nor is it only to do with contraception, abortion, orgasm and sexual equality, important as these things are.

It is an assumed secondariness which dwells in a whole complex of inarticulate attitudes, in smirks, in insecurities, in desperate status differentiation.

Secondariness happens in people's heads and is expressed every time they do not speak, every time they assume no one would listen. It is located in a structure in which both sexes are tragically trapped. The man as much as the woman, for each time he tries to break through, he meets the hostility of other men or the conflicting demands of those women who prefer the traditional sex game.

It is only women who can dissolve the assumptions. It is only women who can say what they feel because the experience is unique to them.

Men, you have nothing to lose but your chains. You will no longer have anyone to creep away and peep at with their knickers down, no one to flaunt as the emblem of your virility, status, self-importance, no one who will trap you, overwhelm you, no etherealised cloudy being floating unattainable in a plastic blue sky, no great mopping up handkerchief comforters to crawl into from your competitive, ego-strutting alienation, who will wrap you up and SMOTHER you.

There will only be thousands of millions of women people to discover, touch and become with, who will say with a Vietnamese girl, "Let us now emulate each other," who will understand you when you say we must make a new world in which we do not meet each other as exploiters and used objects. Where we love one another and into which a new kind of human being can be born.'

25th London, UK The Dialectic of Christmas

Fred Halliday, writing in the *Black Dwarf* towards the end of 1968, reflects on the significance of Christmas:

'From earliest childhood we know the stereotypes of Christmas – gifts, turkey and pudding, decorations, snow, festivity and drink. Yet the very familiarity of Christmas and its yearly occurrence tend to preclude a critical and full understanding of its role in our society. Moreover it might prove excessively morbid to lay the cold hands of analysis on what is par excellence the occasion for light hearted enjoyment and alcoholic oblivion.

'But this very universality and magnitude of Christmas make it the major communal festival of late capitalist society, lived by all and understood by none; and the festivals of late-capitalism, no less than those of feudal and tribal societies, serve important functions in preserving the cohesion and unity of those societies. They are occasions of exuberance in a world of repression, and so they are both festivals in spite of repression and festivals of repression.

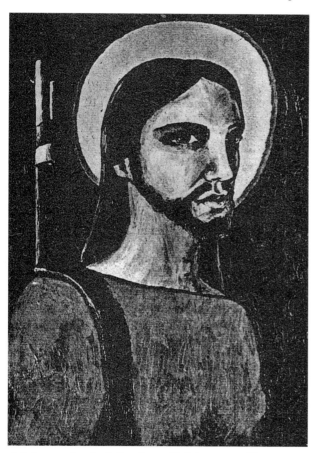

A Cuban poster depicting Jesus Christ as a guerilla.

'Herein lies the dialectic of Christmas. Christmas has inspired some of the greatest works of western music and painting, and no one can deny that Christmas expresses the deepest aspirations of suffering men – a longing for peace, happiness, good food, social equality and the free giving of commodities. In the deepest winter and at the end of the year, all these forces are annually released. The expression of these liberating emotions is, however, controlled by social ritual, as it has been since pre-historic times. And the function of ritual is to provide a controlled way in which human emotions can be resolved without destroying the structures against which they are reacting.

'The liberation of Christmas is controlled by the very institutionalisation of its expression. People should be able to choose when they rave it up and give presents and love each other: yet Christmas ordains and ritualises them. One is pressured into celebrating these at one date in the year to stop one from expressing them for the rest of the year. The expression of freedom in this form is an expression of unfreedom. The happiness of Christmas masks the unhappiness of society.

'Here lies the dialectical significance of Christmas. The desire for happiness is marshalled to defend the instruments of misery and the ideological symbols of myth are carefully used to drown the critical and liberating content of the Christmas festival. To smash the institutionalisation of happiness is to release men from myth, from the need to displace salvation onto gods or charity, and to realign man's hopes on conscious historical action. Within the apparently innocuous shell of Christmas is found both oppression and the longing for liberation and revolution. The Puritans banned it; the Cubans postponed it; we can transcend it. This involves the release of the revolutionary potential now marshalled by late-capitalist forms. In the meantime, we can, of course, enjoy it.'

Make love, not war.

Epilogue

Of History and Happiness

History and happiness
Are similar:
They happened –
Or are prone to happen
Or will happen, burstingly.
Or: they have not happened
O history o happiness.
(David Shapiro, 'A Note and Poem
by Joe Ceravalo in a Dream'
in *After a Lost Original*)

Every epoch, era, generation and milieu has its own political syntax, its own way of thinking, but all periods are not equally intense. The political, cultural and sexual turbulence that characterized 1968–75 left its mark on all of us who lived through those years. Some of the foot-soldiers of the period are now in positions of influence and authority. Not all of them look back on their past with affection.

Others utilize the skills honed on the barricades or in the peace movements in Presidential residences. The three most dramatic examples of this are found in Washington DC, Rio de Janeiro and Colombo.

In May 1969, Hillary Rodham, President of the Wellesley College Government Association, addressed her classmates thus at Wellesley's 91st Commencement:

'For too long, those who have led us have viewed politics as the "art of the possible". The challenge which faces them and us now is to practise politics as the art of making what appears impossible, possible. As the French students wrote on the walls of the Sorbonne: "Be realistic! Demand the impossible!" We cannot settle for less.'

Much of this was forgotten on the way to the Governor's residence in Arkansas. What remained was obliterated as she was safely ensconced in the White House. Now politics was not even the art of the possible, but holding on to power at all costs.

Fernando Henrique Cardoso, who was one of Brazil's most gifted Marxist intellectuals during the sixties and seventies, burst on to the political scene of his country in the late eighties as its fiscally orthodox Finance Minister. At the time of writing, he is the elected President of Brazil. His opponent was the charismatic workers' leader Lula. Once the author of seminal texts published in the *New Left Review* such as 'Dependent Capitalist Development in Latin America', Fernando Enrique Cardoso has now become a passionate neo-liberal, stabilizing the Brazilian currrency by tying it to the dollar.

Wellesley College Government elections, February 1968. Presidential candidates (left to right): Nonna Noto, Hillary Rodham (the victor) and Francille Rusan. Before the age of power haircuts.

In May 1968 a young Sri Lankan student, Chandrika Bandaranaike, participated in the upheavals of the Latin Quarter in Paris and was excited by the sight of ten million striking workers and factory occupations. Now, as President of Sri Lanka, she is even tougher on the trade unions than her right-wing predecessor and austerity is the order of the day.

The past, no doubt, still haunts this triumvirate, but they have little time to think about who they once were. They live for the present.

When American radicals of the sixties stopped troop trains, burnt money on the floor of the Stock Exchange and attempted to levitate the Pentagon, they and others like them the world over were challenging power, trying to recreate a public dialogue which Democracy claimed to favour, but which then, and even more so now, was denied in practice.

There was an urgency and an intensity that came to an end in 1975 with the fall of Saigon to the National Liberation Front and the overthrow of the fifty-year-old fascist dictatorship in Portugal. Both were formative events for Left and Right.

Much has changed since. Under the aggressive leadership of Ronald Reagan and Margaret Thatcher the United States mounted a new offensive. It succeeded beyond its wildest ambitions in the period that began in 1989 and saw the total collapse of the Soviet system and with it the eclipse of socialism as a viable alternative for millions throughout the world. This is not a view shared by the entire Left today. There are some for whom the fall of official communism simply represented a clearing of the decks, so that now we have capitalism pure and unbridled. The enemy need no longer be seen through the tainted spectacles of bureaucratic tyranny. There is an attractive simplicity in this outlook, yet it is pure fantasy.

Rebuilding hope and the belief in an alternative to what exists today will not be easy. And it will take time. Also, there is the awkward question of agency. The big battalions of the industrial working class have been transformed beyond recognition by this latest phase of capitalist rationalization. They exist still in China, in Brazil, in South Korea and South Africa, though even in these countries the post-1989 collapse of communism has brought with it a certain fatalism and acceptance of the social *status quo*. They will fight to improve their conditions, but the horizon beyond that is still murky.

And now it is back with a vengeance to profit and to each for him- or herself and the permanent mocking of those who still believe in the duty of the modern state to provide equality and social justice in equal measure for all its citizens. It is not just Marxism or socialism, but even the social democracy advocated by Eduard Bernstein and Anthony Crosland, not to mention the paternal liberalism of John Maynard Keynes or the universalist values of the Enlightenment, that are all now regarded as hopelessly utopian. Any talk of nurturing a common culture based on the collective interests of the majority is regarded as an incurable and absurd sickness. We are told that we live in a 'culture of difference' where the most important question is our own identity. It follows that a hedonistic self-contemplation is the creed that the youth of today are exhorted to embrace.

A system that fears the noise of discontent usually encourages an abdication from participatory politics. In this way it sows the seeds of despair and creates a soil in which hatreds – based on the 'culture of difference' – flourish. Turkish and Vietnamese families are burnt alive by young German neo-fascists on both sides of a Wall which no longer exists except in German hearts; the French National Front preaches open hatred of North African immigrants in France and barely a week goes by without an incident involving violence against Algerians, Moroccans and other Africans; Ethiopians selling beads have been beaten and, on occasion, killed by the normally tolerant Italians; racist killings continue in contemporary Britain; and there are more blacks in American prisons today than there were in Apartheid South Africa. The litany is endless.

A politics that is truly alive does not live by yesterday's clock or even today's, but by tomorrow's. Those who came to maturity in the sixties and seventies did believe in a better future and attempted in the best way they could, with numerous mistakes and foolishnesses, to struggle for a better world. They failed, but defeat does not necessarily invalidate the whole experience. Today we can ask ourselves what it all meant. How did we live in those days? And if we could begin again would we have behaved any differently?

Overall, the answer to this last, critical question is: no. Some of the things that sounded utopian and absurd in 1968 sound right today. The fact that the Soviet Union has collapsed does not solve the problems that confront Capital on a global scale. It is unlikely that the capitalist summer will last for ever.

Generally speaking, we were justified in the way we acted. We were happy in the knowledge that we were helping to shape history. Happiness comes in different ways, but the joy referred to here has little to do with the cocaine-induced variety so common in the hedonistic culture of today, which is, in reality, an attempt to mask the profound melancholy that lies at the core of contemporary capitalism. The 'don't worry, be happy' generation of MTV enthusiasts are many things. They may be amiable and content-free, but they are also, alas, deeply unhappy. Drugs, drink, conspicuous consumption and the videosphere are not palliatives but an anaestheic which helps to mask the painful realities of everyday life.

We were happy because we carried within our collective self a vision of a better future. Not for ourselves, but for the oppressed throughout the world: for everyone. That hope determined most of our priorities. Ours was not just a soft happiness or rapture (that too was omnipresent and many rooms were conditioned with the scent

A clandestine gathering of dissident socialists outside Leningrad (now St Petersburg) greet the dawn of *perestroika* in 1985, their faces filled with hope.

of marijuana), but one that was linked to taking risks, to danger, to sacrificing one's own life if it would help to further the cause of humanity. This feeling, while probably less pronounced in Britain, was strong in most of Europe *and* the United States, which was the power at the heart of the evil empire.

Our sclerotic culture discourages independent thinking and dissent. We are told that, since no alternative exists, any critique of existing capitalism is beside the point. The change in mood is reflected in the growing narrowness of the agenda that shapes the content of much of television and the national press. There are regional variations – the Germans and the French have still managed to preserve serious newspapers – but all the trends point in the other direction, towards an increasing trivialization of social and political problems and a concentration on consumerism, sex scandals and crime. What is this if not a dumbing-down process, a message to the young that they need not look beyond their own navels? This process is deeply anti-democratic, for it preserves a monopoly on real information for a tiny élite.

A culture that lacks intransigent, permanently questioning heretics and a layer of ruthlessly critical and restless romantics is doomed to reproduce Sancho Panzas. Such a culture will, sooner or later, wither away, and young and old alike will begin to develop an alternative which reaches the part that most of the media avoids like a disease: the brain.

Heretics are indeed a threat, for they encourage explosions of thought which challenge the complacency of our rulers, discomfort the comfortable and irritate minions of every stripe. Heretics are hostile to the rigid crust that coats every dogma. They challenge the quiescence that permits a society to become stagnant.

To attack the way in which free-market economics is being forced upon Russia and Eastern Europe by global financial institutions under the control of the United States, is immediately to be branded as a whinger or a dinosaur. Moreover, it invites being told to stop this foolish bleating since freedom has a price and that is what the unfortunate citizens of the former Soviet Union and Eastern Europe have to pay if they are to progress.

But what if these people were to unite in order to achieve a world that is closer to their hearts? Some of them have done so by voting for the old Communist Parties, in the lame half hope, half belief that at the very least these parties would provide a safety net for the poor as they did in the past. For doing so the people of Poland, Hungary and Russia have been denounced by liberal commentators in Britain and the United States. With understanding smiles, the pundits in the West console one another with the thought that a democratic culture cannot be built overnight: one day even the poor wretches lately emerging from communism will learn to distinguish between terroristic totalizers and those who have brought them real freedom.

We are living through a period of transition, in a time when hope has been banished and fear seems to have colonized the entire world. Whereas hope requires us to be active, fear creates apathy, passivity, caution and conservatism. It locks people into nothingness. In such an atmosphere it is hardly surprising that there is a tendency to mimic the laws of the jungle, to return to the most primitive forms of self-preservation. But this can only be a very short-term solution.

People have always dreamt of the possibility of a better life. The following lines were written not by Marx or Robespierre or Trotsky but put into the mouth of a plebeian by Shakespeare in *Coriolanus*:

FIRST CITIZEN: We are accounted poor citizens; the patricians good. What authority surfeits on would relieve us: if they would yield us but the superfluity, while it were wholesome, we might guess they relieved us humanely; but they think we are too dear: the leanness that afflicts us, the object of our misery, is as an inventory to particularise their abundance; our sufferance is a gain to them.

Let us revenge this with our pikes, ere we become rakes; for the gods know I speak this in the hunger for bread, not in thirst for revenge.

Steve Bell

Till we meet again …

Sources

The publishers have used their best efforts to contact the copyright holders of all materials quoted and illustrated in this publication and to include full acknowledgements, however, any further information would be gratefully received.

Periodicals and newspapers
Das Argument, West Berlin, 1968
Black Dwarf, London, 1968
Guardian, London, 1968
Great Speckled Bird, Atlanta, 1968
Intercontinental Press, New York, 1968
Konkret, Frankfurt, 1968
New Left Review, 1968–72
Le Nouvel Observateur, Paris, 1968
Observer, London, 1968
The Nation, New York, 1968
Quaderni Piacentini, Rome, 1968
Quaderni Rossi, Rome, 1968
Ramparts, San Francisco, 1968–9
Rouge, Paris, 1968
The Times, London, 1968
Village Voice, New York, 1968
World Outlook, New York, 1968

Books and essays
Atelier Populaire, *Texts and Posters*, London, 1969
Tariq Ali, *Pakistan: Military Rule or People's Power?*, London and New York, 1969
Tariq Ali, *1968 and After*, London, 1978
Tariq Ali, *Can Pakistan Survive?*, London, 1983
Tariq Ali (ed.), *The Stalinist Legacy*, London, 1984
Tariq Ali, *Street Fighting Years*, London, 1987
Perry Anderson, 'Components of the National Culture', *New Left Review*, no. 50
Paulo Flores d'Arcais and Franco Moretti, 'Paradoxes of the Italian Political Crisis', *New Left Review*, no. 96
Robin Blackburn and Alexander Cockburn, *Student Power: Problems, Diagnosis*, Action, London, 1969
Bui Tin, *Following Ho Chi Minh*, London, 1995
Wilfred Burchett, *Vietnam Will Win*, New York, 1968
Daniel Bensaid and Henri Weber, *La Répétition Générale*, Paris, 1968
Daniel Bensaid and Alain Krivine, *Mai Si!*, Paris, 1988
John Berger, *Ways of Seeing*, London 1968
Julien Besançon, *Les Murs ont la Parole*, Paris, 1968
Stig Bjorkman, Torsten Manns and Jonas Sima, *Bergman on Bergman*, New York, 1993
Gérard Chaliand, *The Peasants of North Vietnam*, London, 1969
Eldridge Cleaver, *Soul on Ice*, New York, 1968
Bernadette Devlin, *The Price of My Soul*, London, 1969
Ronald Fraser, *1968: A Student Generation in Revolt*, London, 1988
Ronald Fraser, 'Spain on the Brink', *New Left Review*, no. 96
Erich Fried, *100 Poems Without a Country*, London, 1978
Eduardo Galleano, *Memory of Fire*, London, 1987

General Vo Nguyen Giap, *The Military Art of People's War*, New York, 1970
Che Guevara, *Reminiscences of the Cuban Revolutionary War*, London, 1968
David Halberstam, *The Making of a Quagmire*, London, 1965
Frigga Haug, *Beyond Female Masochism*, London, 1992
David Horowitz, *Containment and Revolution*, London, 1967
George Jackson, *Soledad Brother*, London, 1971
Boris Kagarlitsky, *The Thinking Reed*, London, 1988
Alain Labrousse, *The Tupamaros*, London, 1973
Jean Lacouture, *Ho Chi Minh*, London, 1968
Ernest Mandel, *Europe versus America: The Contradictions of Capitalism*, London, 1968
Ernest Mandel, *Marxist Economic Theory* (two vols), London, 1968
Ernest Mandel, 'Lessons of May', *New Left Review*, no. 52
Herbert Marcuse, *Negations*, London, 1968
Herbert Marcuse, *Eros and Civilisation*, London, 1969
Gavan McCormack, 'The Student Left in Japan', *New Left Review*, no. 65
Ralph Miliband, *Parliamentary Socialism*, London, 1967
Juliet Mitchell, 'Women: The Longest Revolution', *New Left Review*, no. 40
Robin Morgan, *Sisterhood is Powerful*, New York, 1970
Robin Morgan, *Going Too Far*, New York, 1977
Michael Myerson (ed.), *Memories of Underdevelopment: The Revolutionary Films of Cuba*, New York, 1973
Huey. P. Newton, *Revolutionary Suicide*, New York, 1995
Jirí Pelikán, *The Secret Vysocany Congress*, London, 1971
D. Plamenic, 'The Belgrade Student Insurrection', *New Left Review*, no. 53
João Quartim, *Dictatorship and Armed Struggle in Brazil*, London, 1971
Angelo Quattrocchi and Tom Nairn, *The Beginning of the End*, London, 1968
Robin Alison Remington (ed.), *Winter in Prague*, Massachusetts, 1969
Witold Rodzinski, *The People's Republic of China*, London, 1988
Sheila Rowbotham, *Dreams and Dilemmas*, London, 1983
Sheila Rowbotham, *The Past is Before Us*, London, 1989
Michele Salvati, 'The Impasse of Italian Capitalism', *New Left Review*, no. 76
Patrick Seale and Maureen McConville, *French Revolution 1968*, London, 1968
Richard Soler, 'The New Spain', *New Left Review*, no. 58
Leslie B. Tanner (ed.), *Voices From Women's Liberation*, New York, 1970
Clyde Taylor, *Vietnam and Black America: an Anthology of Protest and Resistance*, New York, 1973
Constantine Tsoucalas, 'Class Struggle and Dictatorship in Greece', *New Left Review*, no. 56
Petr Uhl, *Le Socialisme Emprisonné*, Paris, 1980
Peter Weiss and Gunilla Palmstierna-Weiss, '*Limited Bombing' in Vietnam*, London, 1969
Richard West, *Sketches from Vietnam*, London, 1968
Raymond Williams et al., *May Day Manifesto*, London, 1968

Picture credits

Picture sources are followed by page numbers and, where necessary, the position of the image on the page.

Tariq Ali 186–187, 189, 196, 197, 216

Associated Press Photo 108, 109, 166, 175

Atelier Populaire 86, 96, 102, 103 (left), 103 (right)

Bruno Barbey/Magnum Photos 92–93, 104, 131

Steve Bell 217

Black Dwarf 8, 18, 45, 57 (right), 62 (left), 83 (top), 99, 112–113, 184 (main picture), 184 (inset), 200–201, 205, 206, 208, 211

Committee to Unsell the War 124

Corbis-Bettmann/UPI 16, 20, 24, 26 (main picture), 27, 28, 29, 33 (left), 38, 41, 54 (main picture), 62 (right), 66–67, 69, 70, 73 (top), 74, 75, 77, 78 (bottom), 81, 82, 87, 95, 98, 106–107, 132, 149, 150, 154–155, 157, 159, 163, 164, 180

Czech News Agency 54 (inset), 55, 134, 135

David King Collection 6, 34–35, 40, 48, 191, 192

EDIMEDIA 91, 94, 100, 101, 105, 118 (top)

Evergreen Review, Inc. 17

GAMMA/Frank Spooner Pictures 90, 97, 141, 146, 147

Franz Goess 140 (top), 140 (bottom)

Guildhall Press 199

Hulton-Deutsch Collection 50–51, 64, 145, 183

Hulton Getty 83 (bottom), 120, 138–139, 177

Interfoto/S.O.A. 37, 47 (top)

Keystone 57 (left)

Library of Congress, Washington DC 19, 65, 73 (bottom), 117 (right)

Roger Malloch/Magnum Photos 125

Fred W. McDarrah 153

Gary Yanker 25, 72, 80, 156, 160, 209

Popperfoto 14–15, 39, 118 (bottom), 126, 127 (bottom), 185

Poster Prints Inc. 212

Private Collection/Index/Bridgeman Art Library, London/New York 170–171

Marc Riboud/Magnum Photos 84

Rouge 182, 202, 203

Stern/S.O.A. 79

Topham Picturepoint 21, 23, 32, 33 (right), 43, 47 (bottom), 61 (top), 68, 78 (top), 89, 117 (left), 127 (top), 137, 143, 144, 167, 195

Wellesley College Archives 214

W.F.D.I.F. 53, 61 (bottom)

Janine Wiedel 122–123, 161

World Outlook 26 (inset), 36, 168 (top), 168 (bottom), 169 (top), 169 (bottom), 172

Acknowledgements

Thanks for this book are due, first and foremost, to Sarah Polden at Bloomsbury, whose unremitting enthusiasm for this project ensured its birth and completion. Tim Foster and Sally Smallwood entered into the spirit of the sixties in their design studio. Anny Chettleborough trawled through numerous archives to find the photographs. Richard Dawes copy-edited the text and made many useful suggestions. In that sense, this was a truly collective undertaking.

Our thanks also to friends whose personal libraries became invaluable sources for us as this book got under way: Richard Gott and Vivien Ashley, Marion Kozak, Peter Gowan, Robin Blackburn, Sheila Rowbotham, Fred Halliday, Adrian and Celia Mitchell and Christopher Logue.

We owe a very special debt to two veterans of the sixties in Glasgow, Tony Southall and Gordon Morgan, archivists of the socialist and labour movement, who responded warmly and promptly to our requests by mailing us original copies of political magazines unavailable elsewhere.

Index

Page numbers in *italic* refer to the illustrations